PERILOUS
DESERT

INSECURITY
IN THE SAHARA

MW00777977

PERILOUS DESERT
INSECURITY IN THE SAHARA

CARNEGIE ENDOWMENT
FOR INTERNATIONAL PEACE

WASHINGTON DC ▪ MOSCOW ▪ BEIJING ▪ BEIRUT ▪ BRUSSELS

EDITED BY
FREDERIC WEHREY & ANOUAR BOUKHARS

© 2013 Carnegie Endowment for International Peace. All rights reserved.

No part of this publication may be reproduced or transmitted in any form or by any means without written permission from the Carnegie Endowment.

Carnegie Endowment for International Peace
1779 Massachusetts Avenue, N.W.
Washington, D.C. 20036
202-483-7600, Fax 202-483-1840
www.ceip.org

The Carnegie Endowment does not take institutional positions on public policy issues; the views represented here are the authors' own and do not necessarily reflect the views of the Endowment, its staff, or its trustees.

To order, contact:
Hopkins Fulfillment Service
P.O. Box 50370, Baltimore, MD 21211-4370
1-800-537-5487 or 1-410-516-6956
Fax 1-410-516-6998

Cover design by Mission Media
Composition by Cutting Edge Design
Printed by United Book Press

Library of Congress Cataloging-in-Publication Data

Perilous desert: insecurity in the Sahara / Frederic Wehrey and Anouar Boukhars, editors.
    pages cm
    Includes bibliographical references and index.
    ISBN 978-0-87003-403-9 (pbk.) -- ISBN 978-0-87003-404-6 (cloth) -- ISBN 978-0-87003-405-3 (electronic)
    1. Security, International--Sahara. 2. Security, International--Sahel. 3. National security--Sahara. 4. National security--Sahel 5. Sahara--Politics and government. 6. Sahel--Politics and government. I. Wehrey, Frederic M. II. Boukhars, Anouar.

    JZ5588.P45 2013
    355'.033066--dc23

                                2012044405

Contents

Foreword

While the world's attention was fixed on the momentous events in Tunisia, Egypt, and Libya after the outbreak of the Arab Awakening, the desert states to the south were undergoing their own transformations with major global implications. Long overlooked by policymakers and scholars, the broader Sahara region has always possessed an underappreciated geopolitical significance. And changes should not be ignored.

At the intersection of the Mediterranean, African, and Arab worlds, the states of the Sahara suffer from a "perfect storm" of afflictions—weak governance, rampant corruption, endemic poverty, ethnic and societal cleavages, and inaccessible terrain—that give room for transnational crime and Islamist militant groups to proliferate and flourish. The region's role as a key transit route for African labor migrants and narcotics trafficking has sparked alarm among European governments. But for much of the past decade, it has been the threat of terrorism, embodied by al-Qaeda in the Islamic Maghreb, that has dominated the Western discourse and approaches to the region.

The significance of the region's insecurity became painfully apparent and the Sahara finally catapulted to the top of policy agendas in 2012 following a series of high-profile events—a coup in Mali followed by the seizure of the country's north by al-Qaeda and affiliated factions, the murder of the U.S. ambassador to Libya in Benghazi by a local Islamist militia with links to al-Qaeda, a French military intervention in Mali, and the seizure of Western hostages at an Algerian gas facility by a multi-national group of militants.

The incidents point to a new front in the struggle against al-Qaeda—what some have called "an arc of instability" stretching from Western Sahara to Somalia and north into the Sinai. While the dangers are certainly real, it is important to understand each militant group's local context and how its agenda feeds off local frustrations, regardless of any professed ties to al-Qaeda.

In many respects, the Malian and Libyan crises epitomize the structural problems faced by the entire region. Weak and corrupt states dealing with pronounced ethnic and societal tensions are unable or unwilling to stop terrorism and crime. Until these underlying problems are addressed, attempts to reduce insecurity will largely fail. But finding solutions is complicated.

Perilous Desert provides in-depth analysis of the factors shaping the Sahara and offers an important foundation for developing policy responses to this troubled region. Leading experts detail the simmering conflicts in the region and assess the role of governments, regional heavyweights—particularly Algeria—and Western powers in both combatting the region's unrest and at times exacerbating it.

The book fills a void in current thinking about the region's problems, providing insight that is necessary to prevent these problems from spilling beyond the Sahara's borders. Canvassing a broad swathe of territory, the authors draw extensively on firsthand interviews—not only in the urban capitals but also in the provinces and ungoverned spaces where the effects of terrorism, crime, and ethnic unrest are most deeply felt—to identify the roots of the challenges. Only from such comprehensive and multidisciplinary assessments will lasting and effective solutions emerge.

Policymakers in and out of the region will find the book's conclusions critical for understanding the transformations under way in the Sahara and crafting solutions that will actually work.

–Marwan Muasher
Vice President for Studies
Carnegie Endowment for International Peace

Introduction

Frederic Wehrey

ong-forgotten swathes of northern Africa burst into the international spotlight in March 2012 when Malian army officers, outraged at their superiors' handling of an uprising in the north by members of the Tuareg ethnic group, toppled the country's democratically elected government. In the ensuing chaos, a coalition of radical Islamists with links to al-Qaeda in the Islamic Maghreb (AQIM) co-opted and later hijacked the Tuareg opposition, carving out an "emirate" in northern Mali.

Within a matter of weeks, a country once lauded as an oasis of democracy amid the region's arid authoritarianism became a junta-led failed state and a terrorist safe haven. Fearing that the Islamists were poised to capture the capital, French military forces intervened in January 2013, followed quickly by militants' dramatic seizure of Western hostages at an Algerian gas facility.

Further north, postrevolutionary Libya was enjoying a tenuous euphoria following its successful parliamentary elections in July 2012. The relative calm was shattered with the murder of the U.S.

ambassador to Libya, J. Christopher Stevens, and three of his colleagues at the American mission in Benghazi. The attack by a local Salafi brigade prompted the West to take a closer look at al-Qaeda's long-standing interest in exploiting Libya's post-Qaddafi landscape. It also shed light on the weak capacity of the Libyan central government, which is relying on independent revolutionary brigades to try to keep control of the country.

These events stand as stark reminders of the deep-rooted instability that plagues the countries of the broader Sahara region. The territory stretches from Africa's Mediterranean coast through the Sahara Desert to the upper reaches of sub-Saharan Africa. It encompasses the tract known as the Sahel—a thin belt that runs from the Atlantic Ocean to the Red Sea along the southern edge of the desert. The most insecure parts of this region are on the southwestern periphery—Mauritania, Mali, Niger, and Western Sahara—with Libya and Algeria key players in the north. Some of these societies are among the poorest in the world.

While observers of the Sahara have long been aware of the witches' brew of problems the region faces, there have been few attempts to unpack the complex interactions between the forces at work. Drawing on extensive fieldwork, the authors attempt to fill that gap. They focus on emerging areas of conflict on the tattered frontiers of the Sahara and Sahel, with contributions unearthing the complex roots of insecurity. Across each of these territories, weak and corrupt central governments combine with ingrained ethnic and socioeconomic divisions to produce a region that is home to extensive illicit cross-border networks and breeds radical Islamism.

At the center of the instability is state weakness. Many state institutions are fragile and ineffective, and many governments cannot exercise authority over vast tracts of difficult terrain. In Libya, the country's fragmented security landscape has handed power and authority to local militias, some of which have explicitly Islamist leanings. In the southern border region, the central government is virtually absent. Mali, Mauritania, and Niger are all afflicted with similar problems.

Corruption is another key issue. Mauritania is a prime example. Wherever the state's presence is minimal—which is in many places, especially in the peripheral parts of the country—the opportunities for different stakeholders to pursue self-interested goals increase. At the center itself, political infighting and factional rivalries further undermine the institutional capacity of the government. Though often overlooked, corruption lies at the root of the crisis in northern Mali as well. The Malian government's cynical collusion with organized crime—particularly kidnapping for ransom—has fueled instability.

Many states are unable to provide for their citizens' basic needs given their high levels of poverty and corrupt systems that favor the privileged few. Large segments of society have limited voice in government and access to social safety nets. As a result, whole communities become isolated from the center and disaffected. Across the region, this absence of inclusive state institutions has exacerbated long-standing **ethnic and societal divides**. Closely knit ethnic communities stretch across state borders and allegiance to kinsmen is often stronger than allegiance to the state.

Such fissures are particularly acute in Moroccan-controlled Western Sahara, where discontent among ethnic Sahrawis and socioeconomic protests have reached unprecedented levels. In Libya, the marginalization of the country's Tabu and Tuareg minorities is fueling unrest along the country's southern periphery. Moreover, these ethnic groups, long underserved by the Qaddafi regime, have weak ties at best to the central government. They rely more on cross-border tribal links than the state, making their integration into Libyan society difficult. On their return to northern Mali after the conflict ended in Libya, Tuareg, who have long agitated for independence from the south, spurred the rebellion that would topple the Malian government. Meanwhile, rapid urbanization in Mauritania has broken down traditional structures of authority, and, when combined with high unemployment, this has created a new pool of underclass, disaffected youth.

These underlying forces have allowed **illicit networks** to flourish across the region. Aggrieved ethnic groups who are marginalized from political and economic resources are frequently drawn to crime. For instance, in the refugee camps near Tindouf that are run by the Polisario (the movement that has long fought for Western Sahara's independence), displaced Sahrawis are increasingly turning to illicit smuggling. In northern Mali and Niger, there are no alternative sources of income and employment that could rival those of contraband and drug smuggling. Among the Tuareg and Tabu of western and southern Libya, smuggling and black market activity have long substituted for formal, legitimate employment. And along Libya's often ungoverned borders, criminal networks and cross-border tribal communities have stepped into the vacuum left by the weak state to take control of territories on the periphery, further enabling the flow of illicit goods and migrants across the broader region.

Given the enormity of these problems, it is easy to see why **radical Islamism** has found fertile soil in the Sahara. Discontent among Sahrawis in the Moroccan-administered Western Sahara has provided new opportunities for AQIM to expand its recruitment efforts beyond its traditional base in Algerian refugee camps controlled by the Polisario.

In eastern Libya the rise of Salafi extremism that fueled the attack in Benghazi is inextricably linked to Qaddafi's legacy of economic and political neglect of the region. Among the region's urbanized, unemployed youth and marginalized ethnic groups, Salafism has an especially powerful magnetism. This is particularly true in Mauritania, where the egalitarianism of Salafism has proven an appealing counterweight to the more hierarchical, caste-based system of Sufism. Sensing an opportunity, AQIM has found an attractive base of supporters and recruits among the region's disenchanted. And in Mali, the government's collusion with organized crime provided a major source of AQIM's cash flow and has funded the group's spread across the region.

Yet the terrorist organization has also encountered pushback, often from like-minded Salafi groups, more moderate Islamists, and tribal/ethnic communities. In Mauritania, for example, moderate Islamists have stood up to extremist forces, and an effective counter-radicalization program was launched by the Mauritanian government. In northern Mali, there are significant tensions between the AQIM affiliates and more nationalist Tuareg groups like the Movement for the National Liberation of Azawad.

Although the authors approach these issues through the lens of security, their conclusions are broader and holistic, delving deeply into the structural maladies that fuel conflict. Above all, solutions must take the region's complex forces into account; simply throwing money at these deeply embedded and interlinked problems will not make them go away.

Ultimately, local and regional solutions must carry the day, backed up by carefully tailored outside support. This is especially critical in northern Mali, where neighboring Algeria has a central role to play. Among regional states, Algiers alone possesses the strategic clout, military power, and political ties to northern Mali's protagonists that are essential for conflict management and resolution.

Moreover, even well-meaning foreign assistance, if applied uncritically and without conditionality, can be counterproductive. In Mauritania an excessive reliance on foreign aid has hobbled the development of inclusive state institutions. In Mali, unconditional support to the regime of former president Amadou Toumani Touré exacerbated state corruption and complicity with AQIM and transnational criminal networks. And perhaps most importantly, outside assistance that relies exclusively on a broad-based counterterrorism response—treating the symptoms rather than the under-lying structural weaknesses—is destined to exacerbate the very problems that the West is trying to resolve.

CRETE
(GREECE)

Mediterranean Sea

TUNISIA

Zuwara
Zawiya
Tripoli
Misrata

Baida
Darnah

Zintan

Nafusa Mts.

Gulf of Sidra

Benghazi

Libyan Plateau

TRIPOLITANIA

Sirte

Sidra
Ras
Lanuf

Brega

Zuwaytina

EGYPT

LIBYA

Sabha

FEZZAN

CYRENAICA
(BARQA)

Libyan Desert

Al-Qatrun

Kufra

ALGERIA

Sahara Desert

LIBYA

AFRICA

CHAD

SUDAN

⬡ National capital
● Town or village
═ Major road
--- Traditional provincial
    boundary
-·- International
    boundary
🌊 Dry salt lake
🛢 Oil terminal
···· Intermittent river

0   200 mi
0   300 km

LUCIDITY INFORMATION DESIGN, LLC

01

The Struggle for Security in Eastern Libya

Frederic Wehrey

A Restive Region

Libya held its first parliamentary elections in sixty years on July 7, 2012. Despite sporadic violence, the polling went remarkably smoothly, defying predictions of both an Islamist landslide and a widespread boycott.[1] Contrary to many assumptions, the country is not headed toward a territorial breakup or a descent into widespread communal strife. Rather, it faces endemic instability resulting from a number of localized struggles over identity, power, and resources in the country's western, southern, and eastern regions. Troublingly, those conflicts are straining the nascent state's capacity, deterring foreign investment, and possibly stunting the emergence of democratic institutions. These conflicts are also empowering potent revolutionary brigades—that is, the numerous armed fighting units that were formed during the course of the anti-Qaddafi struggle, usually on the basis of neighborhood, town, or locale[2]—that the transitional government, bereft of an effective police and army, has been forced to co-opt to quell the fighting.

The most pressing of these local conflicts is the deteriorating security situation in Libya's eastern region of Cyrenaica (henceforth referred to by its Arabic name, Barqa), home of the restive city Benghazi. The roots of eastern grievances run deep and are related in part to the legacy of Qaddafi's policy of marginalizing the region. But missteps by the National Transitional Council (NTC) also fueled suspicion about continued neglect. Added to this are questions about the sharing of oil revenues; the east accounts for nearly 80 percent of the country's oil production and armed groups in that part of the country have already shown the capacity to shut down this production—a form of leverage over the central government in Tripoli. Although the July 2012 elections for the General National Congress (GNC), which replaced the NTC on August 8, represented a referendum of sorts on national unity, the issue of autonomy and federalism is not dead. A number of new federalist parties have sprung up and pro-autonomy armed groups can still play a spoiler role.

In addition to federalist agitation, other subregional conflicts in Barqa have rippled across the country. The region's deeply entrenched Salafi community is undergoing significant upheaval, with debate raging between a current that is amenable to political integration and a more militant strand that opposes democracy. In longtime hubs of Islamism in the east—Darnah, Baida, and, increasingly, Benghazi—Salafi brigades have rallied against elections and launched attacks on both western interests and Sufi sites. The most recent of these attacks was the assault on the U.S. consulate in Benghazi, in which U.S. ambassador J. Christopher Stevens and three other U.S. diplomats were killed. In many respects, Salafi violence has been empowered by the very same security vacuum that has exacerbated communal fighting elsewhere in the country.

Among these conflicts in the east, the most intractable is the ongoing violence in Kufra, a Saharan trade hub that lies far to the south of Barqa's coastal cities but is nonetheless connected to them via tribal linkages and commerce. Here, clashes have erupted between the town's long-marginalized non-Arab African minority, the Tabu, and the Zway, an Arab tribe favored by Qaddafi. Bereft of both legitimacy and the ability to project its authority, the NTC dispatched brigade coalitions and delegations of tribal elders to quell the fighting—both have failed to cement long-term peace.

The multiple sources of eastern instability—federalist activism, Salafi extremism, and ethnic infighting—are best addressed in the long term by an effective constitution and the formalization of the security sector. Obviously, these are priorities that affect the country as a whole, but they have special relevance to the eastern region. By delineating local and national authority over municipal services, budgets, and security, the constitutional process will be a litmus test for consolidating unity between east and west. Similarly, formalizing and integrating the country's numerous revolutionary brigades into the army and police will help end a rising wave of violence in Benghazi, curtail the spread of Salafi militancy, and bring lasting peace to Kufra. It will also help restore eastern confidence in the national government by removing the disproportionate influence the western brigade coalitions have on key ministries.

The Roots of Eastern Distinctiveness

Stretching from the coastal town of Sirte to Egypt and southward to the Saharan border with Chad, the Barqa region comprises a population of 1.6 million—less than a third of the Libyan populace. Ethnically, the area is divided between a largely urban Arab population spread among towns in the mountainous coastal region and a more rural, black minority, the Tabu, who inhabit the south. The region is home to several hundred tribes; by one estimate, the largest concentration in all of Libya.[3] Nearly every tribe in the east has branches elsewhere in Libya, so much so that Barqa is sometimes referred to as a microcosm of the entire country. "The east is 'Libya Minor,'" as one eastern activist interviewed by the author in July 2012 put it.

Despite the prevalence of tribal affinities, eastern distinctiveness has largely urban roots; its epicenter is the area's largest city, Benghazi. There, a thriving merchant class, a long tradition of education, and a pervasive culture of cosmopolitanism combined to produce a distinctly political self-awareness. Added to this is the city's pivotal role in many of the country's defining events. The legendary anticolonial guerilla leader Omar Mukhtar is buried just south of the city in Suluq, the Sanussi monarchy had its seat in Benghazi until 1954, and Benghazi is where Qaddafi himself launched his 1969 revolution, with many of his co-conspirators drawn from eastern families. And of course it was ground zero for the 2011 revolt against the dictator.

There is the widespread sense, therefore, that the city—and the east in general—has long served as the engine of historic change for the whole of the country. "When Benghazi sneezes, Libya catches a cold," goes an old saying in the area. Much of this influence, again, stems from Benghazi's connectedness via familial linkages to the rest of the country, particularly in Misrata, Zawiya, Zuwara, Nafusa, Zintan, and even specific neighborhoods in Tripoli: Tajura, Suq al-Juma'a, and Fashlum.

In the debate over federalism and self-government for the east, these relationships have served dual purposes. For opponents of autonomy, they are reminders of the artificiality of the east's separateness from the rest of the country. For federalism's advocates, these connections serve as alliances and networks of support—almost fifth columns of sympathy. "Benghazi and her sisters" (*Benghazi wa akhawatiha*) is a common refrain among federalists. It is important to note that in the Libyan context, many citizens do not have a common understanding of what is meant by "federalism." For some, it implies decentralized, local governance; for others, outright secession.

Against this backdrop, the long period of neglect during the Qaddafi era was, for many easterners, especially ironic. Although many of his co-conspirators in the 1969 coup hailed from eastern families, Qaddafi realized that future resistance to his rule would ultimately emanate from the east, given the influence of the Sanussi monarchy and the area's powerful Saadi tribes. Shortly after seizing power, he began purging Sanussi officers from the army, dismantling Sufi orders, and expropriating land from Saadi notables and granting it to tribes of lesser status. Although he did not officially declare a capital, he began moving the bulk of government offices from Benghazi to Tripoli and later, in 1977, to his hometown of Sirte. Other institutions of economic and symbolic value were relocated as well: the oil ministry, the Olympic committee, and the Libyan national airline. Even the venerable University of Benghazi—the Arab world's third-oldest university—was considered for relocation. "If the university had wheels, I would move it," Qaddafi is purported to have said.

The development of Libya's hydrocarbon sector added another irritant into the already-combustible mix of eastern grievances. Roughly two-thirds of Libyan oil production comes from the Sirte Basin and the eastern Benghazi region, but oil revenues have had very little effect on easterners' living conditions and infrastructure.

The Movement for Autonomy and Its Opponents

The issue of federalism and autonomy in the east has emerged as a major source of political tension and instability in the post-Qaddafi period. Much of this may have been linked to the temporal character and questionable legitimacy of the NTC, which spurred opposition not just from the east, but throughout the country. At one level, eastern suspicion was rooted in the composition of the NTC and its cabinet. At another, it reflected widespread frustration that even routine administrative services, like passport renewal, required an arduous twelve-hour drive to Tripoli. Regardless, by late 2011 there was mounting concern in the east that the post-revolutionary government would continue the hypercentralization and neglect that defined the forty-two-year reign of Qaddafi.

On March 6, 2012, a conference of 3,000 delegates in Benghazi announced the creation of the Cyrenaica Transitional Council, also known as the Barqa Council. Its head is Ahmed Zubayr al-Sanussi—the great nephew of King Idris and a political prisoner under Qaddafi for thirty-one years.[4] According to a senior official in the council, its second-tier leadership is diverse, comprising over 350 members of tribes, professionals, and ex-revolutionaries (*thuwwar*), represented equally by the far east, the Green Mountains, Benghazi, and Ajdabiya. The council also fields an armed wing, the Army of Barqa (Jaysh Barqa), commanded by Hamid al-Hassi, a former Libyan Army colonel with extensive frontline experience in the revolution.

In its initial statement, the Barqa Council appeared to reject the domestic legitimacy of the NTC entirely, accepting its writ only in the international arena. A senior member of the Barqa Council listed key grievances as the NTC's relocation of Libya's equivalent of the social security administration to Tripoli and the marginalization of easterners on recent lists for graduate scholarships abroad and ambassadorial appointments. The most significant complaint, however, was the NTC's allocation of seats for the GNC—60 for the east, 100 for Tripoli, and 40 for the southwest. In its statement of demands, the Barqa Council called for an election boycott but then shifted to demanding greater representation in the GNC. According to one analyst with a Western nongovernmental organization (NGO) in Libya, the federalists' boycott was only partially grounded in ideology; another reason was that they simply "didn't get their act together in time" to field an effective electoral campaign.

This constant shifting of the goalpost led some observers to criticize the council for deploying what one activist called "a muddled and illogical discourse." There has been additional criticism, even from supporters of federalism, that the council never adopted a mass mobilization strategy or concerted outreach effort. "They never socialized the idea," noted one local politician. "They never peddled it or widened the circle of discussion." An independent parliamentary candidate echoed this: "The problem with Zubayr is he wanted to force federalism on people. He never sought a popular mandate." Much of this was undoubtedly rooted in public perceptions of the council's elite and intellectual roots. (For instance, the council's vice chairman was Abu Bakr Bu'ira, a U.S.-educated professor of management at Benghazi University.)

The council's influence was further undermined when a number of high-profile figures and groups came out in opposition to its March declaration. These included important religious personalities such as the Grand Mufti, Sheikh Sadeq al-Gharyani; the leader of the Brotherhood-affiliated Justice and Construction Party, Muhammad Sawan; the longtime opposition group National Salvation Front; and the powerful east-based coalition the Union of Revolutionary Brigades (Tajammu Sarayat al-Thuwwar).[5]

In the run-up to the election, the Barqa Council began using armed action and violence to call attention to its demands. Most notably, its supporters set up roadblocks along Libya's main east-west artery at a valley known as Wadi al-Ahmar, which marks the administrative boundary between Barqa and Tripolitania. According to Hamid al-Hassi, the closure was in protest of the parliamentary seat allocation. At another level, though, the closure reflected primarily local grievances related to reparations and mine removal. The protesters argued that force or the threat of force was the only means to get the NTC's attention; sources cited the strong-arm tactics of western brigades from Misrata and Zintan, which were successful in securing concessions from the government, as examples of their strategy.

For many Libyans, however, the road closure was a bridge too far—it stopped thousands of citizens from traveling the east-west corridor and forced others to clog the country's already-shaky domestic air service. The closure was followed on July 1 with an attack on the electoral committee's offices in Benghazi by stick-wielding demonstrators—an effort to disrupt the voting by destroying the ballots and other key materials. (Libyan observers in Benghazi at the time referred to the instigators as club-wielding "thugs," or *baltijiya*.) The public response was swift and unequivocal. Benghazi's local brigades mobilized to disperse and arrest the attackers, while the following nights saw massive counterdemonstrations in favor of elections. Public opinion seemed to be tilting sharply against the Barqa Council and its activism. A senior official in the council noted as much in an interview on July 3, arguing that the road closure was finally lifted because, "in the end, we realized we were hurting Barqa more than helping it."

The federalists were dealt the most severe blow when voters in Benghazi handed a victory to party list candidates from Mahmoud Jibril's National Forces Alliance, defying predictions both of a widespread boycott and of a landslide victory for the Justice and Construction Party, which has strong roots in the east.[6] Certainly, there were outbreaks of violence, but not on the scale predicted. In Benghazi, pro-autonomy activists attacked a voting station, and a machine-gun assault on a helicopter carrying election materials killed one official. In Ajdabiya, local police shot dead a pro-federalism protester after he apparently tried to steal a ballot. Just days before the elections, the Army of Barqa shut down the oil terminals at Ras Lanuf, Sidra, Brega, and Zuwaytina.[7]

At the close of voting, however, the mood in the east was one of euphoria and relief. Jibril's National Forces Alliance adopted a conciliatory posture toward the region, offering to form a grand coalition.[8] At a subsequent meeting of independents and smaller party delegates, the so-called "third force" that is unconnected to either the National Forces Alliance or the Justice and Construction Party agreed that the positions of prime minister and chairman/speaker of the GNC should be split between the east and the southwest.[9] In early August, the GNC selected Muhammad al-Magariaf, a longtime oppositionist and the head of the

National Salvation Front, to be its chairman. The selection of al-Magariaf, who hails from Ajdabiya, was greeted with applause in the east—both as a signal of provincial inclusion and as a clean break from the Qaddafi era. Unlike many in the NTC, al-Magariaf was never connected to the dictator's government.

Moving forward, it is clear that the high voter turnout in the east represented an upset for the militant federalists. Added to this, the federalist movement was afflicted by a number of defections in mid- and late-2012. Most notably, a feud emerged between Zubayr and Bu'ira over control of the movement, with Bu'ira breaking away to form his own political party, the National Union Party, on August 2.[10] There were additional indications that the federalists were attempting to work within the framework of Libya's institutions and elected government. For example, as of early 2013, the military wing of the Barqa Council was still nominally under the Ministry of Defense and Hamid al-Hassi had reportedly taken up a position in the office of the Chief of Staff. Most significantly, demonstrations that were planned on the second anniversary of the Libyan Revolution on February 15, 2013, did not materialize on the scale anticipated after a coalition of federalists groups pulled out.[11]

That said, the issue of federalism and decentralization is not dead. Indeed, the underlying grievances of the East that fueled the movement have intensified. In particular, oil-revenue sharing is a key point of contention. Added to this, the government's inability to replace armed brigades with trained police in Benghazi has spurred increasing frustration in the east.

Successful elections do not, therefore, absolve the GNC from remedying the disparities between east and west, building effective governance, and reconstituting the security forces. This imperative is especially pressing in the east's enclaves of militant Salafism.

Salafi Militancy in the East

Since early 2012, a rejectionist strain of Salafism in the east has asserted itself in a number of attacks on Western interests, such as World War II graves, the International Committee for the Red Cross, the U.S. consulate, and a motorcade of the United Nations Support Mission in Libya. Added to this, Salafis have attacked Sufi graves, shrines, and mosques across the country. While these acts hardly represent mainstream Salafi sentiment in the country, they are symptomatic of an intense debate under way between an older generation of Salafis that has embraced political participation and a newer cadre that rejects democracy. In many cases, members of the militant current were residing abroad prior to the 2011 revolt, returned home, and have since been trying to assert themselves through excessive zealotry in the realm of Islamic social mores, eschewing electoral participation, and sending volunteers and material aid to Syria and Gaza.

Salafism in Libya is not a uniquely eastern phenomenon, but it has strong roots in the east, given the area's commingling of religion and politics under the Sanussiya. Partly as a result of developments in neighboring Egypt, the Muslim Brotherhood's influence in the east became great in the 1950s and 1960s. The industrial seaport of Darnah emerged as an especially active hub of Islamism. There, growing religiosity combined with mounting economic woes and the collective memory of the town's prominent role in the anticolonial struggle to produce a trend of jihadi volunteerism that sent thousands of young men to Afghanistan in the 1980s and to Iraq after 2003. A similar dynamic was at work in the poorer sections of Benghazi, particularly the Laythi neighborhood, which earned the nickname "Little Kandahar."

Returning veterans of this war formed the Libyan Islamic Fighting Group (LIFG), which had the explicit goal of bringing down the Qaddafi regime. In the mid-1990s, the LIFG, once a clandestine group, came into direct confrontation with the government, resulting in fierce fighting, mass arrests, torture, and most notably, the incarceration of a significant number of key leaders in the Abu Salim prison in Tripoli. The LIFG subsequently renounced violence, a move that was rooted in the prison experience at Abu Salim, shifts in the personal thinking of key figures, and an amnesty program launched by Qaddafi's son, Saif al-Islam.[12] Without going into the full history of this shift, it is sufficient to note that with the fall of Qaddafi and the holding of parliamentary elections, a significant portion of the LIFG's cadre—known in local parlance as *muqatileen* (fighters)—had adopted democratic participation.

Yet the move into politics also produced splits among the *muqatileen*. One faction, led by Abd al-Hakim Bilhaj, the LIFG's former emir and the ex-commander of the Tripoli Military Council, formed the al-Watan Party. But many more *muqatileen* joined a separate party, the Umma al-Wasat, led by Sami al-Saadi, the LIFG's key ideologue who had once authored a seminal anti-democratic tract. Al-Saadi was joined by another central figure in the LIFG, Abd al-Wahhab al-Ghayid (the brother of the late Abu Yahya Libi, widely regarded as al-Qaeda's number two), who ran successfully as a parliamentary candidate in the southern city of Murzuq. In many respects, this fracturing of the politicized *muqatileen* was related to differences over piety and ideological purity. Sami al-Saadi, who holds a master's degree in Islamic law, is regarded as more of a clerical authority than Bilhaj. The leader of the Taliban, Mullah Omar, is reported to have lauded him as the "sheikh of the Arabs." Similarly, Abd al-Wahhab al-Ghayid is known to be a compelling orator and master of jurisprudence (as was his brother), which was clear during a speech he delivered at a commemorative ceremony for the Abu Salim prison massacre in Tripoli on July 29.

While this current entered politics, a parallel faction was forming representing the second generation of Salafi jihadists. These are the sons and nephews of the first generation, who witnessed the 1990s crackdown and torture of their fathers or were incarcerated themselves and radicalized by their experiences. Some went to Afghanistan and Iraq after 2001, were imprisoned by coalition forces, and were repatriated to Libya by British and American intelligence services. In the tumult of the 2011 revolution, they reemerged as leaders of revolutionary brigades in Benghazi, Darnah, and other eastern cities.[13]

Unlike Bilhaj and his cohort, though, this group never relinquished their militant view. A key player is Abd al-Hakim al-Hasadi, who formed the Darnah Brigade in the early stages of the revolution, which was later renamed the Abu Salim Martyrs' Brigade. At some point, al-Hasadi was joined by Sufyan bin Qumu, another veteran of the LIFG, who was associated with Osama bin Laden in Sudan and fought with the Taliban before being arrested by Pakistani authorities and turned over to the United States.[14] Qumu reportedly trained the brigade but later had a falling out with the force, perhaps because of his explicit links to al-Qaeda. Another, more shadowy figure associated with this current is Abd al-Basit Azuz, a former veteran of the anti-Soviet jihad in Afghanistan, who fled Libya for Syria in the 1990s, then lived for a period in the United Kingdom before moving to the Afghanistan-Pakistan border in 2009.[15] According to one report, he was personally dispatched by Ayman al-Zawahiri to Libya in the wake of the 2011 revolts to establish an al-Qaeda foothold in Darnah. An undated online video (probably from the spring of 2012) shows Azuz speaking at a rally in Darnah in the presence of Salim Derby, who was al-Hasadi's successor as the commander of the Abu Salim Martyrs' Brigade and a fellow veteran of the LIFG.[16]

As of mid-2012, the Abu Salim Martyrs' Brigade had become a force unto itself in Darnah. It began closing down beauty parlors and enforcing strict social mores in the city. In Darnah's central court, it hung up a banner proclaiming Islamic law.[17] Outside the city, in the foothills of the Green Mountains, it is reputed to run a training camp for volunteers in Syria. There are also indications that it is asserting itself through criminal enterprises such as drug smuggling and illicit weapons trafficking to Gaza. On March 2, 2012, the Abu Salim Martyrs' Brigade was reported to have assassinated Muhammad al-Hassi, a former colonel in the Libyan army who was in charge of internal security in Darnah and in line to be the head of the Darnah branch of the Ministry of Interior's new security force, the Supreme Security Committees (SSCs). It is likely that the brigade viewed him as a threat to both their lucrative black market activity and their control of the town's overall security. In any event, on April 11, the brigade had effectively been assigned to the SSCs. The brigade's new commander, Fathi al-Sha'iri, hails from Darnah's most prominent tribe.

In many respects, this institutionalization of the Salafi jihadists marked another phase in their development, a branching off by an even more radical group that coalesced under the name of Ansar al-Sharia, which announced its establishment in April. It is purportedly led by the aforementioned Sufyan bin Qumu in Darnah and is composed of more hardline elements of the Abu Salim Martyrs' Brigade who opposed the brigade's incorporation into the SSC. It is reported to field roughly 300 members and, like the Abu Salim Martyrs' Brigade, is said to maintain a small training camp in a forest outside of Darnah. In an April interview with a jihadist forum, Qumu argued that the brigade was in the forest to guard the city's "steam plant."[18]

An Ansar al-Sharia Brigade also exists in Benghazi, led by Muhammad Ali al-Zahawi.[19] According to the group's Facebook page, al-Zahawi is a former political prisoner under Qaddafi who fought in the battle for Benghazi on March 19 with Rafallah Sahati (a prominent LIFG veteran who was killed in the battle), assumed command of the Rafallah Sahati Brigade, then went on to lead a contingent of eastern fighters in the defense of Misrata. On the political front, he is one of the founders of the High Authority for the Protection and Achievement of the February 17 Revolution and the Society for Islamic Dawa and Reform. According to its pamphlets, Ansar al-Sharia aims to unify all Islamist groups in Libya, wage jihad against "tyrants and polytheists," and eliminate secular courts in the country.[20] Al-Zahawi also made a rare public appearance on local television to condemn the July 7 elections as un-Islamic and to forbid participation in them.[21]

While similarly hardline in its views, the group and its leaders deny any linkages to Qumu's Ansar al-Sharia Brigade in Darnah. The Ansar al-Sharia in Benghazi operates openly in the city and reportedly performs some public service functions such as guarding a hospital, but has refused to fall under the Ministry of Interior's authority. Ansar al-Sharia vehicles and leaders were reportedly present in the initial assault on the U.S. consulate in Benghazi on September 11, 2012, although the group made a statement steadfastly denying involvement while at the same time praising the culprits. In mid October, Libyan authorities announced that a key suspect in the assault was Ahmed Abu Khattala, the leader of the shadowy Abu Obeida bin Jarrah Brigade, but described in press reports as associated with the Ansar al-Sharia. Other reports cite U.S. officials who described the attackers as having linkages to al-Qaeda in the Islamic Maghreb (AQIM) and an Egypt-based jihadist network.[22] While details remain shadowy, these reports show the growing ability of Salafi groups in eastern Libya to form linkages with like-minded militants across North Africa and the Sahel.

Ansar al-Sharia in Benghazi made its most visible entrée into eastern politics in early June, when it organized a rally for likeminded Islamist brigades in support of Islamic law. On the morning of June 7, over 150 vehicles representing fifteen brigades (eleven based out of Benghazi), paraded along the city's waterfront. According to one of the commanders of the participating brigades the parade was "meant to intimidate those who do not want God's law." Yet the rally met with fierce opposition. By late afternoon, groups of civil society activists, including large NGOs and women's groups, had appeared on Benghazi's waterfront to oppose the rally. Many bore flags and placards emblazoned with "Libya is Not Afghanistan."[23] Importantly, the Benghazi counterdemonstration was not an isolated incident. Throughout the east, there has been burgeoning opposition and outreach to Salafi militancy from a range of societal actors.

Local Counterweights to Salafi Militancy

In each of the enclaves where it has enjoyed support, the Salafi rejectionist current has also encountered opposition from civil society activists, tribes, and religious figures. This opposition has been particularly evident in Darnah, a city that, despite its long-standing notoriety as a hotbed for Islamism, has a robust educated class and a thriving NGO scene. Voter turnout in Darnah during the GNC elections was relatively high and Islamists did not make strong gains. Over 140 NGOs operate in Darnah, of which 60 are led by women. A number of liberal theater groups that challenge the Islamic orthodoxy of Ansar al-Sharia have also sprung up— the most notable of these is a troupe called Breeze of Freedom (Nasim al-Huriya). Darnah's university has become a particularly contested area in the struggle, with Salafi groups attempting to impose social restrictions on students. At the same time, it has emerged as a sort of neutral ground for mediation and conflict resolution. A prominent faculty member, Adl al-Unaybah—also a member of Darnah's local council—has emerged as a key mediator with the area's Salafi groups. According to several interlocutors, al-Unaybah convinced the Abu Salim Martyrs' Brigade to affiliate themselves with the SSC. He reportedly tried a similar approach with Ansar al-Sharia but was unsuccessful.

Aside from these interlocutors, there are religious mediators. These clerics hail from the same Salafi milieu as the rejectionists and were perhaps themselves incarcerated at Abu Salim prison, but they evince a more moderate outlook.[24] Chief among these is the Grand Mufti of Libya, Sheikh Sadeq al-Gharyani. Appointed as Grand Mufti by the NTC in May 2011, al-Gharyani has emerged as one of the NTC's foremost conflict mediators, not just on religious issues, but on tribal fighting in the south and west. On the Salafi issue, he has played a central role in condemning the desecration of Sufi shrines.[25] Former *muqatileen* who have joined Bilhaj's al-Watan Party have also played a role in outreach. According to one member of al-Watan: "We try to talk to Ansar al-Sharia. We tell them: 'You can protest, but bring your women and children, not weapons. Don't wear Afghan clothing.' We tell them, 'you should talk to the media.'" The Libyan Muslim Brotherhood is another counterweight; it maintains a robust media network in the east that frequently posts condemnations and counterpoints to Salafi militancy.

Yet the tribes have proven to be the strongest counterweights to Salafism in the east. Tribal elders (known in the local dialect as *wujaha*) have engaged in outreach to the Salafists, attempting to woo them into local councils and incorporate their brigades into the formal security services. And their voices have weight. In an April 2012 interview, Qumu stated that he would obey the dictate of the *wujaha* to integrate Ansar al-Sharia into the Libyan Army or SSC.[26] The tribes have also been a source of extraordinary pressure, which was illustrated on two occasions. First, following the killing of Muhammad al-Hassi, his tribe, the al-Shalawiya, removed Abu Salim Martyrs' Brigade checkpoints in Darnah and briefly chased the brigade out of town for three days. Second, the killing spurred a major conference of eastern tribes south of Darnah sometime in late June. It was agreed that the tribal elders would prevent their youth from joining the Abu Salim Martyrs' Brigade, the Ansar al-Sharia Brigade, and likeminded Salafi groups. Moreover, the tribes agreed that they were not responsible for anyone who entered the ranks of these groups; if a tribal member who joined was killed or detained by police or security services, the traditional tribal law of retribution would not apply.

The results of the elections have further put the Salafi rejectionists on the defensive by revealing that the majority of the Libyan electorate, even in eastern Islamist enclaves like Darnah, is focused on pragmatic, technocratic agendas for developing the country, rather than on piety, charity, and social justice—the traditional selling points of the Islamists. In many respects, the Salafis have yet to find a niche or a compelling cause that will resonate in Libya. Much of this has to do with the country's already-conservative social mores and piety; alcohol is banned and many women adopt the hijab. The more radical elements of the Salafi movement have therefore taken to destroying Sufi shrines and graves that they regard as idolatrous and un-Islamic. These incidents provoked an unprecedented public outcry against the Salafis, as well as the Interior Ministry for failing to prevent the attacks and allegedly permitting them. By many accounts, this violence is not a sign of the Salafis' influence in Libyan society, but rather their isolation and marginalization. "I met with several of the Ansar al-Sharia members," noted one local activist. "They seemed scared. They are constantly under fire because of public anger over their attacks on Sufi sites."

In the wake of the Benghazi consulate attacks, this dynamic was apparent in full force. On September 21 and 22, hundreds of protesters demanded that the government evict Ansar al-Sharia and other Islamist brigades from Benghazi as part of a massive "Save Benghazi" campaign. Other protests soon erupted in Tripoli and the west. The target of the demonstrators' ire was not only the Salafi armed groups, but the government's ambivalence and toleration of their presence.

The net result was that Ansar al-Sharia fled its compound and ceased its presence on the web. The Ministries of Interior and Defense implored the protestors not to attack the compounds of three key brigades that allegedly fell under its authority: the Libya Shield, the Rafallah Sahati Brigade, and the February 17 Revolutionary Brigade. All three have Islamist leanings, yet were subcontracted by the weak central government to provide essential security tasks in Benghazi, such as guarding polling stations and even protecting the consulate itself. As of this writing, there have been token, but largely unsuccessful attempts by the Ministries of Interior and Defense to exert greater oversight of these brigades. The suspects in the assault, however, still remain at large. Most worrisome, in the midst of Benghazi's worsening security vacuum and the inability of the police to provide order, is the fact that local citizens have reportedly welcomed back Ansar al-Sharia and other Islamist brigades to guard crucial facilities like hospitals.

Given these developments, a key priority in the wake of the U.S. consulate attack will be to build policies of inclusive governance, development, and security sector reform in the east. This holds true not just for Barqa's urban coastal areas, but also on the Saharan periphery where a long-forgotten conflict has raged in Kufra since February 2012.

The Tabu-Arab Conflict in Kufra

A longtime hub of trans-Saharan commerce, human labor, and narcotics trafficking, Kufra is a remote town located approximately 540 miles from the coast, in the tri-border area between Egypt, Sudan, and Chad. Of its estimated population of 43,500, the majority are ethnic Arabs from the Zway tribe. Around 10 percent are ethnic Tabu, a group which is found mostly in Chad but also in Libya—in Sabha, al-Qatrun, and Kufra. Since February 2012, fighting between the Tabu and Zway in Kufra has left over 200 killed.

The Zway-Tabu conflict has rippled across Barqa and the whole of Libya on multiple levels. Citing indiscriminate attacks by the Zway and the NTC's inability to stop them, Tabu leader Issa Abd al-Majid threatened to boycott the GNC elections, demanding an international peacekeeping force be stationed in Kufra, and for Tabu representatives to be given seats in the country's cabinet.[27] He has warned of setting up a separate Tabu state in the south as well.

Members of the Zway have also threatened to declare a semiautonomous zone if the fighting continues. Unlike the Tabu, the Zway have a powerful economic lever at their disposal: oil. With vast fields under their sway, they can plausibly claim to control up to 17 percent of Libya's oil output; Zway tribesmen serve as security guards at several refineries and processing stations.[28] On multiple occasions the tribe has threatened to shut down oil production if the NTC did not intervene in Kufra.[29]

A Struggle Over Identity and Resources

The current conflict in Kufra reflects a confluence of national, ethnic, local, and economic factors. At one level, the fighting is a contest over the town's lucrative smuggling networks—by various accounts, the violence erupted in February 2012 when Tabu guards arrested Zway smugglers or when a Zway shopkeeper was killed in a Tabu armed robbery. More broadly, the conflict is a struggle by the Tabu to undo the vestiges of Qaddafi's discriminatory policies that deprived them of citizenship, housing, and medical care and condemned them to serf-like status under the Zway. Qaddafi's policies of Arabization fueled Tabu grievances with the state. During the Libyan-Chadian war (1975–1994), the Tabu in Kufra fell under further suspicion as fifth columns for Chad, while the Libyan government showered the Zway with arms and money to enlist them as state proxies. Added to this, Tabu refugees from northern Chad fled to Kufra, further upsetting the tenuous balance of power between the two groups.

Throughout the late 1990s and into the 2000s, the Tabu in Kufra saw their livelihoods decline precipitously, with the majority of Tabu confined to ghetto-like conditions in the districts of Swaydiya and Qaderfi. In 2007, Qaddafi withdrew Libyan nationality from many Tabu in Kufra, effectively depriving them of health care, housing, jobs, and education. In response, local Tabu formed the Front for the Salvation of Libyan Tabus; widespread rioting and protests ensued. In 2008, the regime suppressed a major Tabu uprising in Kufra, deploying helicopter gunships and tanks.[30] During the 2011 revolt, however, the Zway and the Tabu temporarily shelved their differences and fought together against Qaddafi.

But in the aftermath of Qaddafi's ouster, the conflict reemerged. Each side feels increasingly disenfranchised, believing that the other is quickly gaining economic and political advantage. The absence of the state as a mediator and the general security vacuum has only intensified this perception. Flush with heavy weaponry from the area's local arms depots, Tabu and Zway brigades have mobilized to provide local security and have wrestled for control of cross-border smuggling routes. On this front, the Tabu appeared to have seized the advantage with the tacit endorsement of the government. Suspicious of the Zway as longtime Qaddafi supporters, the NTC invested authority in Issa Abd al-Majid to monitor and guard the southeastern border. In effect, the NTC handed him a near monopoly over the area's illicit economy.[31] Emboldened by this newfound wealth, the Tabu are attempting to reclaim their citizenship, demanding better social services and access to political power. Many complain that, rather than addressing these demands, the government is simply continuing the discriminatory policies of the Qaddafi era.

This perception has been undoubtedly worsened by the contentious cross-border dimension of the conflict. In the wake of Qaddafi's ouster, thousands of Tabu from Chad returned to Kufra, many claiming Libyan citizenship. The lack of accurate record keeping has meant that it is impossible to verify claims. In the run-up to the July 7 GNC elections, the registration of roughly 1,000 Tabu voters in Kufra was rejected by the NTC on the grounds of fraudulent citizenship—approximately 15 percent of Kufra's 7,000 Tabu. While the move undoubtedly had justification in some cases, it inflamed an already-tense situation.

Added to this, many Libyan media outlets and Zway leaders in Kufra have charged that local Tabu are aided by Chadian and Sudanese militias, specifically the Darfurian opposition group, the Justice and Equality Movement (JEM).[32] In many respects, this accusation is convenient scapegoating for what is ultimately a localized Libyan conflict over power and resources. That said, the JEM does have a history of interference in Kufra's affairs that has exacerbated Zway-Tabu tensions. During the 2011 war, for example, the JEM attacked Kufra and fought with Qaddafi's army against revolutionary forces as far west as Misrata. JEM forces fighting in Brega captured a Zway revolutionary leader from Kufra and spirited him to Darfur; he was released only after a ransom of 100,000 Libyan dinars was paid.

The Government Response: Subcontracting Security and Mediation

Hampered by a lack of capacity to project its authority, the government has relied upon coalitions of local militia to restore security and delegations of tribal elders to negotiate ceasefires. In both cases, this informal strategy has failed to provide lasting peace or address the entrenched roots of the conflict. In some instances it has ended up inflaming tensions even more.

In place of the army, the NTC dispatched a coalition of revolutionary brigades known as the Eastern Libyan Shield to Kufra.[33] (In June, a group of Majabra tribal sheikhs from Ajdabiya stopped a contingent of Ansar al-Sharia fighters from moving south to join the fighting in Kufra.[34]) By many accounts the Shield has ended up aggravating the situation in Kufra by adopting a markedly partisan approach to the fighting, with forces augmented by Zway tribal brigades. On several occasions, the Shield was reported to have shelled the Tabu neighborhood of Qaderfi, causing civilian casualties, and at one point undertook a mass expulsion of Tabu from Kufra that, according to Issa Abd al-Majid, amounted to ethnic cleansing. Some Shield commanders appear to believe they are fighting an influx of African volunteers from Kenya, Somalia, Sudan, Chad, and

Mauritania who have come to assist the Tabu.[35] One of the Tabus' key demands has been the withdrawal of Eastern Libyan Shield forces and their replacement by regular units from the Libyan Army.

As of mid-July, the Shield purportedly withdrew and was replaced by new militia coalitions from the Libyan Army and the Union of Revolutionary Brigades, which is also guarding the border. While this is not a viable, long-term solution, it does appear to have quieted the unrest somewhat; the commanders of these brigades are viewed by both Tabu and Zway as neutral and impartial. That said, there may be other costs to this approach. As in other instances throughout the country, the NTC's policy of "deputizing" the brigades to quell local conflicts or exert control over the borders endowed those forces with an unhealthy degree of autonomy and leverage. The Union of Revolutionary Brigades has been allegedly asking for payment directly from European diplomats in return for preventing migrants from sub-Saharan Africa from traversing Libya and flooding southern Europe.

In tandem with the dispatch of brigades, the NTC sent teams of tribal elders, principally from Ajdabiya, to Kufra.[36] When they failed, other tribal sheikhs from Misrata, Nafusa, and Zawiya were dispatched.[37] As of early August, the elders negotiated a shaky truce that appeared to be largely the result of the Eastern Libyan Shield withdrawing from the area.[38]

At the same time this mediation has been under way, the NTC took nascent steps to control the tri-border region between Sudan, Chad, and Libya. In March 2012, a joint border force was established by the three countries, but its deployment has been plagued by delays.[39] Recent weeks have also seen government efforts to register former Tabu revolutionaries and integrate them into the police and army. But there is reportedly hesitation among many Tabu about joining because of concerns about the army's perceived infiltration by Qaddafi-era holdouts.[40] This highlights the need for reforming the security sector which, in tandem with the drafting of an effective constitution, represents the critical next step for the east.

Next Steps in the East:
The Constitutional Hurdle

In the months ahead, the General National Congress will face tough questions about the balance between central government and local administration. Many of these questions will hinge upon the drafting of an effective constitution. Already, there has been significant debate about the process for drafting this document, with many in the east viewing it as a post-election litmus test for the GNC's commitment to resolving east-west differences. In March 2012, the NTC made a remarkable amendment to Article 30 of the constitution when it decreed the document would be drafted by a 60-member committee—the so-called "Committee of 60"—that would be formed along the lines of the body that drafted the 1951 constitution. Its sixty members would be appointed by the GNC to represent each of Libya's three regions. This was seen as a clear effort to win support from the Barqa region. The amendment does differ significantly from the 1951 precedent by stating that any measure must be passed by two-thirds majority plus one—a caveat designed to prevent a single region from overruling the other two, as happened during the 1951 process.[41]

On July 5, 2012—just two days before the elections—the NTC went even further in an effort to head off the expected boycott from the east. It decreed that the Committee of 60 would be elected by popular vote, rather than appointed. The measure met with widespread support in the east, but there were certainly critical voices as well. Some believed that the constitution-drafting process would become excessively politicized and that the members of the committee should be drawn from legal experts, political scientists, and technocrats rather than popularly elected. Others argued that treating each region as a single constituency would marginalize towns and villages with smaller population densities.[42] In a statement after the election, the NTC appeared to leave the door open to even further modification by stating that the eleventh-hour amendment was not legally binding on the GNC.[43] On February 6, 2013, however, the GNC voted to keep the committee as an elected, rather than an appointed body—a deft move that avoided reigniting a contentious issue in the east.

The committee and the GNC face an ambitious timeline for adopting a constitution. According to a recent amendment, the committee has one hundred and twenty days to draft a constitution and then hold a referendum within thirty days. It will then go to the GNC for ratification and promulgation. Many have pointed to likely turbulence in this process, citing the inexperience of both the committee and GNC delegates, the lack of a clear parliamentary bloc, and the potential to conflate national with municipal issues. Others have called for an extension of the timeline, citing the precedent of the 1951 constitution which was formulated in twenty-five months.[44]

Formalizing the Security Sector

Irrespective of the constitutional timeline, the GNC will face the daunting challenge of rebuilding the country's security sector, a task with particularly dire implications in the east given a recent spike in violence in Benghazi and other cities. In July alone, over thirteen Qaddafi-era officials were killed in Benghazi and surrounding cities. Benghazi also witnessed a string of grenade and rocket-propelled-grenade attacks against a courthouse and prisons, kidnappings, and improvised explosive attacks against local security headquarters.[45] The perpetrators of these attacks remain unknown. Some have attributed them to an Islamist vigilante group with a hit list. It may also be attempts by local brigades to strike at the formal organs of the state security apparatus, which are believed to be staffed by Qaddafi-era officials.

Overlaid on all of this is an ongoing feud between tribal opponents and supporters of the late Abd al-Fatah Yunis, the former minister of interior under Qaddafi who defected to become the opposition's military commander during the revolution. He was assassinated under mysterious circumstances in Benghazi on July 28, 2011, and much of the recent violence was clustered around the anniversary of his death. For instance, on the evening of July 31, masked gunmen stormed the Ministry of Interior building in Benghazi and freed his alleged killer.

Regardless of origin, the attacks point to the urgency of addressing the security situation in the east within the framework of broader security sector reform in the country. Specifically, the numerous revolutionary brigades must be integrated into the regular police and army, and young, ex-revolutionary *thuwwar* must be given opportunities for job training or further education. Much of the work will have to focus on the ad hoc and temporary security bodies that were created or tolerated by the NTC. In some cases, they are billed as holding pens or halfway houses for revolutionary brigades on the road to dismantlement and integration into the police and army. In others, they are bottom-up initiatives by the brigade commanders themselves, to resist the incorporation of their fighters into the army or police and to preserve the cohesion of the brigades—albeit under a different name. The central government will have to find a way to either dismantle those forces or bring them under tighter control.[46] Otherwise, they run the risk of evolving into a sort of shadow state that subverts the development of democratic institutions.

Among these bodies, the most problematic is the Supreme Security Committee, which falls under the Ministry of Interior. Numbers of the force remain murky, with the some estimates ranging from 90,000 to 100,000 members. Ostensibly, the force is composed of revolutionary fighters and is meant to temporarily harness their zeal and fighting experience in the service of transitional security, particularly during the election period. Most ominously, the committees have left the brigade structure intact—entire brigades have joined en masse and their commanders have simply switched hats. In late August 2012, there were worrisome indications that the committees in Tripoli were infiltrated by hardline Salafis who had desecrated Sufi sites in Tripoli and Zliian.[47] Paradoxically, then, the committees are perpetuating the very brigade system the NTC was trying to dismantle, running at loggerheads with other demobilization programs under the prime minister's office and minister of defense.[48]

Among Libyan citizens, the SSCs have hardly engendered confidence or trust. While the local police (which also fall under the Ministry of Interior) are derided as Qaddafi-era holdouts, the SSCs are feared as unruly thugs or derided as misfits. Accusations of torture, kidnapping, and murder are widespread. Increasingly, there are signs of a worrisome formality—the uniforms have gotten more standardized and the SSCs now have a website—that suggest they are not going away anytime soon.[49] Most recently, the SSC in Tripoli forced the GNC to back down by threatening a strike after it had called for the resignation of SSC leaders following the desecration of Sunni shrines in late August.

Equally problematic as the SSCs over the long term is the Libyan Shield coalition of brigades from the east, Misrata, and Zintan that effectively functions as a parallel to the anemic Libyan Army. The Shield has often ended up inflaming tensions in the east because its commanders are seen as being party to the local conflict. In many respects, the force is a bottom-up initiative by brigade commanders themselves, designed to resist the incorporation of their fighters into the official army or police departments and to preserve the structure of the brigades—albeit under a different, more official-sounding name.

One Misrata brigade commander, arguably the most powerful military leader in the city, plans to transform the Shield into Libya's reserve military force, which would operate alongside the country's army, navy, and air force, and would be directly run by Libya's chief of staff. According to his plan, Shield members would train one month a year and receive a stipend and medical benefits for themselves and their families. In exchange, they would hand over their heavy weaponry—artillery, tanks, rockets, recoilless rifles—to the Ministry of Defense. The government would buy back the fighters' medium-size weaponry—the 14.5 and 23 millimeter anti-aircraft guns that were staples of the revolution. All these weapons would be stored in regional "military zones," overseen by local Shield commanders. The scheme is purportedly intended to break up the brigades, since recruits join as individuals, not as part of a group. It is hard not to imagine, however, that it is just an ingenious way of preserving the prerogatives of the regional brigades and positioning the Shield as a hedge against an unfavorable political situation in Tripoli.[50]

Yet another brigade initiative that serves as a counterweight to the Libyan Army is the Supreme Revolutionaries' Committee—a coalition of brigades from Tripoli, Misrata, and the Nafusa Mountains that was announced in late July. The committee has asked the Joint Chiefs of Staff to exclude all army officers that fought on Qaddafi's side from the new Libyan Army. The body also agreed on establishing a "political wing" for the committee that will be responsible for holding ministries and state institutions accountable to combat corruption in the Libyan state.[51]

In the last months of its tenure, the NTC took some steps to demobilize the brigades and integrate their young fighters into society. At the forefront of this effort is an initiative from the prime minister's office called the Warrior's Affairs Commission for Development (known locally as the WAC). The WAC has registered nearly 215,000 revolutionary fighters and collected data on them as well. It functions as a sort of placement service, moving these young men into the police and the army, or sending them on scholarships abroad, furthering their education at home, or giving them vocational training. After vetting and screening, roughly 140,000 are now eligible for placement; what happens to the other 65,000 remains to be seen. According to one WAC official interviewed in September 2012, the implied goal of the committee is to break up the brigades by appealing to individual interest, "We need to appeal to the *thuwwar's* ambitions and desire for a better life. We need to tell him that the brigades cannot offer you anything." Unsurprisingly, the reaction from the brigades has been tepid.

Institutional Development in a Security Vacuum

Although fears of the east's secession and potential autonomy have subsided, many pressing security concerns that will challenge the GNC remain. The recent GNC elections represented a mandate for territorial unity, but there is still the potential that high expectations for economic growth and political inclusion will be unmet. A number of armed groups in the east maintain the capacity to play a spoiler role. Added to this is the mounting scale of assassinations, kidnappings, and bombings that have afflicted Benghazi.

Aside from the security vacuum, the most pressing conflicts within the east are the rise of Salafi militancy and Tabu irredentism. In both cases, the gap between central authority and local governance has exacerbated long-standing tribal and generational conflicts. The weakness of the formal security sector has meant that the state has devolved enforcement and mediation to informal actors—brigade coalitions and tribal elders. These stopgap measures have frequently inflamed the situation and handed an unhealthy degree of leverage to the brigades and tribal leaders.

One of the new parliament's core tasks, therefore, will be to hasten the institutional development of the police and army, as well as the judiciary. Much of this is already happening, unplanned, at the local level. The new government would be wise to harness this momentum, rather than implementing a top-down approach that does not take local considerations into account, which will be regarded as yet more evidence that Qaddafi's centralizing policies are alive and well. In tandem, the GNC must carefully steer the country through the constitutional process. The prospect for deadlock and polarization remains high, particularly on two issues that could animate violence in the east: local autonomy and the role of Islam in legislation.

In many respects, the outside community has limited leverage over these events. Already, a number of multilateral and bilateral efforts are under way to assist the Libyans with strategic planning in the ministries of defense and interior, to train the police, and to hasten the integration of young fighters. For models of constitution writing and decentralized government, the Libyans could benefit from other countries' experiences—the United States, the United Arab Emirates, and Brazil. But for now, they appear to be drawing both positive and negative lessons from their own country's brief experiment—the 1951 constitution. Regardless of which model is used, the new government must restore the periphery's confidence in the center, repairing the political disconnect between the national government in Tripoli and local councils. Only then will the country's numerous brigades be persuaded to relinquish their autonomy.

Notes

Unless otherwise stated, this chapter draws from interviews conducted by the author in eastern Libya in March and July of 2012.

1   For a representative example, see Aymenn Jawad al-Tamimi, "Libya Heading Toward Islamism," *American Spectator*, November 11, 2011. It is important to note that raising the specter of an Islamist advance in Libya was more prevalent among Western than Arab observers, with the latter noting the fractured nature of Libya's Islamist movement as a key check on its strength. Kamel Abdallah, "Ihtimalat Iqamat Dawla Diniya fi Libya" (Possibility of Establishing a Religious State in Libya), *Al-Siyasa al-Dawliya* (Arabic-language international affairs periodical), October 2011.

2   For more on this typology in the Libyan context, see Brian McQuinn, "Armed Groups in Libya: Typology and Roles," *Small Arms Survey Research Note*, no. 18, June 2012.

3   Faraj Najem, *Tribe, Islam and State in Libya*, unpublished PhD dissertation, 241.

4   See the website of the Barqa Council at www.ctc-ly.org.

5   "Creation of Cyrenaica Council Sparks Furious Federalism Row," *Libya Herald*, March 7, 2012. Also, Rafd Taqsim Libya 'ila Fedralyaat, "Rejection of Dividing Libya Into Federal Sates," al-Jazeera.net, July 21, 2011, www.aljazeera.net/NR/exeres/6C403781-A193-45F8-A392-2A900CB1CD4E.htm.

6   "Jibril's Bloc Wins Party Seats in East Libya," Al-Jazeera, July 7, 2012, www.aljazeera.com/news/africa/2012/07/2012711202926521918.html.

7   "Gunmen Close Libyan Oil Terminals Ahead of Vote," *NOW Lebanon*, July 6, 2012.

8   "Libya Leader Threatens 'Force' to Foil East Autonomy Bid," *Jordan Times*, March 8, 2012.

9   Michael Cousins, "Congress Independent Members Mull PM and Chairman Choice," *Libya Herald*, July 28, 2012.

10 "Federalists Launch Political Party," *Libya Herald*, August 1, 2012.

11 "Federalists Pull Out of 15 February Cyrenaica Demonstrations," *Libya Herald*, February 14, 2013.

12 For background, see "Al-Islamiyun fi Libya: Tarikh wa Jihad" (Islamists in Libya: History and Jihad, parts 2 and 3), *Al-Manara*, January 2012.

13 For background on the Islamists' role in the defense of Benghazi see the interview with Fawzi Bu Katif, *Al-Manara*, February 14, 2012; available at www.almanaralink.com/press/2012/02/10675.

14 For more, see Charles Levinson, "Ex-Mujahedeen Help Lead Libyan Rebels," *Wall Street Journal*, April 2, 2011.

15 Nic Robertson and Paul Cruickshank, "Source: Al Qaeda Leader Sends Veteran Jihadists to Establish Presence in Libya," CNN, December 30, 2011; and Nic Robertson, Paul Cruickshank, and Tim Lister, "Growing Concern Over Jihadist 'Safe Haven' in Eastern Libya," CNN, May 15, 2012. Azuz is also cited in an Amnesty International Report for Syria in 1995.

16 See www.youtube.com/watch?v=5ytkhjMd4PQ.

17 See the Abu Salim Martyrs' Brigade's "*shari'a* session" at www.youtube.com/watch?v=LYIF74yCRxw&feature=related.

18 See interview in the jihadist web forum Tamimi: http://tamimi.own0.com/t97883-topic#686380.

19 See www.facebook.com/anssarelsharieah.

20 Ansar al-Shari'a's pamphlet is found at http://a5.sphotos.ak.fbcdn.net/hphotos-ak-ash3/541262_337055756351449_310853968971628_938176_1789504486_n.jpg.

21 *Al-Hurra* TV (Libya), June 19, 2012.

22 Eric Schmitt, "Petraeus Says U.S. Tried to Avoid Tipping Off Terrorists After Libya Attack," *New York Times*, November 16, 2012; and Siobhan Gorman and Matt Bradley, "Militant Link to Libya Attack," *Wall Street Journal*, October 1, 2012.

23 Misbah al-Awami, "Khilal Al-multaqa al-Awal Li-Ansar al-Sharia bi-Benghazi ... Muslahun Yasta'radun Quwatahum ... Wa Makhawif Min Tahu Libya li-Dawla Mutatarrifa" (During the First Gathering of Ansar Al-Shari'a in Benghazi, Armed Men Displayed Their Strength Amidst Fears of Libya Turning Into an Extremist Country), *New Quryna*, June 14, 2012, www.qurynanew.com/36582.

24 For a representative example see the article: Sa'ad al-Na'as, "Ansar al-Shari'a wa Islam" (Ansar al-Sharia and Islam), *al-Watan* (Libya), June 28, 2012.

25 At the same time, some observers have criticized him for ambiguity on the desecration of shrines and for not being forceful enough. For video of his rulings on Sufi shrines, see www.youtube.com/watch?v=-8OZvlDvCkI.

26 See the interview posted in the jihadist web forum, http://tamimi.own0.com/t97883-topic#686380.

27 "Libyan Tabu Tribe Threatens Election Boycott," Associated Press, July 2, 2012.

28 Geographic Services, Incorporated, "Geographical and Tribal Factors at Play in Kufrah, Libya," September 22, 2011.

29 "Zway Tribesman 'Cut' Oil Production," *Libya Herald*, July 4, 2012, www.libyaherald.com/?p=10480.

30 For background on the conflict, see Philip Martin and Christina Weber, "Ethnic Conflict in Libya: Toubou," Norman Paterson School of International Affairs, Carleton University, June 21, 2012, and "Libye: Quand les Toubous se Réveillent," *Jeune Afrique*, May 5, 2012.

31 "Jibril's Bloc Wins Party Seats in East Libya," *Al-Sharq al-Awsat*, July 7, 2012, www.aljazeera.com/news/africa/2012/07/2012711202926521918.html.

32 Shuhood 'Ayan: Hajum Quwat Muslaha min al-Tabu al-Chadiyeen wa Harakat al-Adl wa Masawah 'ala Madinat al-Kufrah" (Eye Witnesses: Attacks by Armed Forces of Chadian Tabus and Justice and Equality Movement on the City of Kufrah), *Al-Manara*, February 13, 2012.

33 There are three branches of the Libya Shield forces: a Western Shield (a Zintan-based coalition), a Center Shield (led by Misrata), and an Eastern Shield (based in Benghazi).

34 "Al-Kata'ib al-Musharika bil-Multaqa al-Awal Li-Ansar al-Shari'a bi-Benghazi Tatwajah 'ila Kufrah" (The participating brigades in the first gathering of Ansar Al-Sharia in Benghazi head to the city of Kufrah), *New Quryna*, June 12, 2012, www.qurynanew.com/36410.

35 See the April 21, 2012, interview with a commander of the Eastern Libya Shield in Kufra, www.youtube.com/watch?v=1mgP6opsyS4&feature=related.

36 "Kufra Mediation Moves Slowly," *Libya Herald*, June 18, 2012.

37 See the April 21, 2012, interview with a commander of the Eastern Libya Shield in Kufra, regarding the Shield's goals in Kufra and the extent of tribal mediation, www.youtube.com/watch?v=1mgP6opsyS4&feature=related.

38 "Kufra Leaders Agree to Meet and End Violence," *Libya Herald*, August 2, 2012.

39 "Sudan, Chad and Libya Establish Joint Patrols to Control Common Border," *Sudan Tribune*, March 9, 2012.

40 "Tebu Fighters in Kufra to Be Integrated Into Security Forces," *Libya Herald*, May 13, 2012.

41 Translation of the amendment provided by the Project on Middle East Democracy (POMED); available at http://pomed.org/wordpress/wp-content/uploads/2012/07/Constitutional-Amendment-No-1-2012-en.pdf.

42 "Harak Mujtama'i fi Benghazi Hawal al-Mu'atammar al-Watani al-'Am wa al-Hay'ah al-Ta'ssissiyah wa Dustur Libya al-Muqbil" (Benghazi Community Enthusiastic About the General National Conference, the Constitutional Drafting Committee, and Libya's Future Constitution), *Al-Manara*, July 26, 2012.

43 Umar Khan and George Grant, "NTC Takes Responsibility for Constitution From National Conference," *Libya Herald*, July 5, 2012.

44 "Harak Mujtama'i fi Benghazi Hawal al-Mu'atammar al-Watani al-'Am wa al-Hay'ah al-Ta'ssissiyah wa Dustur Libya al-Muqbil" (Benghazi Community Enthusiastic about the General National Conference, the Constitutional Drafting Committee, and Libya's Future Constitution).

45 "Benghazi: Jum'a Sakhina wa Ghayib 'Amni Muqlaq Li-Muwatani al-Madina Benghazi" (A Hot Friday and A Troubling Police Absence for the City's Citizens), *Al-Manara*, July 28, 2012.

46 See background on these structures, Frederic Wehrey, "Libya's Militia Menace," *Foreign Affairs*, July 15, 2012.

47 George Grant, "Why the Supreme Security Committee Must Be Brought to Heel—Before It's Too Late," *Libya Herald*, August 29, 2012.

48 Author's interview with U.S. and European defense officials, Tripoli, Libya, July 2012.

49 "Insihab al-Lajna al-Amniya min Shawara' Benghazi wa Mudiriyat al-Amn al-Watani Tu'akid Qudratiha 'ala Bast al-Amn" (Withdrawl of the Security Committee From the Streets of Benghazi and the National Directorate of Security Confirms Its Ability to Establish Security), *New Quryna*, July 24, 2012, www.qurynanew.com/38949. Also, see the Facebook page for the Benghazi SSC at www.facebook.com/#!/ssc.benghazi.

50 Pamphlet on the Libyan Shield provided to the author, Misrata, Libya, June 28, 2012.

51 "Al-'Alan Rasmiyan 'an Ta'ssis al-Majlis al-'Ala Li-Thuwwar" (Official Announcement of the Supreme Council of Revolutionaries), *New Quryna*, July 29, 2012, www.qurynanew.com/39268.

TUNISIA

Mediterranean Sea

CRETE
(GREECE)

N

Rijdalin
Zuwara
Ras Jdeir
Al-'Assa
Jmail
Zawiya
Tripoli

Baida
Darnah

Wazin-
Dabiha
Nalut
Zintan
Misrata

Benghazi

Libyan Plateau

Nafusa Mts.

TRIPOLITANIA

Gulf of Sidra

Sirte

Zuwaytina

Ghadames

Sidra
Ras-
Lanuf
Brega

L I B Y A

EGYPT

Sabha

FEZZAN

CYRENAICA
(BARQA)

Libyan Desert

Murzuq

Al-Qatrun

Al-Wigh

Sahara Desert

Kufra

ALGERIA

Ma'tan
as-Sarah
Air Base

✝ Border crossing
✧ National capital
● Town or village
═ Major road
--- Traditional provin-
cial boundary
-·- International
boundary
🗪 Dry salt lake

OUZOU STRIP

NIGER

CHAD

SUDAN

0   200 mi

0   300 km

02

Borderline Chaos? Stabilizing Libya's Periphery

Peter Cole

Libya's Border Struggles

The fall of the Qaddafi regime created a persistent crisis of governance in Libya's extensive border areas. Close to a year after the regime's collapse, large swathes of territory along Libya's 4,300-kilometer border remain, in many ways, ungoverned and perhaps even ungovernable. Outside population centers, Libya's armed forces have been unable to control migration and trafficking flowing through the country.

As Libya's army and police forces collapsed during the 2011 conflict, large numbers of armed groups, describing themselves as brigades acting in the name of the February 17 revolution, cropped up in their wake.[1] Many had not participated greatly in the fighting against Qaddafi's forces and therefore had few loyalties other than to the communities from which they sprang; this was particularly so in Libya's border territories, which were far from the revolutionary strongholds of Benghazi, Misrata, and the western mountains. The power vacuum formed in Qaddafi's absence triggered localized conflicts over control of border posts and cross-border trade both between rival communities and between the central government and the many brigades.

The brigades, sometimes from faraway communities and in pursuit of their own interpretation of state functions, have seized control of border posts from Libya's armed forces and Interior Ministry and engaged in their own border control activities. Elsewhere, border communities fight for control of trade routes or simply take the opportunity to settle old scores with those they deem to be either non-Libyans or Qaddafi supporters. The killing has subsided, but the border towns remain in a state of frozen conflict, with the Libyan army simply managing and administering shaky ceasefires. As a result of this fighting, some of Libya's border communities, like the Tabu and Tuareg—both non-Arab sub-Saharan ethnic groups— are less inclined than ever to trust or cooperate with the state. Illicit smuggling has increased, and the country is more dangerous and unpredictable for migrants and traffickers.

Libya's incapacity to control its borders poses considerable problems for all its neighbors. Arms and people that transit Libya flow somewhat freely across the wider Maghreb, thanks to closely connected ethnic groups and organized criminal networks tying the region together. The situation is particularly dire in Mali, where Tuareg rebels in alliance with Islamist groups from across the Sahel used weapons procured in Libya to take control of the northern part of the country. All this negatively affects the security of Europe as well, with trafficked goods and people entering the European Union (EU) proper.

For all its failings, during the 2000s the Qaddafi regime could control that traffic to Europe to a degree. Libya was and is one of the key trafficking hubs into Europe, affecting in particular Malta and Italy, whose island of Lampedusa lies a mere 600 kilometers from Libya's shores. In the 2000s, Europe faced a marked uptick in illegal immigration and narcotics trafficking from West Africa, and the EU turned to Libya and other Maghreb states to tighten up their own borders in response.

Like many things in Libya before 2011, the security services that monitored border traffic were under Qaddafi's thumb. Though it was chaotic and disorganized, at times serving Qaddafi's contradictory policy objectives, the system was working to some extent and had developed a degree of predictability that was lost when the regime was overthrown. The new government may have better intentions than the old—one immigration officer stationed on Libya's coastline lauded the change in regime as finally giving him the chance to do his job free of Qaddafi's manipulation of immigration trafficking—but it has far less knowledge of and control over the actors on Libya's borders.

But in truth, no Libyan government ever fully controlled its own borders and the trafficking that passed across them. The incentives to do so simply never stacked up, for either local government officials or Libya's population. Instead, government negligence or discrimination encouraged border communities, shut out of the formal economy, to participate in informal trade and trafficking. Local government officials, sometimes denied more lucrative career paths in government, also took part, lured by the money and flows from illicit trade.

For Libya to create a truly effective border security strategy, it ideally has to do what no Libyan government before it has done and disentangle the web of economic and local interests that exist in Libya's border communities. This requires grappling with deep-rooted communal issues, not least the issue of citizenship, and developing legal alternatives to the black-market economy. Border forces will need thorough restructuring and training, virtually from scratch, with the army taking over the task of surveillance from the various armed groups that now control Libya's borders. Truly reforming the system will be a long process, which means that Libya's restive borderlands will remain an issue for both Libya and Europe for a long time to come.

Qaddafi's Legacy

With no physical barriers forming Libya's border—save the Mediterranean Sea and the minefields that were the legacy of wars fought with Chad in the 1970s and Egypt during the Second World War—and because Qaddafi invested so little in infrastructure and surveillance, Libya's various security services could only monitor, not prevent, migration and cross-border trade. But their ability to carry out even this function has been affected by legacy issues within the security forces that hamper them still.

Under Qaddafi, the task of monitoring borders was carried out by ill-coordinated and competing departments spread across several ministries.

The management of border posts and processing of visas and passports fell to the Interior Ministry's Immigration Department, while the customs regulator, the General Department for Combating Smuggling and Drugs, was part of the Finance Ministry. Patrol of maritime borders and border posts was equally fragmented between the navy, naval coast guard, and Interior Ministry, with, for example, each of these bodies coordinating independently with European border forces. The Interior Ministry itself was siloed, with regional branches operating almost autonomously from each other and from the ministry's central bureaucracy in Tripoli.

Consequently, individual border posts and towns enjoyed large degrees of autonomy. Few officials outside the major cities and ports had computers, and so the ability to access databases for travel documents or international blacklists, for example, was sometimes nonexistent.[2] As a result, there were multiple lines of authority within each post. Facilities were woefully underresourced; border posts were sometimes little more than shacks, lacking even electricity.

Governance of some border territories, notably al-Wigh near the Niger border and the Ma'tan as-Sarah air base near Sudan, was handed over to the army, but this did not provide any centralized, coordinated control either. Qaddafi had deliberately divided and fragmented the force's operations and chains of command. There was no defense ministry, with the army's various branches instead reporting separately to Qaddafi personally via an Interim Defense Committee. The various brigades that made up Libya's armed forces were kept in separate bases with separate communications frequencies and chains of command to Interim Defense. While the official National Army was stationed in and recruited mainly from the east, other brigades stood apart from the rest, with higher pay and better equipment.

This fragmentation allowed Qaddafi to easily override individual ministries or departments responsible for implementing a particular area of policy. A lack of coordination and of clear chains of command left Qaddafi the sole authorized decisionmaker. Border management, therefore, could be as quixotic and contradictory as the dictator's personality. In general, though, Qaddafi successfully exercised some control over the borders.

Under pressure from European countries, and particularly Italy, Qaddafi managed to tighten the security of Libya's maritime borders to prevent smuggling of people and goods to Europe. These efforts were given political impetus by Qaddafi's public abandonment of his weapons of mass destruction program in 2004, and 2007 saw a watershed bilateral agreement with Italy that set up joint maritime patrols, allowing the Libyan and Italian navies to coordinate their efforts. Italian companies also agreed to supply border surveillance equipment. With Qaddafi's support, illegal immigration and narcotics trafficking from Libyan shores to Europe drastically subsided between 2008 and 2010.

In addition, Libya tightened up, though did not substantially update, its archaic laws governing border flows—some of which had been unchanged since the 1950s. In 2004, Libya increased the penalties levied against smugglers, the people being smuggled, and others violating immigration requirements, and laws governing the employment of foreigners were tightened in 2007.[3] In 2010, it further increased penalties imposed upon those who entered or stayed in Libyan territory without the required permissions; illegal migrants, whether trafficked willfully or not, were subjected to either a 1,000 Libyan dinar fine (today around $800) or indeterminate imprisonment.[4] The government also redefined Libyan nationality rules to make Libyan citizenship distinct from citizenship of other Arab countries for the first time since 1954. With such changes, Libya did little to observe or entertain European insistence on human rights for migrants, and European powers did not insist strongly on such delicate issues at a time when tentative progress was being made elsewhere in relations with Qaddafi. Migrants "pushed back" from Europe were usually left to an uncertain fate.[5]

This toughening up of Libya's legal system and maritime security radically benefited Europe. Italy in particular was able to implement a so-called "pushback" policy in May 2009 that allowed the government to deport illegal immigrants directly back to Libya without independently assessing their asylum claims, according to one former Italian diplomat. The resulting radical drop in arrivals in Europe from over 37,000 in 2008 to 4,300 in 2010 illustrated just how effective such agreements could be for European powers.[6]

Still, Qaddafi was not fighting the traffickers by sealing Libya's borders but by applying pressure primarily on sea routes from Libya to Europe. Europe secured the cooperation of a government that was so intimately bound up with illegal trafficking that it was able to influence and control it, "turning off the taps" of migrant flow to Europe at Qaddafi's will. And with policymaking so dependent upon Qaddafi's whims and preferences, and his use of different branches of the security services to pursue different policy aims, confusion and frustration spread lower down the ranks, where no one was sure what "official" policy was.

One former member of Qaddafi's internal security force who worked on efforts to counteract illegal migration—interviewed after his defection to the February 17 revolutionary movement—complained bitterly that coordination between the coast guard, the Interior Ministry, and the military prisons that housed captured migrants was so bad that some of those captured while attempting maritime crossings were released. On more than one occasion, the officer suspected, instructions given to one branch would contradict the processes followed by another. Both Libyan government officials and diplomats believed that trafficking boats to Europe were allowed to continue whenever Qaddafi found it suitable. One officer interviewed suspected that some arrested migrants were deliberately released back into the arms of human traffickers operating in the port town of Zuwara, a key hub for migrants traveling by boat to Europe; he also alleged that some were recruited into the military.

Libya's Black Market

Though Qaddafi could stem flows of migrants across Libya's maritime borders, the regime never succeeded in increasing its control over its southern border. Partly, this was the result of policy calculation. A police officer in the far southern town of Murzuq told of the varying degrees of commitment with which the army in the nearby military base of al-Wigh would pursue human traffickers entering from Niger, advising traffickers of current policy according to Qaddafi's calculations and orders at the time. But failure to control the southern border also reflected a structural issue, which was the close web of personal relationships between local government officials, between Qaddafi's middlemen and representatives who oversaw them, local community notables, and trafficking networks. It will be extremely difficult for the new government to address this entrenched system of state subversion and gain full control of the country's borders.

The movement of and trade in goods across borders, usually for significant markups when the traffic occurred between far-flung communities, was—and continues to be—the bedrock of the local Libyan economy, with roots far deeper than the Libyan state. Indeed, Libya's legal system still does not clearly criminalize some aspects of the trafficking economy and does not fully comply with the UN Convention on Transnational Organized Crime, particularly where collusion with local authorities is concerned.

Throughout Qaddafi's state, a host of incentives motivated actors at nearly every level of society to participate in the black market. Interviews with Libyan immigration officials, smugglers, and local officials provide an overall picture of how the system worked, although the corroboration of specific points is not always possible. Essentially, all interviewees agreed that both government officials and the local population had incentives to allow smuggling to continue. Land-border officials regularly held up and examined border traffic, whether illegal or legal, for multiple days, but the imposition of such obstacles was driven as much by incentives to enact a kind of toll—since with small payments, traffic could either bypass the border altogether or expedite customs inspections—as it was by the desire to enforce procedure. Though local officials obstructed traffic, their livelihoods were enriched by its continuance.

Qaddafi's government relied on the empowerment of trusted individuals who, by being in Qaddafi's confidence, were able to route around the relatively powerless government apparatus. Those individuals were well placed to profit from the informal economy in Libya's major cities and administrative centers. For example, Colonel Masoud Abdul Hafidh, the governor of Sabha, a military zone under Qaddafi, collected tariffs from smugglers operating within his jurisdiction, as did community leaders from the Arab Zway community, heavily supported by Qaddafi, in Kufra.[7] Qadhadfa community leaders themselves controlled trade in some goods.[8]

Similarly, locals too had many incentives and opportunities to collaborate with and participate in cross-border trafficking. According to interviews conducted with Libyan merchants and smugglers in Sabha earlier this year, at the small end of the scale, it was normal for Libyans traveling south to bring excess amounts of (heavily subsidized) fuel and food with them, and return with white goods, drugs, cigarettes, or alcohol, the distribution of which was heavily restricted in Libya. Larger commercial-scale ventures arbitraging food and fuel could be extremely profitable, but that required a more substantial investment. In the south of the country, cross-border trips, depending on the destination, took anything from fifteen days to a month, with the more committed smugglers managing a maximum of two trips per month. While a single trip could net anything from 100 to 10,000 or more Libyan dinars (approximately $8,000) this amount would be expected to be distributed among three to four families participating in the voyage, as well as safe house operators en route, interviewees explained. The amounts earned would be relatively small for the risk and time involved in undertaking the voyage (the risks from banditry were highest of all), though it would still significantly outweigh the few hundred dinars a month available through salaried state employment.

In particular, the socioeconomic position of the Tabu and Tuareg facilitated such activities. Both Tabu and Tuareg habitually socialized with and married their kin from other clans in different communities and countries. This strengthened their ties to relations in Chad, Niger, Mali, Algeria, and Mauritania. Tabu and Tuareg traveled regularly across borders to visit relatives and move livestock herds for grazing or for sale. In doing so, it was common for them to circumvent the official border crossings in order to avoid multiday delays. For some members of these groups, as well as Arab communities such as the Awlad Suleyman and Warfalla, who also had relatives across the Sahel, that type of movement relatively easily transitioned into the transit of goods back and forth. Border posts would normally be informed of this traffic, and often the illegal routes would not stray far from official roads or border posts.

The informal economy was thus recognized by border officials, and even regulated, but not controlled. Individual officials would benefit from kickbacks and the locals would benefit from the fast transit of goods. Indeed, recruits from the Tabu and Tuareg were present in the low-level ranks of the police and army, and many shared the same economic and citizenship issues as their kin working the black-market economy. Normally, this kind of illicit trade proved more lucrative than state employment, helping to thoroughly inculcate the black-market system into Libyan society.

The human trafficking economy was also well-established, providing both tariff income, a labor pool, and even military recruits to the state. Previously, human traffickers operated some of the more established and well-traveled routes into Libya. On the southern border, migrants tended to enter either through al-Wigh and Qatrun from Niger and western Africa, through a particular valley in the Tibesti mountains from Chad, or to Kufra from Sudan and eastern Africa. Once there, migrants were placed in safe houses; they would normally then work to supply the funds required for onward movement to the northern coast, where, again, many would either settle or work in order to provide funds for onward movement. The trafficking networks were therefore not only well-established but integrated into the local economy, and though the state often knew of their existence, the incentives to clamp down on such networks were not always clear. Illegal labor was also used to provide many state services that Libyan nationals would not touch.

With the fall of the Qaddafi government, migrant trafficking increased significantly. While some armed groups on the border tolerated and even participated in the trafficking, some revolutionary brigades engaged in roundups and attempted to disrupt the trade. Similarly, trade in illicit goods, not least the weaponry raided from Qaddafi's army stores, drastically increased, while also triggering fighting between ethnic communities in the south.

The same incentives that permit cross-border trade of goods and people—a lack of alternative employment, poor state salaries, strong cross-border communal ties, the expense and effort needed to thoroughly monitor Libya's land borders—that existed under Qaddafi persist today. And given the dearth of economic alternatives for many in southern Libya, that is unlikely to change in the near future. All of this makes securing Libya's border regions very difficult.

The Fall of the Regime and Its Consequences

The collapse of the Qaddafi regime upset an order that had held for forty-two years. Regional governors fled, and any community that had benefited in some way from Qaddafi's policies, such as the Qadhadfa tribe or the Tuareg, found themselves subject to challenges and competition from previously disadvantaged groups. The south also saw an influx of armed groups from the north, only partially disciplined and coordinated, some of which attempted to police or control trafficking. The resulting uncertainty had profound consequences both for the state's ability to manage Libya's borders and for the fate of communities that live there and engage in cross-border activities.

The surviving border management bureaucracy attempted to continue its work much as before, despite the death or flight of the Qaddafi family, a significant cadre of military generals and officers, and leading decisionmakers within the Interior Ministry. Yet they were challenged by a variety of armed groups that had taken control of border crossing points as Qaddafi's forces withdrew or collapsed. The earliest ports in the east to come under rebel control—including Benghazi airport, Tobruk seaport, and the land-border crossing of Salloum—did so immediately after the defection of the eastern division of the National Army, before armed civilian groups had a chance to coalesce. But thereafter, as the National Army took a backseat during much of the fighting, subsequent borders and ports fell to civilian groups.

Libya's interim government, the National Transitional Council (NTC), was able to do little to influence the activity of these groups, and it could not replace them. As a stopgap measure, the NTC's interior and defense ministers registered and officially sanctioned the local military councils and the myriad of brigades across Libya's borderlands. In reality, however, they were sometimes little more than local youth, some with military training, who had banded together to protect their towns from whatever eventuality lay in store for them.

The brigades that had formed and fought during the 2011 movement to overthrow Qaddafi were quite different. Those brigades, based essentially in Benghazi, Misrata, Zintan, and recently Tripoli, had merged into large, well-organized coalitions spread across the country.[9] They moved into Libya's central and southern hinterland aiming to protect key infrastructure and monitor conflicts emerging in border communities. By April 2012, they had formalized and legitimized their operations with the Ministry of Defense, calling themselves the Libyan Shield Forces.[10]

In turn, the National Transitional Council and the Libyan Shield Forces attempted to fold the local groups manning Libya's borders into a "Border Guard." But the armed groups controlling Libya's borders lacked the kind of centralized management and recognized military leadership that the Libyan Shield Forces and the revolutionary brigades of Misrata, Benghazi, and Zintan possessed. Without such structures, any project aimed at coordinating these local groups meant little in practice, particularly given the meager infrastructure and communications available on Libya's far-flung borders. While the armed forces' new chief of staff, Yusuf al-Manqoush, was able over the course of 2012 to assert his executive authority over the field operations of the Libyan Shield Forces, he was not able to do so over the armed groups on the border. This was also because the NTC itself resisted giving Manqoush the legal authority to rein in those forces; it was feared that if he was given that authority, the chief of staff would become too powerful compared to the nascent Defense Ministry.

In February, the NTC in its wide-ranging Law No. 11, which redefined the relationship of the Defense Ministry to the chief of staff, made the deputy minister of defense, Siddiq Mabrouk, the head of the Border Guard—and the ministry authorized units from local border towns such as Murzuq, Zuwara, Kufra, and elsewhere to act in its name.[11] This gave armed groups controlling local border posts a semblance of legitimacy in the form of registration and brought them nominally under the authority of the Interior Ministry, though such formalities meant little in practice. Meanwhile, the Interior Ministry departments responsible for administrative procedures such as customs and travel documents inspection were, for the most part, permitted to return to work. This state of affairs, unsatisfactory though it was, allowed the NTC to save face with the armed groups that effectively controlled Libya's territory.

But Mabrouk's command and control over the Border Guard, as the defense minister himself acknowledged in an interview in April 2012, was often little more than nominal.[12] The authorization of guard units was largely a temporary political compromise to satisfy local communities in control of border posts and not a genuine effort to build an effective force. The fact that the Interior Ministry and its Immigration Department remained in organizational disarray, with key decisionmakers removed, equipment lacking, and central and regional units noncommunicative with each other, did not help.

Consequently, Libya's borders came under parallel, duplicated management, with the old official government departments going through the motions, while local networks observed, or carried out, duplicate border management activities side-by-side with them. As a consequence of poor management during the Qaddafi years, each post was shorn of connections to any kind of central command within the Interior Ministry, a problem compounded by the fact that the regular units now working in those posts did not trust official channels. Each post therefore operated on its own, obeying local dynamics. In the far-flung land borders, particularly those in the south across which most illegal human and commercial traffic flowed, the Interior Ministry was sometimes unable to deploy people at all, or had only token representation.

Armed groups took advantage of this dearth of official leadership to take control of border territories and posts. Misratan civilian fighters, during the lengthy siege of their town in April 2011, took control of Misrata's sea ports and airports. After Tripoli fell in August 2011, fighters from Zintan gained control of the international airport.[13] Zuwaran fighters took the Ras Jdeir border crossing with Tunisia—one of the country's busiest—from retreating Qaddafi forces, according to residents of Zuwara, Rijdalin, and Jmail, and other border posts fell to different groups, like the Tabu.

The Interior Ministry was able to deploy customs officials and immigration officers in Ras Jdeir, but brigades from the nearby town of Zuwara operated their own checkpoints. The same held true in other land-border areas. Throughout 2011 and 2012, the NTC attempted to withdraw certain armed groups from major ports and airports without success. Notably, attempts to pull back Zuwaran military brigades from the Ras Jdeir met with violent opposition. Likewise, attempts to dismiss Zintani brigades from Tripoli airport foundered repeatedly, though in May the forces did withdraw, only to be replaced by other militia brigades from Misrata.[14]

While informally, brigades and military councils acknowledged the material gains they made from controlling border crossings, some were also genuinely motivated to support the state. In an effort to demonstrate their own credibility, local military councils and their brigades took on a variety of roles typically reserved for the state, including border management, customs authority, and the detention of illegal immigrants, and pursued their own interpretations of those functions with zeal. The brigades claimed from the army the right to monitor borders, with the army decidedly ill-equipped to play any kind of advanced role doing so. This led to conflict as armed groups belonging to particular communities claimed the right to police areas used by neighbors for smuggling. And it further raised uncertainties for border communities attempting to control their trade and livelihood.

Zuwara, for example, created its own "Border Guard" unit in late March 2012 with other heavily pro-revolution armed groups from Nalut and Zawiya designed to cover the crossing at Ras Jdeir and the desert immediately south of it. The Zuwaran units set up a checkpoint at Al-'Assa, an area located in territory considered to belong to a rival neighboring town, Rijdalin. Like the Zuwarans, the Rijdalinis also engaged in cross-border trafficking with their kin in Tunisia. Rijdalini men attacked and captured the Zuwarans, prompting three days of fighting in early April 2012. At the same time, a similar unit in the south was set up in Murzuq, southern Libya, again prompting deep suspicion and tension with local Tabu armed groups, not least the man initially charged with putting the Border Guard unit together, Abdul Wahhab al-Gayed, who had background in the Libyan Islamic Fighting Group. (In August 2012, al-Gayed took a seat in Libya's General People's Congress, the successor organization to the National Transitional Council, leaving the southern Border Guard unit on hiatus.)

Fighting was not simply triggered by armed groups' attempts to dominate trafficking routes, but also by the zealous arresting of smugglers. For instance, in May, the arrest of a Tunisian fuel smuggler near Zuwara by an armed group that attempted to confiscate both fuel and the smuggler's vehicle led to demonstrations by Tunisians so severe that Tunisia's government was forced to close the border crossing. Further skirmishes at the Wazin-Dabiha border crossing with Tunisia in August also led to the closure of that border crossing—then reinforced with armed groups.

Libya did succeed in making some diplomatic progress with its neighbors on new bilateral agreements on border security. In February 2012, Libya concluded a tripartite agreement with Chad and Sudan on border surveillance and security,[15] which was followed by two similar agreements with Algeria in March and April.[16] Libya signed another such deal with Tunisia in March,[17] but to date, no such agreement has been reached with Niger, which still hosts a number of exiled members of the former Libya regime. Still, with no coherent army or Interior Ministry to implement such agreements, they again are worth little more than the paper they were written on.

At bottom, neither the state nor the irregular armed groups holds the technology or the experience to adequately monitor Libya's open borders. The new government must begin to address some of the deep-seated local grievances that perpetuate this broken system.

Ethnic Dissent and Border Control

As it attempts to regain control of its borders, Libya must deal with the hopes and fears of its sizable cross-border populations in the south—specifically the Tabu and Tuareg, Libya's Sahelian non-Arab minorities.

The communal conflicts of 2011–2012 that have erupted across Libya's lengthy southern borders have generated much anxiety among the Tabu and Tuareg. In both cases these communities have fallen back on their own kin as a social safety net, and while they took opposing stances during the revolution, both have come to wholly distrust what has come after it. Their response has been to preserve their own armed groups, their own free movement across borders, and their autonomy.

The consequent lack of cooperation either with the Libyan army or with revolutionary brigades has made the notion of border policing little more than a fiction or aspiration. Both communities readily acknowledge that the borders are in practice wide open, but until their own local interests are addressed, neither is prepared to help address the interests of the Libyan state in securing these borders.

A History of Exclusion

The Tabu number approximately 350,000 spread across southeast Libya and northern Chad and Niger, while the Tuareg number roughly 1.2 million across Mali, Niger, Algeria, Libya, and Burkina Faso (no adequate census data on the Tabu's total numbers or the Tuareg's numbers in Libya exist). At present, the Tabu have taken effective control of much of the southern borderlands, stretching from Kufra in the far east to Qatrun and al-Wigh, south of Sabha. While their networks are wide-ranging, their standing within Libyan society is a point of contention.

In 1954, shortly after its creation as an independent state in 1951, Libya's first and only census was carried out,[18] and in the same year, the state stipulated requirements for Libyan nationality and citizenship that remain largely unchanged, being defined as dependent on the parents' descent and/or on birth in the territory. With much of the population illiterate when the citizenship law went into effect, proof rested on the presentation of handwritten "family books," which are still kept by Libyan households today (and were used, for example, in voter registration during the

2012 elections). For the marginal, nomadic Tabu and Tuareg populations, however, only a few were settled enough in the 1950s to even acquire family books. As a result, large numbers remained and still remain paperless.

Cultural and ethnic differences compounded the exclusion of the Tabu and Tuareg from the modern state, particularly their tradition of marrying into families that are of the same ethnic group but well removed, geographically and genealogically. That preference complicated their ability to integrate into Arab Libyan society, though some achieved a measure of integration, through either education and employment in a sector such as oil or the military or through service to a family (whereby a Tabu or Tuareg dedicated to a particular family becomes part of the fabric of a particular tribe or town). (Such cases, however, do not sway Libyan prejudices toward either ethnic group or the issues of exclusion they face.) The preference to marry and trade within their respective ethnic groups made it much harder for Tuareg and Tabu to conclusively prove Libyan citizenship under laws drafted primarily in the Arab cultural context. Moreover, the Tabu and Tuareg, with their close economic and social connections to their counterparts in other countries in the region, were increasingly viewed as the "other" by Libya's Arab population and even the Qaddafi state. History books printed under Qaddafi, for example, acknowledged the Amazigh origins of the Tuareg and Berber Libyans, while ignoring the Tabu entirely; many Libyans interviewed say the Tabu were considered "African," "Chadian," and "not Libyan."

Undoing this state of affairs requires substantial engagement with the root issues of Tabu and Tuareg irredentism.

The Tabu

The Tabu once shored up and supported the Libyan army—the bodyguard of King Idris, Libya's ruler from 1951 until 1969, included many Tabu recruits. The distrust that Tabu armed groups currently hold toward the Libyan army and government is a more recent development, deriving in large part from the legacy of Qaddafi's intervention in Chad from 1978 to 1987.

In the 1970s, Qaddafi offered the paperless Tabu an easy route to Libyan citizenship in exchange for their political support in Libya's territorial claim over the Ouzou Strip—a stretch of territory running along the Libya-Chad border that made up a key part of Tabu homelands. Qaddafi occupied the strip in 1972, and by 1977, Libya was supporting Tabu Chadian insurgents against the Chadian government in Ndjamena.[19] Meanwhile many Tabu lacking citizenship papers, whether authentically "Libyan" or not, had been granted citizenship by the Libyan government from 1973 onward on the condition that they register in the Ouzou Strip, thus cementing Libyan claims to the territory and encouraging a new generation of Tabu of Chadian origin to enter the armed services and become naturalized Libyans.

Tabu fortunes changed after the political alliance between Qaddafi and Tabu Chadian insurgents broke apart. In 1978, after being repelled by French troops stationed in Chad, the Tabu insurgents' leader, Goukouni Oueddei, expelled Libyan military advisers from the Ouzou Strip and reached out politically to France. Though Qaddafi and Oueddei continued to attempt to cooperate after the insurgents entered a national unity government in Chad in 1980, by 1981 relations between them had deteriorated swiftly. With Libyan military deployment in Chad ever-increasing, Qaddafi turned instead to solicit the support of Arab elements within the unity government against the Tabu, who too had become members of that government. By the mid-1980s, Qaddafi, still trying to consolidate his military presence in Ouzou, was in head-on conflict with Goukouni Oueddei and the Tabu in the so-called Tibesti war.

Because blood relations between Libyan and Chadian Tabu were so close, the Chadian wars meant that Qaddafi's government ceased its initial support for Libya's Tabu, and instead pursued the "Arabization" of Libya's south. In the 1980s, the Libyan government began to encourage the repatriation of Libyan Arab tribes that had settled in Chad and Niger—Awlad Suleyman and Warfalla tribes in particular. In Sabha, these groups settled in large tent cities and vociferously supported Qaddafi's policies and his interventions in Sahelian affairs. In Kufra, Qaddafi began patronizing the Zway, an Arab group that had long fought with the Tabu over farmland and water resources. Tabu neighborhoods in Sabha and Kufra were demolished, and residents were compelled to move into poor slums on the towns' outskirts or further south into the desert. Chadian refugees entered the country, raising communal tensions still further. Worse, after the Ouzou Strip was awarded to Chad in 1994 by the International Court of Justice,

Tabu who had registered in the strip found their papers frozen, leaving them marginalized to this day, living in quasi-legal slums, and unable to secure new jobs. Those who had low-paying state jobs were reliant on keeping them to avoid deportation.

This history of discrimination and political manipulation underscores the position of the Tabu today. Moves by Qaddafi's government in 2007 to withdraw citizenship from Tabu in Kufra prompted the formation of a new opposition group, the Front for the Salvation of Libyan Tabu led by Issa Abdul Majid Mansour, and in 2008 a significant uprising in Kufra ensued, suppressed by the Libyan army. Thereafter, the forcible eviction of Tabu from Kufra and the destruction of their homes continued, according to the Society for Threatened Peoples, which described the Libyan government as pursuing a deliberate policy of ethnic cleansing.

Unsurprisingly, the Tabu joined the revolt against Qaddafi early on, while the Arab tribes so favored by Qaddafi in the south—the Zway, Awlad Suleyman, many Warfalla in Sabha, not to mention the Qadhadfa tribe—stayed loyal. But in joining the uprising, the Tabu ensured from the beginning that they secured enough concessions and compromises to protect their interests in the uncertain times ahead. On May 23, 2011, Qaddafi's government issued an official decision granting the Tabu registered in Ouzou citizenship en masse as a means of enlisting support against the rebels.[20] The Tabu accepted the decision, and with it large numbers of weapons from the governor of the military zone in Sabha.

With these concessions, the Tabu promptly began securing their historical lands, throwing their lot in with the rebel movement. Kufra had been fought over throughout April, with Issa Abdul Majid taking final control of the town on May 6. The NTC allowed Issa to maintain control of the Kufra region, extending to the southeastern borders with Sudan and Chad. In the country's south, Tabu began taking control of the southern borderlands. The military base at al-Wigh, southeast of Sabha near the Niger border, fell in June, followed by the border town of Qatrun, the desert plateau of Umm Aranib, the town of Zweila, and finally the town of Murzuq. Sabha itself fell on September 20 with the coming of substantial numbers of rebel forces from the north. In the political vacuum that followed the collapse of the regime, the Tabu attempted to consolidate their gains. With, the Tabu claimed, promises by the NTC to honor

Qaddafi's May 23 decision, the Tabu began submitting citizenship applications to the Libyan government. In Kufra, Qatrun, and Murzuq, the Tabu took control of the local military councils; they also secured large numbers of weapons from al-Wigh airbase. Tabu from Chad and the Ouzou Strip, and those Tabu who had registered in the Ouzou Strip in the 1970s, returned to Kufra and other Tabu strongholds. By the time of Qaddafi's death on October 23, 2011, the Tabu de facto controlled much of the southern border, including land entry points.

Naturally enough, the Tabu's change in fortunes generated hostility among Libyan Arabs of the south who still viewed the Tabu as non-Libyans. Economic rivalries over smuggling routes combined toxically with the tensions over ethnicity and citizenship. In Kufra, Issa Abdul Majid Mansour's seizure of border areas upset the balance of power with the Zway, who under Qaddafi had collected tariffs on smuggled goods and run some safe houses. A shooting incident that led to the death of a Zway man at the hands of a Tabu militia in early February 2012 sparked a full-blown conflict between Zway and Tabu that quickly escalated to the use of rocket-propelled grenades and anti-aircraft weapons.[21] A ceasefire wrought by local notables repeatedly broke down in April and June 2012 over similar disputes.

Another conflict was sparked in Sabha in March 2012 when members of the Awlad Buseif, an Arab community, accused a Tabu of stealing a car. The local military council, dominated by the Awlad Suleyman, who had supported Qaddafi's marginalization of the Tabu during the 1980s and 1990s, intervened in the dispute. Making matters worse, local council authorities claimed that the Tabu and Awlad Suleyman were at the same time in competition over cross-border trade, with armed groups from both sides capturing convoys belonging to each other. A planned reconciliation gathering at the People's Hall (a Qaddafi-era municipal building) degenerated into a firefight, followed by five days of intense combat. Residents from across Sabha converged on and shelled Tabu shantytowns; at least 147 died and approximately 500 were wounded.[22]

The effect of the clashes was to polarize both communities and make Libya's border areas even more ungovernable. Tabu military groups felt that the Libyan army, which followed the Libyan Shield into Kufra to monitor agreed ceasefires in both towns in early March 2012, privately favored Arab Libyans over them. The Libyan Shield Forces were accused of being equally partisan.[23] With fears that elements in both would use the security vacuum to ethnically cleanse the Tabu from the area, Tabu militias held fast to their territory and their weapons. Issa Abdul Majid Mansour himself turned from being the NTC's ally in the area to an outlaw when his followers refused to put down their arms, fleeing instead to the borderlands. Charges from Libyan media that Tabu have since been supported by Chadian and Sudanese armed groups, while probably largely untrue (one Tabu noted that Libyan Tabu were better-armed than their southern counterparts),[24] are also hard to disprove. They also raise the initial, charged question of which Tabu are "Libyan" and which are not.

While the security consequences of the Tabu's irredentism are all too evident in the south today—Libya's borderlands from Niger through to Sudan remain largely outside state control—the political consequences appear milder. The Tabu have organized politically, with offices in Tripoli mounting a small effort to lobby the government, but they have few political demands beyond the redress of citizenship issues and the provision of better jobs and services. Secession or unification with Tabu areas in neighboring countries is extremely unlikely; Tabu homelands are resource-poor and though contiguous are not connected by roads or other infrastructure.

The Tabu also claim that the possibility of radicalization against the state appears low. Some Tabu activists have asserted, in interviews with the author, that 2004 saw a purported attempt by Abdul Raziq Boraq, a courier working on behalf of al-Qaeda, to sound out Tabu loyalties, but the Tabu appear to have been unreceptive to such efforts. The 2011 conflict in the south saw the return and rise to prominence of many former Afghanistan fighters and mujahideen—Kufra, for example, saw the return in May of Mustafa Bu Juful, a Zway mujahid from Benghazi who had fought in Afghanistan and was subsequently killed fighting in Sirte. But few if any such returnees are known to be Tabu in origin, while comparatively many come from Arab communities resident in the south. Tabu issues are therefore comparatively unlikely to be internationalized, making a political solution all the more within the reach of the Libyan government.

The Tuareg

The Tuareg have also faced discrimination, born of different historical circumstances. Large numbers of Tuareg immigrated to Libya in the 1970s following a large-scale drought in the Sahel and political persecution in Mali.[25] Their Berber roots (the name *Tuareg* is cognate with the Berber name for Fezzan province, Targa) conflicted with Qaddafi's insistence on Libya's Arab identity. However, with Qaddafi's "turn" toward Africa as a source of political support and economic influence during the 1990s, when Libya was under Western sanctions, he began increasingly to recruit Tuareg of Malian and Nigerien origin into the armed forces, with Tuareg entering standing brigades. These included the Tarq brigade, based in Awbari; the Fars brigade, based in Sabha; and to a lesser extent, the well-known 32 or Khamis Brigade, headed by Khamis al-Qaddafi, one of Qaddafi's sons. Tuareg were a part of the short-lived Islamic Legion, one of Qaddafi's early military projects aimed originally at unifying the Sahel and deployed extensively in Chad in the 1980s, and they also made up a second such brigade of roughly 5,000 named the Black Battalion, which was, according to some, also deployed in Chad.[26] Successive Tuareg rebellions in Mali and Niger during the 2000s led to closer relations with the Qaddafi government, with Qaddafi supporting the Tuareg as a mediator with the Nigerien and Malian governments.

Though Qaddafi cannot be said to have liberally armed the Tuareg, they certainly sought such support from the Qaddafi regime, and further waves of settlement and integration into the Libyan armed forces occurred during the 2000s. In 2005, Qaddafi rolled out a separate, reduced category of citizenship aimed, in practice, primarily at these Tuareg. Relations with neighboring Arab groups remained tense, as with the Tabu, but with the added complication that many Libyans saw the Tuareg as supporting the regime throughout the uprising against Qaddafi. In fact, though some Tuareg did come across from Niger and Mali to fight for the Libyan army on a paid basis, for many, such experiences were short-lived. While some loyalists fought until the end, many Tuareg who had settled in Libya and even enlisted in the armed forces simply moved back to Mali and elsewhere soon after NATO's imposition of a no-fly zone over Libya in March 2011. Being somewhat less settled than the Tabu, the Tuareg could—and did—abandon their posts in the armed forces and leave the country. Though many left, many communities remain in the southwest and, as with the Tabu, come under ethnically motivated attack.

This had implications across the region. In Mali in particular, returning Tuareg fighters fueled a rebellion in the north of the country and forged links with al-Qaeda in the Islamic Maghreb,[27] relying on strong support from Tuareg in other countries. In return, the Libyan Tuareg were able to supply other Tuareg—according to those with knowledge of the black market in Sabha, as well as what can be deduced from the Tuareg rebellion of 2012 in Mali[28]—with the kind of weaponry that secessionists had long unsuccessfully sought from the Qaddafi regime.

While the Tabu came into bloody conflict with Arab neighbors in 2012, the Tuareg largely did not. This is at least partly because the few towns with substantial Tuareg populations, such as Ghat and Awbari in the far southwest, did not have substantial Arab Libyan populations. However, the Tuareg did suffer from the perception of having fought on Qaddafi's side, and therefore faced discrimination and attack in the post-Qaddafi era. In the far west town of Ghadames, where resident Tuareg and Arab Ghadamesiyya (local Ghadames residents) came into conflict soon after the fall of Tripoli. There, the Ghadamesiyya had their own armed group that had the backing of the NTC, and so set up their own military and local council to govern the area. Tuareg attacked the city in September 2011, claiming that Ghadamesiyya were destroying homes and making unfair arrests; seven or eight died in the subsequent fighting.[29] The root causes of the conflict—the status of the councils or of wrongdoers whom both sides wanted to see brought to justice—remained unresolved and clashes continued through the first half of 2012.

The Tuareg in Ghadames are choosing to rely on de facto autonomy and on securing their own defenses rather than placing their faith in the interim government or local community notables' attempts to negotiate peace between the Tuareg and the Ghadamesiyya—five of which have come to naught.[30] While women and children were allowed to stay in Ghadames to use schools and facilities, most men have been evicted and have relocated to small nearby towns.[31] Others have simply fled to Algeria or further afield. Tuareg are putting their hopes on creating an entirely new town, which they name al-Waal, as the only sustainable solution. Some Tuareg representatives and local leaders note, privately, that the Tuareg rebellion in Mali will help deter their further marginalization more than any peace initiatives, and they are stockpiling weapons accordingly.

Conclusion

Tackling the economic incentives that lie behind smuggling, the corruption of local border guards, and the seizure of border posts by armed groups requires addressing deep, difficult socioeconomic issues that have plagued Libya's south for as long as it has existed. The competing security solutions—whether high- or low-tech—that various countries have offered to the Libyan government would help, but any security solution can be subverted if enough incentives compel the actors involved to do so.

Securing the borders of the vast country therefore requires the reform and formalization of the security sector as well as investment in training, equipment, and infrastructure for border security posts. As important is the reform of the country's administrative system, so that clear lines of authority within and between departments can be established for the first time and government ministers start to cooperate at the executive level. The constitution-writing project in which Libya is about to engage is an excellent opportunity to clarify lines of authority at the ministerial level and create the necessary new institutions.

Clearer lines of authority and a better-equipped workforce will help give Libya's security forces some momentum. But dealing with the armed brigades with which the security forces must work in parallel is a deeper issue. The September 11, 2012, attack on the U.S. consulate in Benghazi has encouraged the Libyan government to take a harsher line with the brigades, but at root the issue is not just one of toughness, but of politics. The brigades' justifications for remaining apart from the state are numerous, but the most common themes are a distrust that the new state is sufficiently reformed from the old, a disrespect for the army's and police's "weakness," and, in the case of Tabu and Tuareg groups, that their communities face a racially motivated threat. Those justifications, one by one, must be removed.

The economic incentives for local communities to seek income from cross-border trade must be swept away too. This involves sponsoring development and tackling social issues that have been neglected since Libya's creation as a modern state. Tabu and Tuareg citizenship claims must be thoroughly redressed, and both communities must be offered a political and economic stake in the new Libya, including the provision of education programs and jobs. The imposition of tolls and tariffs by border police, and the sometimes-arbitrary holdup of travelers for several days, should end, as all such things encourage informal routing around border posts. Those stripped of their citizenship for ostensibly political reasons while they continue to hold lawful employment with the Libyan state should be rewarded appropriately. The use of non-Libyan (or legally ambiguous) Tabu and Tuareg citizens as auxiliaries in the armed and police forces, if it is to continue, must also be placed on clear legal footing in order to finally put an end to the Qaddafi government's tacit encouragement and manipulation of such issues for political purposes.

The end goal for Libya should be to steadfastly undermine and remove the deeply entrenched incentives to engage in illegal or quasi-legal cross-border activity—something that can only be achieved by creating a stable and prosperous south. The recent conflicts in the country have opened the eyes of many Libyan officials and conflict negotiators—in some cases, for the first time. They must not be forgotten as Libya's new government starts to grapple once again with its own borders.

Notes

1. Libya's armed groups are frequently described in the media as "militias." While convenient, the nomenclature is arguably misleading and inaccurate. In the Libyan context, the equivalent (*milishiyyaat*) tends to describe an exclusively non-state group, whereas Libya's armed groups (brigades) either sprang up as part of a revolutionary effort or were since formed with the sanction, if not blessing, of the National Transitional Council and the defense and interior ministries. Neither are they exclusively civilian, counting many former military officers among their number. Since in Libya they are termed "brigades" (*kata'ib*), the same nomenclature is used here. For further taxonomy of armed groups in Libya see International Crisis Group, *Divided We Stand: Libya's Enduring Conflicts*, Middle East/North Africa Report no. 130, September 14, 2012, www.crisisgroup.org/~/media/Files/Middle%20East%20North%20Africa/North%20 Africa/libya/130-divided-we-stand-libyas-enduring-conflicts; and Brian McQuinn, "Capturing the Peace," *Small Arms Survey*, 2012.

2. The European Union, which carried out a needs assessment after the revolution, during which border stations were looted, noted a similar dearth in capacity. See European Union, "Integrated Border Management Needs Assessment for Libya," May 31, 2012.

3. Ibid.

4. For further details, see European Union, "Integrated Border Management."

5. Having not ratified the 1951 UN Convention on Refugees (the Geneva Convention) or its 1967 protocol, Libya neither made efforts to coordinate or agree with it. Migrants were rarely informed of their rights in detention; there was no legal basis for the application of rights as defined in international law, and responsibility for their custody and its duration was ill-defined. According to reports by UNHCR and Amnesty International, beatings, rapes and other infringements of rights continued.

6. Luiza Bialasiewicz, "Borders Above All?" *Political Geography* 30 (2011): 299–300; Amnesty International, "Libya of Tomorrow: What Hope for Human Rights?" For a summary of European policy at the outset of the 2011 conflict in light of its reliance on Qaddafi for border security, see Nicole Koenig, "The EU and the Libyan Crisis: In Quest of Coherence?" Istituto Affari Internazionali Working Paper 11/19 (July 2011).

7. See Frederic Wehrey, "The Struggle for Security in Eastern Libya," Carnegie Paper, Carnegie Endowment for International Peace, 2012, http://carnegieendowment.org/files/libya_security_ 2.pdf.

8. Wolfram Lacher, "Organized Crime and Conflict in the Sahel-Sahara Region," Carnegie Paper, Carnegie Endowment for International Peace, 2012, http://carnegieendowment.org/files/sahel_ sahara.pdf.

9. For a case study of how this process occurred in Misrata, see McQuinn, "Capturing the Peace."

10. For more on this process, and on the emergence of local military councils and other armed groups, see International Crisis Group, *Divided We Stand*.

11. Ministry of Defense documents viewed by author, Sabha, May 2012 and Zuwara, May 2012.

12. See notes from a television interview with the defense minister broadcast on Libya al-Hurra, April 28, 2012, subsequently provided to the author.

13. See "Libya Government Takes Control of Tripoli Airport," Agence France-Presse, April 20, 2012, www.google.com/hostednews/afp/article/ALeqM5gncFJ7cqs4lduDcUVQp54zuwsJVA? docId=CNG.fbce75d2eba2ecc24710f72328c3b9d9.301.

14. Author observations, Tripoli International Airport, August 2012. See also J. Cole, "Despite Airport Incident, Henry Kissinger Is Wrong About Libya," *Informed Comment* blog, www. juancole.com/2012/06/despite-airport-incident-henry-kissinger-is-wrong-about-libya.html.

15 See European Union, "Integrated Border Management."

16 Ibid.

17 Ibid.

18 See *Maslahat al-Ihsa' wal-Ta'dad* (General Population Census of Libya), 1954.

19 For more on Libya's Chad campaign, see Kenneth Pollack, "Arabs at War: Military Effectiveness, 1948–91," *Studies in War, Society and the Military*, 1991.

20 Document viewed by author, May 2012.

21 Wehrey, "The Struggle for Security in Eastern Libya."

22 See "Libya Names Military Governor in Conflict-Ravaged South," Bloomberg, April 1, 2012, www.bloomberg.com/news/2012-04-01/libyan-tribal-clashes-leave-147-dead-health-minister-says.html.

23 See International Crisis Group, *Divided We Stand*.

24 Wehrey, "The Struggle for Security in Eastern Libya."

25 For background, see International Crisis Group, *Mali: Avoiding Escalation*, Africa Report no. 189, August 2012.

26 Interview with author of International Crisis Group report, *Mali: Avoiding Escalation*.

27 Lacher, "Organized Crime and Conflict in the Sahel-Sahara Region."

28 See International Crisis Group, *Mali: Avoiding Escalation*, for background on the consequences of the 2011 Libyan conflict on the 2012 Tuareg rebellion in Mali.

29 Author interview with foreign conflict mediator in Ghadames, May 2012.

30 Rebecca Murray, "Tackling Conflict on Libya's Margins," Al Jazeera, August 10, 2012, www.aljazeera.com/indepth/features/2012/08/201287122322275927.html.

31 Ibid.

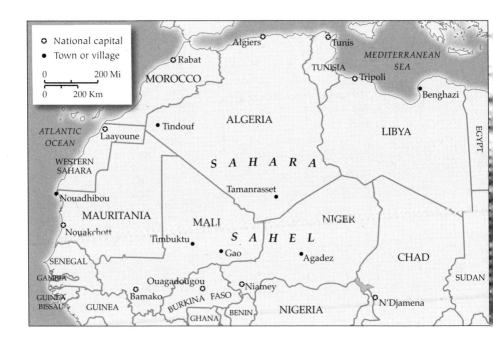

National capital
Town or village

0   200 Mi

0   200 Km

ATLANTIC
OCEAN

MEDITERRANEAN
SEA

Algiers

Rabat

MOROCCO

Tunis

TUNISIA

Tripoli

Benghazi

LIBYA

EGYPT

Tindouf

ALGERIA

Laayoune

WESTERN
SAHARA

S A H A R A

Tamanrasset

Nouadhibou

MAURITANIA

MALI

NIGER

Nouakchott

Timbuktu

S A H E L

Gao

Agadez

CHAD

SENEGAL

SUDAN

GAMBIA

Ouagadougou

Niamey

GUINEA
BISSAU

Bamako

BURKINA FASO

N'Djamena

GUINEA

GHANA

BENIN

NIGERIA

03

Organized Crime and Conflict in the Sahel-Sahara Region

Wolfram Lacher

The Growing Impact of Organized Crime

Over the past decade, the United States and Europe have become increasingly focused on security in the Sahel and Sahara region—defined here as Mauritania, Mali, and Niger, as well as adjacent areas in Algeria and Libya—for fear that the territory could become a new safe haven for extremist groups linked to al-Qaeda. These fears appeared to have been borne out by the 2012 insurgency in northern Mali that saw northern cities fall under the control of two groups closely linked to al-Qaeda in the Islamic Maghreb (AQIM)—Ansar Dine and the Movement for Tawhid and Jihad in West Africa (MUJAO).

Meanwhile, the growth of organized criminal activity in the region received much less attention. External observers and Malian government officials readily acknowledged the importance of drug trafficking, but focused above all on the involvement of AQIM while ignoring or downplaying the links of state officials and political leaders to criminal networks. Moreover, Western policymakers primarily perceived the regional al-Qaeda franchise as a terrorist group, despite the fact that its most notorious activity consisted of abducting foreign nationals to extort ransoms.

In order to understand the crisis in northern Mali and more broadly the growing instability of the region it is necessary to go beyond the role of AQIM and other jihadist organizations. Rivalries over the control of smuggling and state officials' tolerance of criminal activity by political allies allowed extremist groups to flourish. The complicity and involvement of Malian officials, and the willingness of Western governments to pay ransoms, also caused the kidnapping industry to thrive. Moreover, these factors were key to the dynamics that caused the eruption of renewed conflict in northern Mali in 2012.

Researching organized crime is a task fraught with problems and pitfalls. In the Sahel, accusations and rumors about the actors involved abound, but little hard evidence is available. In various interviews the author carried out in Nouakchott and Bamako in July 2012, interlocutors were quite willing to make accusations against specific individuals, who were in most cases players in the conflict in northern Mali. Though it was often difficult to establish whether the accusations were valid or were weapons used to discredit political enemies, triangulation of information provided by multiple sources from different political backgrounds and with different agendas allows the author to feel reasonably confident of the accuracy of this analysis. Unless otherwise noted, the conclusions drawn here are based on those conversations and research in Mauritania and Mali, in addition to research in Libya in 2012.

The Rise of Organized Crime in the Sahel

The Sahel and Sahara region is far from a pivotal area for transnational organized crime. The importance of organized criminal activity there stems from the fact that there are few alternative activities that produce similar profits and rapid enrichment. This particularly applies to three undertakings that have expanded significantly since around 2003: smuggling of Moroccan cannabis resin, cocaine smuggling, and kidnapping for ransom. Individuals and networks involved in these activities have converted their wealth into political influence and military power. Contraband trade in licit goods, which had developed across the region in previous decades, laid the institutional basis for the development of these high-profit activities.

The Origins and Evolution of Illicit Regional Flows

While the bulk of commercial flows across the Sahara are in licit goods, which often rely on informal arrangements with security and customs services, the boundaries between licit and illicit trade are blurred. Long-standing commercial and social networks that are frequently based on families and communities specializing in trade are spread across trading hubs in different countries; those networks have been growing closer since decolonization in the 1960s. From the 1970s onward, the links that had survived the collapse of the long-distance caravan trade in the late nineteenth century began to expand, thriving on contraband of subsidized Algerian and Libyan goods traveling to northern Mali and Niger.[1]

Like consumer goods imported to Mauritanian ports and traded through Timbuktu in Mali by Arab merchants, these flows bypassed the official customs system in a process that led to the establishment of informal arrangements between traders and officials. In parallel, exports of camels from Mali and Niger to Algeria and Libya grew, often relying on the same networks. While this trade was dominated by Algerian and Libyan merchants, Malian and Nigerien Arab traders increasingly established themselves in the sector.[2]

During the 1990s, cuts to Algeria's subsidy budget caused a partial economic slump, but the embargo imposed on Libya stimulated contraband; in addition, conflicts in Algeria, northern Niger, and Mali turned the region into a major arms trafficking hub. Weapons smuggling was sometimes run by the same networks controlling contraband, as illustrated by the case of Hadj Bettou, who during the 1980s and early 1990s dominated contraband and weapons smuggling in southern Algeria, benefiting from the protection of senior security officials.[3] Contraband from Mauritania, Algeria, and Libya continues today and has intensified with the conflict in northern Mali, where supplies in food and petrol now overwhelmingly come from Algeria. The illegal sale of subsidized Algerian fuel to Mali is managed by local officials in the Algerian administration and security apparatus.[4] The regional trade in weapons has increased as a result of the conflict in Libya and growing demand from northern Mali since early 2012.

Cigarette smuggling in particular has greatly contributed to the emergence of the practices and networks that have allowed drug trafficking to grow. The smuggling of cigarettes to North African markets began to thrive in the early 1980s, and it developed into a large-scale business controlled by a few major players. Cigarettes, imported through Mauritania, supplied a large portion of the Algerian and Moroccan markets, while those imported through Cotonou in Benin and Lome in Togo were routed through Niger and Burkina Faso to Libya and Algeria. In 2009, the United Nations Office on Drugs and Crime (UNODC) estimated that cigarettes smuggled along these routes accounted for around 60 percent of the Libyan tobacco market (or $240 million in proceeds at the retail level) and 18 percent of the Algerian market (or $228 million).

The key actors in this trade are legal cigarette importers and distributors, who import their merchandise from free trade zones such as Dubai. The trade is therefore best interpreted as a deliberate strategy by tobacco companies to circumvent tax regimes or break North African state monopolies on cigarette distribution.

This system has led to the erosion of the customs services because of corruption and collusion between smugglers and state officials. For part of its journey, the merchandise is transported in large trucks on the main roads, with the connivance of Malian and Nigerien security officials. In Libya, cigarette smuggling is controlled by networks in the security apparatus dominated by members of the Qadhadfa tribe. In the triangle between Mauritania, Mali, and Algeria, Sahrawi networks—often with the direct involvement of officials in the Polisario movement, which seeks independence for Western Sahara—trade subsidized Algerian goods and humanitarian aid southward and cigarettes northward to Algeria and Morocco.[5] Cigarette smuggling has also contributed to the emergence of smaller gangs of smugglers charged with transporting the merchandise from Mauritania, Mali, and Niger into Algeria. Mokhtar Belmokhtar, the former AQIM commander who orchestrated the dramatic seizure of Western hostages at the In Amenas gas facility in Algeria in January 2013, is widely reputed to have long run a cigarette smuggling racket across the Sahara.[6]

Like contraband of licit goods and cigarette smuggling, the migrant business also helped spawn the emergence of carriers in the region specializing in off-road transport or in establishing arrangements with corrupt officials. Irregular migration flows from sub-Saharan Africa to North Africa and on to Europe grew beginning in the early 1990s. Gao in northern Mali and Agadez in neighboring Niger, which are also hubs for cigarette smuggling, emerged as major hubs for migrants' journeys to Morocco (via Algeria) or Libya.

Across the Sahara, the migration business did not produce transnational networks on a significant scale. Irregular migration across the region generally follows a "pay-as-you-go" rather than a "full-package" system. That is, as outlined by the UNODC, one group or network does not typically manage the entire process; transportation and the negotiation of bribes with customs and police officials typically takes place in several separate legs across Niger and Mali, with Algerian or Libyan carriers taking over at the borders. Only in Libya was the control of migration and its profits monopolized by members of one tribe—the Qadhadfa—with close links to the security apparatus.[7] The emergence of multiple militias controlling parts of the Libyan territory has made the country more dangerous for migrants, who now risk being intercepted in many different locations.

The Development of Drug Smuggling

During the last decade, the smuggling of legal merchandise based on price differentials between countries and avoidance of taxes was supplemented by the smuggling of illicit drugs. Two distinct flows across the Sahel have expanded rapidly, their diverse routes intersecting at times: since around 2005 that of South American cocaine to Europe, including via Libya and Egypt, and that of Moroccan cannabis resin to Libya, Egypt, and the Arabian Peninsula.[8] The growth was driven by rising demand in Europe and the Mashrek, as well as by tightened controls along the Moroccan-Algerian border, off the coasts of Spain and the Canary Islands, and in European airports, which made routes across the poorly controlled Sahel region appealing to smugglers.

The cocaine trade from South America to Europe via West Africa expanded rapidly in 2005–2007, and it remains important, despite a contraction after 2008. The UNODC estimated that around 14 percent of Europe's cocaine—or 20 tons, amounting to a wholesale value of $1 billion in Western Europe—transited through West Africa in 2008. Most of the cocaine passing through West Africa on its way to Europe first arrives in one of the coastal states—notably Guinea and Guinea-Bissau, as well as Togo, Benin, and Ghana—and is then either transported by air or boat. Alternatively, cocaine is sent by air couriers to Europe, including from airports in the West African interior. Bamako, Ouagadougou, and Niamey airports are among the hubs for air couriers, some of whom transit via Algiers airport. These routes remain active, as seizures during 2011 and 2012 at these airports underline.[9] Mauritania briefly emerged as a major transit country for air, sea, and overland transport in 2007–2008, the two biggest seizures made in Nouadhibou airport in May 2007 (630 kg of cocaine) and in Nouakchott in August of the same year (830 kg of cocaine).[10] Since 2008, however, Mauritanian annual seizures have drastically declined.

The overland routes across the Sahel and Sahara toward Europe are diverse, and there is little evidence for sustained major flows on any single route. Cocaine is transported from the coastal hubs—in this case, Guinea or Mauritania—overland to northern Mali and on to Morocco, Algeria, or Libya (via Algeria or northern Niger for Libya). Several reports that aircraft were being used to bring cocaine to northern Mali suggested that the overland route acquired greater importance during 2009 and 2010, at the same time seizures along the West African coast declined. By far the most spectacular of these reports was the discovery of a Boeing 727 carcass that had either crashed on takeoff or been set on fire near the town of Tarkint in Gao Region in November 2009. The plane, subsequently nicknamed "Air Cocaine" by the media, was registered in Guinea-Bissau and had taken off from Venezuela. According to the state prosecutor in the ongoing investigation, the plane carried between 7 and 11 tons of cocaine that was subsequently smuggled overland to Morocco by a network including Spanish, French, Moroccan, Malian, and Senegalese nationals.[11] While there is no evidence that a transaction of this magnitude was anything more than a one-off incident for northern Mali, there have been several reports of smaller aircraft being used to carry cocaine from the coastal hubs to Mali's north.[12]

Since early 2011, however, there have been no incidents in the region that could indicate how cocaine smuggling routes and volumes have evolved since the collapse of the regime in Libya and since the eruption of conflict in northern Mali in early 2012. It is likely that overland smuggling across the Sahel and Sahara has declined because smuggling across West Africa dropped and the overland routes are by and large dependent on the hubs in coastal states.

In contrast, all available evidence suggests that the other major flow, of Moroccan cannabis resin toward Libya, Egypt, and the Arabian Peninsula, continues unabated. Moroccan production, considered the world's largest or second largest, was estimated by the UNODC to be 877 tons in 2008. The Mauritanian intelligence services reportedly estimate that around one-third of Moroccan production transits the Sahel states, partly to circumvent the Algerian-Moroccan border.[13] Cannabis resin arrives in Mauritania overland (via Algeria or Western Sahara) or by boat, and then takes either a northern route to enter Mali in its far north, or it is transported along the Nouakchott-Nema road to enter Mali in Timbuktu Region.

The cannabis resin trade is dominated by mixed networks of Moroccan, Sahrawi, and Mauritanian nationals—as well as, allegedly, Algerian army officers—until it arrives in northern Mali. Across northern Mali and Niger, the bulk of cannabis resin smuggling is run by networks from Malian Arab communities that can often draw on family and tribal ties in Mauritania and Niger.[14] In some cases, Sahrawi cannabis resin smugglers with close ties to the Polisario have been known to take cocaine to Morocco on their way back from Mali.[15] From northern Mali, cannabis resin smuggling routes partly overlap with those serving the cocaine trade, traversing northern Niger or southern Algeria toward Libya. The drugs are then either exported to Europe via the Balkans or transported to Egypt and Israel. Another route runs via Chad and Sudan to the Arabian Peninsula.

Seizures of 2 tons of cannabis resin off Nouadhibou (western Mauritania) in January 2012 and of 3.6 tons in Timbedra (eastern Mauritania) in May 2012 show that this trade is thriving. Instability in Libya and conflict in northern Mali does not appear to have disrupted this route, with 4 tons of cannabis resin seized in Tripoli in May 2012, suggesting that the city has become a major hub for the trade.[16]

There is little evidence to support allegations of direct AQIM involvement in drug smuggling. AQIM does not appear to be an actor in reported clashes between drug smugglers in the region. In addition, the link allegedly established by a court in New York between AQIM, the Colombian FARC, and cocaine smugglers does not hold: the case involved an undercover U.S. Drug Enforcement Administration agent presenting himself as a FARC representative to three Malian nationals, who in turn asserted they could arrange protection from AQIM for a cocaine shipment across the Sahara. There is nothing to suggest that this was anything more than a false claim made to impress their supposed business partner. It is plausible, however, to assume that AQIM, as other armed groups in northern Mali, has sought at times to impose transit fees on drug smugglers or lent its protection to smuggling convoys.

Kidnapping for Ransom

The rise of kidnapping for ransom in the region was closely linked to, and a main driver of, AQIM's growing presence in the Sahel. Since the end of the Tuareg rebellions in northern Mali and Niger in the mid-1990s, the so-called "residual banditry" affecting the Sahara included occasional kidnappings of foreign nationals for political or financial ends. The abduction of 32 European tourists in 2003 in southern Algeria—seventeen of whom were freed on Algerian territory, while the fifteen remaining hostages were released in northern Mali after six months of captivity—was a novelty both in its scope and with regard to the responsible party. The kidnappings were carried out by the Algerian insurgent Salafist Group for Preaching and Combat, which in early 2007 changed its name to al-Qaeda in the Islamic Maghreb. However, the case remained a one-off incident for several years. Excluding an attack on the Mauritanian border post of Lemgheity in 2005, there was little evidence that the group had a significant presence, leading some observers to question whether it was a fact or fiction.[17]

This changed in December 2007 when four French tourists were killed by AQIM members in southern Mauritania. Soon afterward, in early 2008, a series of kidnappings across the region began. By April 2012, 42 foreign nationals had been targeted; of those, 24 were released, five were killed while being taken hostage or in captivity, and thirteen were still being held hostage as of the end of August 2012. The locations of these abductions included southern Algeria, Tunisia, Mauritania, Niger, as well as northern Mali, but in all cases the hostages were held and released in northern Mali by AQIM or, beginning in late 2011, by the AQIM offshoot Movement for Tawhid and Jihad in West Africa. The kidnappers focused on nationals of states that were known to be willing to negotiate ransom payments.

Political motives to spread terror played a limited role in AQIM's hostage takings. Although political demands were at times voiced by AQIM in messages posted on the Internet, available evidence suggests that all releases of Western nationals were secured through ransom payments, in some cases coupled with the release of prisoners linked to AQIM or MUJAO by Mali or Mauritania. In a number of instances, attempted rescues or the refusal to pay ransoms led to the death of hostages.[18]

Reports of ransom payments are never officially confirmed by the governments concerned and media reports vary on the amounts involved, although most range between $1.5 and $4 million per hostage.[19] The only reliable information in this respect comes from the Swiss. In 2009, the Swiss government authorized the use of $5 million in relation to the negotiations over the release of three of its nationals, of which $2 million appears to have been set aside for the ransom payment.[20]

Kidnapping for ransom has developed into a highly lucrative industry that has allowed AQIM to become a significant political and military force in the Sahel and Sahara. Extrapolating from available information, the income derived by AQIM, MUJAO, and associated mediators from kidnappings is likely to have totaled between $40 million and $65 million since 2008, paid mostly by Western governments. At the same time, repeated hostage takings have caused tourism in the Sahel and Sahara to collapse, thereby further limiting opportunities for employment and profit outside of criminal activity.

The Impact of Organized Crime: Collusion, Corruption, and Competition

The link between organized crime and conflict is obvious in the kidnapping-for-ransom business operated by AQIM and MUJAO. However, tensions related to the growing drug traffic, and the erosion of state institutions through complicity with organized crime, played even more important a role in the dynamics that led to the outbreak of conflict in northern Mali in January 2012. Officials' collusion with organized crime of all sorts has been present to varying degrees across the region.

In Mauritania, the final years of former president Maaouya Ould Sid'Ahmed Taya's rule (1984–2005) saw the high-level involvement of security officials and businessmen in contraband and weapons smuggling. Ould Taya's rule was based on an alliance between members of the Smacid, Ouled Bou Sba, and Rgeybat tribes, and these tribes' control of smuggling activity was a key building block in their coalition.[21]

The major cocaine seizures of 2007 and 2008 demonstrate the linkages between regime figures and the drug trade. The seizures coincided with a period of political instability, and senior figures wielded arrests on drug charges as a tool in power struggles within the ruling elite. Sid'Ahmed Ould Taya, the former president's nephew and Interpol liaison officer in Mauritania, was arrested in connection with a 2007 cocaine smuggling transaction at Nouadhibou airport, as was Sidi Mohamed Ould Haidallah, the son of another former president.

The current Mauritanian president, Ould Abdel Aziz, took power following a 2008 military coup, and with the consolidation of this rule, seizures and arrests have receded, making it difficult to discern whether high-level involvement continues. Some incidents have certainly raised eyebrows, including the president's decision to reduce the prison sentences of five convicted cocaine smugglers in February 2011 and a Nouakchott appeals court's inexplicable decision to release 30 convicted smugglers in July 2011. While the verdict was subsequently reversed, several key high-level players had fled in the meantime.[22] In another case, a cannabis resin smuggling network dismantled in January 2012 sought to evade checkpoints using special permits allegedly issued by the former head of police,[23] and a retired senior military officer was allegedly linked to a May 2012 cannabis resin seizure in Timbedra. Moreover, the Mauritanian security and judicial apparatus clearly stops short of investigating the sudden fortunes amassed by some individuals in recent years, many of which are suspected of being built on drug smuggling. But there is insufficient evidence to conclude that smuggling is today managed by senior Mauritanian officials as a political resource, as it was during the final years of Ould Taya's rule.

The boundaries in Niger are similarly murky. Contraband of licit goods and irregular migration takes place openly and with the full connivance of the authorities. Moreover, the fact that seizures of drug and weapons shipments are rare in northern Niger, a major transit area for both, cannot be explained simply by the Nigerien security forces' limited capacities. At least in some cases, the government has turned a blind eye to drug and weapons smuggling in order to preserve stability in the north.

The most prominent recent example was the release of the former Arab rebel leader Abta Hamidine in March 2012. Hamidine had been arrested in June 2011, following a clash between the Nigerien army and a convoy carrying explosives and weapons from Libya, apparently destined for delivery to AQIM in northern Mali. Also implicated in the case was Aghali Alambo, a former Tuareg rebel leader who had been appointed adviser to the president of the Nigerien legislative assembly (after spending time in Libya leading Nigerien Tuaregs fighting for Muammar Qaddafi). He was briefly arrested in March 2012 and then set free shortly afterward, along with Hamidine, in a move that appeared designed to prevent Hamidine's and Alambo's associates from taking up arms against the government.[24]

The collusion also stretched to southern Algeria and Libya. In Algeria, the complicity of senior officials appears to be organized at the provincial (*wilaya*) rather than the national level.[25] In Libya, smuggling was managed by senior officials until the demise of the Qaddafi regime; since then, arms smuggling out of Libya to Egypt, Tunisia, Algeria, and the Sahel has been thriving and has created vested interests that will be difficult for any future Libyan government to dismantle. Moreover, rivalries over the control of illicit activity have helped fuel violent conflicts in southern Libya between militias along tribal lines.

But nowhere in the region were state institutions more implicated in organized crime than in northern Mali. The former Malian leadership tried to use organized crime as a resource for the exercise of influence in the north by allowing its local allies to engage in criminal activity. It eventually lost control over the conflicts this generated, while the rule of law and the legitimacy of state institutions were eroded through complicity with organized crime.

The State–Organized Crime–Conflict Nexus in Mali

Organized crime truly began to take hold in northern Mali at the time of a rebellion led by several Tuareg officers from Kidal, a northern region bordering both Niger and Algeria, that began in May 2006. While the outbreak of the rebellion was due to wider political grievances, rivalries over the control of smuggling gradually became more prominent in the dynamics of the conflict. The rising profits to be made from drug smuggling spawned a drive by different networks to control smuggling routes or to impose transit fees on smugglers from other groups.

The Malian leadership deliberately exploited these tensions to exert its influence by playing leaders from certain communities against others and relying on select tribes to keep the north under control. To counter the Ifoghas and Idnan Tuareg rebels, the leadership around the then president, Amadou Toumani Touré, allied itself with those rebels' rivals—primarily leaders from the Arab Berabiche and Lamhar tribes, as well as from Imghad Tuareg tribes.

From August 2007 onward, only a small group of rebels drawn from a subsection of the Ifoghas continued to fight, repeatedly attacking Berabiche and Lamhar drug smuggling convoys. Clashes related to cocaine smuggling played out in 2007 and 2008.[26] Sometimes state officials directly intervened, as Lieutenant Colonel Lamana Ould Bou, a Malian army officer with close ties to the then head of state security, did in a clash in August 2007 over a cocaine shipment, arranging the return of the shipment in exchange for a large payment.

Prominent Arab figures from the Timbuktu and Gao regions sought to protect their business interests by establishing militias. That stance aligned with the interests of the Malian leadership, which remained intent on mobilizing Arab leaders to fight the rebels. The irregular forces, financed by businessmen like Dina Ould Daya and Oumar Ould Ahmed, were thus temporarily headed by members of Mali's military, such as Colonel Mohamed Ould Meydou and Lieutenant Colonel Bou.[27]

The relationship between the state, local notables and businessmen, and the drug trade can be seen in the supposedly huge November 2009 cocaine shipment transported to northern Mali by plane. According to an Algerian journalist with close links to the security apparatus, after landing in Tarkint, north of Gao, the shipment was most probably handled by Lamhar notables, including Tarkint mayor Baba Ould Cheikh, who was close to the Malian leadership. Prominent Lamhar businessmen Cherif Ould Taher and Mohamed Ould Laghwinat were also likely in attendance.[28]

Tensions came to a temporary head in January 2010. Then, an armed group made up of Ifoghas and Kounta had seized a large cocaine shipment transported by government-aligned Lamhar and Imghad smugglers. Members of the Lamhar tribe responded by kidnapping the leader of the Kounta Arabs in Gao Region.[29]

Such smuggling-related conflicts had a wider political dimension as well. The rift exposed by the latter incident corresponded to the division between the Malian leadership's allies and its enemies. Moreover, the Lamhar and Imghad tribes had historically been vassals of the Kounta and Ifoghas, respectively. And this was not the first time that conflicts involving contests over the vassal relationship had erupted. Clashes broke out during the 1990s, including after the end of the Tuareg rebellion in northern Mali.[30] Over the next decade, Lamhar leaders used their wealth derived from smuggling to increase their political influence in Gao Region, including through local and national legislative elections.[31]

A similar process occurred in Timbuktu Region, where Berabiche leaders involved in smuggling began to play a more prominent political role. Figures associated with drug smuggling successfully lobbied the Malian leadership for the creation of a separate administrative region (Taoudeni) and several new districts in an administrative reform adopted just before the outbreak of the most recent rebellion. In addition, profits derived from smuggling were often invested into livestock and associated infrastructure, such as wells, fueling tensions between communities over resources.

State Complicity With AQIM

The alliance between the Malian leadership and local notables based on organized crime also applied to AQIM's kidnapping-for-ransom business. These arrangements go a long way to explain why the Malian security apparatus by and large stopped short of confronting AQIM and its practice of using northern Mali as a safe haven for its hostage cases.

When the European tourists were abducted in 2003, the Malian and European governments relied on a former Tuareg rebel leader and current head of AQIM-linked Ansar Dine, Iyad Ag Ghali, and Tarkint's mayor, Baba Ould Cheikh, to act as intermediaries in the ransom negotiations. Beginning in 2008, the same figures would surface time and again as mediators in hostage cases, in some cases competing with each other, in others cooperating. In addition to Baba Ould Cheikh and Iyad Ag Ghali, this included Ibrahim Ag Assaleh—a member of the National Assembly for Bourem (a district that includes Tarkint) and later a leading figure in the Tuareg rebel National Movement for the Liberation of Azawad (MNLA)—and Mustafa Ould Limam Chafi, special adviser to the Burkinabe president.[32]

Although there is no hard evidence, it is generally assumed that successful intermediaries took a significant cut of the ransom payments and shared this with their political protectors in the Malian (or Burkinabe) leadership. U.S. diplomats observed in May 2009 that "an enormous influx of cash likely linked to the Canadian and European hostage crisis" had complicated the local elections in Tarkint, where several of the intermediaries were themselves running. Lamhar militiamen and suspects in kidnapping cases had shown up in the town on election day to intimidate voters.[33] For the Malian leadership, backing certain mediators was, at the least, a way of rewarding its allies in the north—and, possibly, a source of financial gain for senior officials.

Complicity between security officials and AQIM went beyond collusion in ransom negotiations as evidenced by the June 2009 assassination of Lieutenant Colonel Lamana Ould Bou by AQIM. Several sources, including Malian army officers, consistently explained the death as related to an arms deal with AQIM gone awry. Bou had been known to feed information to AQIM, as had several other Berabiche army officers, many of whom had close relations with relatives and fellow tribesmen in the group.[34]

By the fall of 2010, Malian officials' complicity with AQIM and drug traffickers had emerged as a major obstacle to regional security cooperation. After the Mauritanian army suffered heavy casualties during a raid in northern Mali in September 2010, the Mauritanian defense minister visited Mali's capital to demand in vain that a Malian army officer suspected of having informed AQIM about the offensive be prosecuted. Several Algerian journalists, operating as mouthpieces for the regime, publicly pointed to the Malian leadership's complicity, as did senior Algerian officials in talks with U.S. diplomats.[35] The Mauritanian army continued to fight AQIM in northern Mali, restricting cooperation and information sharing with the Malian army to a minimum. Hostage deals in which European states successfully pressured Mali and Mauritania to release convicted kidnappers or AQIM members further undermined regional cooperation, with Algeria and Mauritania protesting strongly against Mali's release of their nationals.

In northern Mali, the government lost all credibility in view of widespread evidence of collusion with AQIM and organized crime. Northern leaders, including future key players in the Tuareg rebel MNLA, publicly denounced such collusion.[36] Even former senior government officials recognize today that complicity with criminal interests had "entirely taken over government policy in the north" in the final years of President Amadou Toumani Touré's rule. This was the context in which the return of Tuareg fighters from Libya altered the balance of power in the north and thereby paved the way for a new rebellion.

Organized Crime and Current Conflict Dynamics in Mali

The current conflict in Mali is not exclusively or even predominantly a clash between competing criminal networks. Other interests and grievances contributed to the eruption of the conflict in January 2012. Nevertheless, actors involved in organized crime play leading roles and wield decisive political and military influence.

This is most obvious in the alliance that has dominated the conflict—that of Tuareg rebel leader Iyad Ag Ghali and other members of the Ifoghas tribal establishment with AQIM. By all accounts, Ag Ghali made a pact with the AQIM leadership after his ambitions for leadership in the Tuareg rebellion were thwarted in January 2012.[37] In doing so, he was able to build on the business relations he had established with AQIM through various ransom negotiations since 2003.

AQIM's financial and military power, acquired principally through its kidnappings for ransom, is likely to have been central to Ag Ghali's tactical considerations. Perhaps equally important was the fact that AQIM continued to hold several hostages at the outbreak of the conflict, meaning that major future revenues were to be expected. In the rapidly evolving balance of power between various armed groups in the north, AQIM emerged as the key arbiter due to its financial clout. The alliance allowed Ag Ghali's Ansar Dine movement to rapidly supersede the MNLA as the main Tuareg military force. Close observers of developments in Timbuktu and Gao between May and July 2012 generally agree that AQIM commanders were the real decisionmakers behind Ansar Dine and, to a lesser extent, the AQIM offshoot MUJAO.

MUJAO in Gao

MUJAO emerged as the main force in Gao in May and June 2012, illustrating the role of criminal interests even more clearly. The group, whose two most prominent public figures have close ties to AQIM, first surfaced in October 2011, claiming the abduction of two Spaniards and an Italian from the Tindouf refugee camps in Algeria's far southwest.[38] At first, the group represented a hard core of jihadist and criminal elements, but it quickly became a front for drug smugglers from Gao. While the group does include some convinced jihadists, it only became a powerful force through its integration or association with organized crime networks—and they are likely to see MUJAO as a convenient temporary instrument.

The bulk of MUJAO's core membership was drawn from Lamhar Arabs in Gao Region—at least until July 2012, when it began a wider recruitment effort. Local sources consistently named a handful of Lamhar businessmen with known involvement in drug trafficking and kidnapping for ransom as MUJAO's real masters and financiers—including Cherif Ould Taher and Mohamed Ould Ahmed "Rouji." Prominent Lamhar and Songhai notables and businessmen such as Mohamed Ould Mataly, Baba Ould Cheikh, and Ali Badi Maiga also quickly adapted to and supported the joint MUJAO–Ansar Dine–AQIM administration in Gao to protect their interests.[39]

The group appears to be doing well financially. MUJAO likely made a significant profit in return for its release of an Italian and two Spanish hostages in July 2012. It also gained in prestige following the Burkinabe-mediated deal, as three suspects in the kidnapping case who were imprisoned in Mauritania and Niger were also released as part of the agreement.

Before the French-led intervention in northern Mali in January 2013, the group managed to gain the support of the wider Gao population by using its financial clout to distribute food to the people.[40] It also claimed responsibility for suicide attacks targeting Algerian security forces in March and June 2012, as well as the capture of seven Algerian consular officials in Gao in April. Whether the group's quarrels with Algeria are related to its smuggling activities is open to speculation.

AQIM and Arab Militias in Timbuktu

A somewhat different situation has prevailed in Timbuktu, where, as in Gao, criminal networks and jihadist militants initially entered into an alliance. The government-allied militias protecting the town split in late March 2012 as MNLA and Ansar Dine forces neared. One group of forces led by Colonel Mohamed Ould Meydou left Timbuktu while others remained to negotiate Timbuktu's handover. The forces that remained were led by three prominent businessmen reputed to be involved in cannabis resin smuggling who had been key to the militia mobilization effort since 2008: Oumar Ould Ahmed, Dina Ould Daya, and Moulay Ahmed. According to several consistent accounts, they delayed the MNLA's takeover of the town and in the meantime allowed AQIM to enter the city and take control.

Subsequently, however, AQIM ordered the militia out of town. The forces that were expelled then emerged as the National Liberation Front of Azawad (FNLA), seeking to distance themselves from the Islamist groups controlling Timbuktu.[41] When the Berabiche community held a meeting at the Malian-Mauritanian border in June 2012, notables and army officers publicly attacked the FNLA's leaders as known drug smugglers who shared responsibility for the escalation of conflict in northern Mali and had willingly handed over Timbuktu to AQIM. Consequently, the FNLA was isolated among the Berabiche community at the meeting.[42]

Before the French intervention, the group, which has changed its name to Arab Movement of Azawad, apparently considered that its interests were best served by dissociating themselves from the jihadist groups without confronting them. The group remains a force to be reckoned with, as are the smuggling-related interests it represents.

Fluid Dynamics

While the role of criminal networks is clear in the above groups, the dynamics at play here are ever-evolving. The lines between groups are often blurry, alliances are temporary, and networks overlap. The boundaries between the MNLA and Ansar Dine, for instance, remain fluid, making further reconfigurations within the Tuareg movements likely. The Ifoghas leaders backing Ansar Dine have continually—and often successfully—sought to rally the support of other Tuareg rebel leaders and fighters, including several notables from the Kidal region. Those important political and military players are reputed to be involved in drug smuggling and have at times switched their loyalties between the MNLA and Ansar Dine.[43] The formerly government-allied Imghad militias, some of which have joined Ansar Dine while others fled to Niger under the leadership of Colonel Elhadji Gamou and were inactive as of July 2012, have also often been associated with drug smuggling.

Current conflict dynamics are characterized by tactical alliances in which networks involved in kidnapping for ransom and drug smuggling play a decisive political and military role. Some of these networks currently call the shots in radical Islamist movements, most obviously in the case of MUJAO. Others maintain an ambiguous relationship with such movements, such as in the case of the FNLA's and Ansar Dine's relations with AQIM. Their aversion to clear and open positions in the current stage of the conflict betrays a readiness to rearrange their alliances once doing so becomes opportune, in order to promote their political and business interests. These groups are constantly looking for the next most-advantageous arrangement.

This poses a dilemma for the Malian government, as well as northern community leaders siding with the government: Should they seek the support of notables and businessmen involved in criminal activity and allied with the armed groups that controlled northern Mali in order to weaken AQIM and MUJAO? Or would such alliances with criminal interests undermine the credibility of their enterprise, likening it to the former Malian leadership's approach to the north? Many politicians in the north believe a temporary alliance with drug traffickers commanding armed groups is unavoidable if the jihadist elements hiding in the vast desert and mountains of northern Mali are to be defeated.

Conclusion

Though the entire Sahel and Sahara region is affected by state-criminal collusion, the role of organized crime in northern Mali's descent into conflict is particularly vivid, and it offers lessons not just for Mali's donors but also for neighboring states.

Organized criminal activity escalated in northern Mali during a period when the country was a major recipient of foreign assistance from the United States, the European Union (EU), and individual EU member states. External security-related aid was heavily focused on counterterrorism and state capacity, with donors providing training and technical assistance. Leading donors—particularly the United States and France—grew increasingly frustrated by the Malian leadership's reluctance to tackle AQIM but saw this mainly through the lens of counterterrorism, paying much less attention to the wider problem of state complicity with organized crime.

As the situation deteriorated, the EU began promoting a major push to expand the state's administrative and security presence in northern Mali known as the Special Program for Peace, Security, and Development of North Mali. Like other donor assistance in the security domain, the plan was primarily designed to boost state capacity but neglected the fundamental political issue of state collusion with organized crime. Moreover, despite donors' increasing frustration with the Malian leadership's inaction vis-à-vis AQIM, they did not exert stronger pressure on the government by leveraging the substantial development aid allocated to Mali.

As West Africa's supposed democratic success story, Mali remained the region's "donor darling" until the regime crumbled under a mutiny of low-ranking officers in March 2012. Arguably, the takeover of the state and politics in the north by criminal elements could have been avoided had donors used their influence to push for officials involved in organized crime to be prosecuted or dismissed. Donors' strong and largely unconditional support for the regime of Amadou Toumani Touré, accused by Mauritania and Algeria of failing to tackle AQIM, merits critical self-evaluation.

A possible implication for donors from the Malian trajectory is that greater attention should be paid to the risks of state collusion with organized crime in Mauritania and Niger. Concentrating on capacity building in the judicial and security sector is the right approach only as long as there is political backing from governments for combating criminal activity—and in Mali, this was clearly not the case. Focusing more on the drug and weapons trade in Mauritania and Niger should impact Mali, given that most flows transiting the country also pass through these two neighbors.

In Mauritania, donor support since 2009 has been largely based on the Ould Abdel Aziz regime's tough approach to counterterrorism, after what had been perceived as a lenient stance by his predecessor. But that focus is too narrow. Donors should balance that approach by placing greater emphasis on action against corruption and organized crime.

In Niger, the government is treading carefully in its approach to the thriving smuggling networks in the country's north because upsetting the vested interests at stake can easily provoke renewed instability in the region. As in Mali and Mauritania, Niger's government finds itself having to choose between allowing its political allies to benefit from smuggling and risking that a zero-tolerance policy spawns the rise of hostile smuggling networks. To help address this problem, donors could encourage and support a strategy that makes the political accommodation of influential players in Niger's north contingent upon their disengagement from the illicit economy and commitment to containing drug and weapons smuggling. Across the region, donors could also support initiatives to promote public debate and the dissemination of information on criminal activity through media outlets, in order to undermine the political backing criminal networks receive from the state or community.

But tackling the smuggling networks in Mali itself will be impossible as long as the north is outside government control. In northern Mali, extremist Islamist groups draw their power from their alliance with local criminal networks and business interests, and any approach to the conflict must include strategies to break these alliances. In all likelihood, this will have to include the co-optation of some criminal elements by the Malian government or guarantees from the state and from their communities that they will be shielded from prosecution.

The local northern communities should be at the heart of any future approach. Many of these communities hold the criminal actors responsible for the collapse of state institutions there, which has resulted in the isolation of those actors. Such pressure from local communities is likely the most effective means of containing criminal networks.

Ultimately, any settlement to the conflict should tackle the practices and structures that allowed state complicity with organized crime to thrive. Those practices include the maintenance of government-allied militias that were given a green light to engage in smuggling, and the absence of strong judicial and legislative checks and balances on the executive at the regional and local level.

It may be tempting for outside forces looking to take action now to recommend a decisive crackdown on smuggling to cut off funding sources and disrupt criminal networks. But zero-tolerance policies toward smuggling are not only unrealistic given the huge expanses over which these networks stretch and the security forces' limited resources; they are also counterproductive. In northern Mali and Niger, there are no alternative sources of income and employment that could rival those of contraband and drug smuggling. The collapse of tourism in parallel with the development of the kidnapping industry has further aggravated the situation, and the return of that income source will likely take many years even once the situation has stabilized and abductions cease. Until there are viable economic alternatives, clamping down on smuggling would further alienate local communities from their states.

There may be no definitive way to break up these criminal networks quickly. But beyond encouraging domestic political solutions, there are two areas over which external actors can perhaps wield a degree of influence: kidnapping for ransom and regional cooperation. Western governments have been playing an overwhelmingly negative role by paying ransoms and supplying what is most likely AQIM's and MUJAO's most important source of financing. Hiding behind the secrecy that surrounds the deals, Western governments have contributed to the growth of mafia-like networks linking the kidnappers with the intermediaries. Negotiators and their supposedly highly placed political backers also profit from the deals. Western forces have undermined regional cooperation by pressuring governments into releasing suspects or convicted criminals as part of the agreements, repeatedly irritating other governments in the region that had sought the detention of these individuals for crimes committed on their territories.

While outright rejection of ransom payments—let alone their criminalization, which was proposed by Algeria—is unrealistic, there is a clear need for a coherent international approach to the issue. Western governments should refrain from pushing regional governments to release criminals as part of ransom deals. They should also work to exclude any intermediaries from the negotiations and the ransom payments and pressure regional governments to prosecute intermediaries benefiting from such payments.

In addition, the distrust between the former Malian leadership and Mauritania, as well as Algeria, is a major obstacle to security cooperation in the region, including on organized crime. Further, Algeria is split between its desire to assert its pivotal role in tackling the issue and its reluctance to take the lead, a stance that will also continue to pose a challenge. But the demise of the regime of Amadou Toumani Touré represents an opportunity for improved regional security cooperation, including on organized crime. Western governments should seize the opportunity by supporting regional initiatives to improve cooperation, rather than try to play a leading role themselves.

Notes

1   Emmanuel Grégoire, "Sahara Nigérien: Terre d'Echanges," *Autrepart* 6 (1998): 91–104; Judith Scheele, "Tribus, États et Fraude: La Région Frontalière Algéro-Malienne," *Études Rurales* 184, (July–December 2009): 79–94.

2   Judith Scheele, "Circulations marchandes au Sahara: Entre Licite et Illicite," *Hérodote* 142 (3/2011): 143–62.

3   Ahmed Rouadjia, *Grandeur et Décadence de l'Etat Algérien* (Paris: Éditions Karthala, 1994), 349–52.

4   Saad Lounes, "Kidal, 49ème wilaya d'Algérie," June 14, 2009, http://saadlounes.unblog.fr/kidal-49eme-wilaya-dalgerie.

5   Alain Antil, *Contrôler les Trafics ou Perdre le Nord: Notes sur les Trafics en Mauritanie*, Note de l'Ifri, 2010.

6   Amel Blidi, "Un pacte entre la maffia de la cigarette et les terroristes," *Le Quotidien d'Oran*, April 3, 2005.

7   Interviews, Tripoli, June 2012; also see Jean-François Bayart, *Global Subjects: A Political Critique of Globalization* (Cambridge: Polity, 2007), 56f.

8   Information on the routes used is partly drawn from Jean-Luc Peduzzi, *Physionomie et enjeux des trafics dans la bande sahélo-saharienne*, Note de l'Ifri, 2010; as well as Simon Julien, "Le Sahel Comme Espace de Transit des Stupéfiants. Acteurs et Conséquences Politiques," *Hérodote* 142 (3/2011): 125–42.

9   See, for example, "Saisie de près de 1,5kg de Cocaïne à l'Aéroport International Houari-Boumediene," *El Watan*, May 17, 2012; "Plus de deux Kilogrammes de Cocaïne saisis à l'Aéroport d'Alger," *El Watan*, May 10, 2012; "Huit Stewards d'Air Algérie Arrêtés pour Trafic de Cocaïne, des Fils de 'Personnalités' Protégés," *Dernières Nouvelles d'Algérie*, November 15, 2011, www.dna-algerie.com/interieure/huit-stewards-d-air-algerie-arretes-pour-trafic-de-cocaine-des-fils-de-personnalites-proteges-2.

10 "Saisie Record de Drogue à Nouakchott," Radio France Internationale, August 14, 2008.

11 Adam Thiam, "Air Cocaïne: L'étau se resserre, Interpol recherche Ibrahima Gueye," *Le Républicain*, May 11, 2011; "Affaire dite du 'Boeing de la drogue': Le Procureur Sombé Théra interjette appel contre la décision du juge d'instruction," *Le Prétoire*, July 2, 2012.

12 Julien, "Le Sahel Comme Espace de Transit des Stupéfiants," 132.

13 Peduzzi, *Physionomie et enjeux des trafics*, 6.

14 Julien, "Le Sahel Comme Espace de Transit des Stupéfiants," 128–29.

15 "Démantèlement du réseau de trafic de drogue nommé Polisario," *Jeune Afrique*, December 20, 2010; "Le Mali traque dans le désert des trafiquants de drogue et leur marchandise," Agence France-Presse, September 14, 2011.

16 "Dun al-Kashf an Jalibiha: al-Lajna al-Amniya al-Ulya fi Tarabulus Tadhbut Arbaa Atnan min al-Mukhadharat w Taqum bi I'damha" [Without revealing their importers: the Supreme Security Committee Tripoli seizes and destroys four tons of drugs], almanaralink.com, May 29, 2012.

17 International Crisis Group, *Islamist Terrorism in the Sahel: Fact or Fiction* (Brussels: International Crisis Group, 2005).

18 "Droudkal aurait demandé 10 Millions de dollars pour la libération d'Eden Dyer," *Ennahar Online*, June 16, 2009, www.ennaharonline.com/fr/news/2159.html.

19 See, for example, "Les otages auraient été libérés contre une rançon," Agence France-Presse, November 2, 2008; "8 millions d'euros de rançon pour libérer les otages espagnols?" *Le Nouvel Observateur*, August 24, 2010; "Italian Maria Mariani Free After 14 Months as al-Qa'ida hostage in Sahara desert," Agence France-Presse, April 18, 2012.

20 Délégation des finances, *Sixième séance ordinaire de la Délégation des finances des Chambres fédérales*, www.parlament.ch/f/mm/2009/Pages/mm-findel-2009-11-19.aspx.

21 Antil, *Contrôler les Trafics ou Perdre le Nord*.

22 Afrique drogue, "Mauritanie: un trafiquant de drogue français en cavale," September 16, 2011, http://afriquedrogue.blogs.rfi.fr/article/2011/09/16/mauritanie-un-trafiquant-de-drogue-francais-en-cavale.

23 "Mauritanie-Drogue: La bande qui a détrôné le General Ould El-Hadi," *Alakhbar*, June 18, 2012.

24 "Niger: Aghali Alambo et Abta Hamidine, inculpés d'actes terroristes, libérés," Afrik.com, April 2, 2012, www.afrik.com/article25219.html; "Reportage Exclusif: Abta Hamidine s'apprêtait à livrer les quatre otages français au clan Kadhafi," *Aïr Info*, June 29, 2011.

25 See, for example, "Policière égorgée à Adrar: Les soupçons se dirigent vers un réseau de trafiquants et des policiers," *Tout Sur l'Algérie*, July 23, 2010, www.tsa-algerie.com/divers/policiere-egorgee-a-adrar-les-soupcons-se-dirigent-vers-un-reseau-de-trafiquants-et-des-policiers_11662.html.

26 Scheele, "Tribus, Etats et Fraude, 87–88."

27 Interviews, Berabiche and Tuareg leaders, Nouakchott, July 2012; "Prominent Tuareg's View of Arab Militias, Rebellion, and AQIM," Diplomatic Cable, U.S. Embassy, Bamako, March 18, 2009, www.wikileaks.org/cable/2009/03/09BAMAKO163.html.

28 Salima Tlemçani, "Au Sahel, narcotrafiquants et terroristes se partagent le terrain," *El Watan*, November 1, 2010.

29 "Kidnapping and Liberation of Kounta Leader Illuminates Political Fissures in North," Diplomatic Cable, U.S. Embassy, Bamako, February 1, 2010, www.wikileaks.org/cable/2010/02/10BAMAKO52.html.

30 Baz Lecocq, *Disputed Desert: Decolonisation, Competing Nationalisms and Tuareg Rebellions in Northern Mali* (Leiden: Brill, 2010), 311–33; and Georg Klute, "Hostilités et alliances: Archéologie de la dissidence des Touaregs au Mali," *Cahiers d'Etudes Africaines* 137 (35) 1995: 55–71.

31 Scheele, "Tribus, Etats et Fraude."

32 "Affaire des otages européens détenus au Mali: Le président malien nomme un militaire comme médiateur," *Le Quotidien d'Oran*, August 14, 2003; "Quand le Mali négocie avec le GSPC," *Liberté*, November 3, 2008; "No thanks from Canada for freeing hostages: negotiator," Agence France-Presse, October 12, 2009; "Deux émissaires du président malien d'Amadou Toumani Touré auprès de la nébuleuse salafiste Al-Qaïda au Maghreb ont joué un rôle central," *Jeune Afrique*, March 6, 2010; "The Liberation of AQIM's Austrian Hostages: An Inside View," Diplomatic Cable, U.S. Embassy, Bamako, November 14, 2008, www.wikileaks.org/cable/2008/11/08BAMAKO888.html; "A Familiar Name Surfaces in Search for Canadian Diplomats' Kidnappers," Diplomatic Cable, U.S. Embassy, Bamako, February 23, 2009, www.wikileaks.org/cable/2009/02/09BAMAKO106.html.

33 "Electoral Tensions in Tarkint: Where AQIM, Arab Militias, and Tuaregs Meet," Diplomatic Cable, U.S. Embassy, Bamako, May 8, 2009, www.wikileaks.org/cable/2009/05/09BAMAKO280.html.

34 "Berabiche and AQIM in Northern Mali," Diplomatic Cable, U.S. Embassy, Bamako, April 17, 2008, www.cablegatesearch.net/cable.php?id=08BAMAKO371.

35 "Cinq algériens arrêtés à kidal: QG d'Al Qaîda et barons de la cocaïne au nord du Mali," *El Watan*, February 21, 2010; "Algeria Says Bamako Summit Key to Regional Campaign Against AQIM," Diplomatic Cable, U.S. Embassy, Algiers, October 25, 2009.

36 "Mali: une complicité en haut lieu avec les trafiquants de drogue et Aqmi," *Jeune Afrique*, November 21, 2011; "Mali: les autorités annulent une réunion sur le narcotrafic," *RFI*, October 6, 2011.

37 Interviews, Nouakchott and Bamako, July 2012. See also International Crisis Group, *Mali: éviter l'escalade* (Brussels: International Crisis Group, 2012), 12–19.

38 "Some Things We May Think about MUJWA," *The Moor Next Door*, May 30, 2012; http://themoornextdoor.wordpress.com/2012/05/30/somethings-we-think-about-mujwa.

39 Interviews, Songhai leaders, Bamako, July 2012; "Brèves de Gao: Le conseil des sages sur le banc des accusés," June 20, 2012, www.maliweb.net/news/la-situation-politique-et-securitaire-au-nord/2012/06/20/article,74405.html.

40 "Nord du Mali: le Mujao a marchandé la libération des otages européens," *RFI*, July 19, 2012.

41 "Le groupe armé arabe FNLA dit avoir quitté Tombouctou sur injonction d'Aqmi," Agence France-Presse, April 28, 2012.

42 Interviews, Berabiche leaders, Nouakchott and Bamako, July 2012; "Mali: la communauté arabe s'oppose aux groupes islamistes," *RFI*, June 5, 2012.

43 See, for example, the role of Deyti Ag Sidimou, as described in "Les hommes influents d'Ansar Dine: Qui sont-ils?" *La Dépêche*, July 23, 2012.

04

The Paranoid Neighbor: Algeria and the Conflict in Mali

Anouar Boukhars

Influence and Instability in Mali

The collapse of the old order in Mali came faster than anyone expected. Less than three months after the crisis erupted there in January 2012, the Malian army was unceremoniously defeated as it tried to quell an insurrection in the north, driven back south by an assortment of loosely aligned armed groups. A military coup on March 22 sent President Amadou Toumani Touré into hiding.

The crisis has created a major challenge for Algeria. Given its status as a regional military power and its intimate knowledge of the conflict dynamics in Mali, the country is expected to take the lead in solving the conflict. But preoccupied with a looming leadership transition, faced with popular disenchantment at home, and fearful of possible blowback from military intervention in Mali, Algeria has been more timid, hesitant, and ambivalent than the international community wants it to be. This posture is also attributed to the country's strict and inflexible adherence to the principle of nonintervention.

With more than $200 billion in foreign currency reserves, a massive military budget, battle-tested security forces with combat experience in counterterrorism, and influence in regional and international organizations, Algeria should logically use its military power and political influence to foster regional stability and sincerely coordinate a regional effort to fight terrorist groups in the Sahel. In Mali in particular, these resources could be put to very good use in mediating the conflict and in exerting pressure on the armed groups in the north. But so far, the military resources Algeria has applied have not equaled its capabilities. Algerian foreign policy seems torn between the country's desire to be cast and recognized as a regional leader and its reluctance or inability to use the significant tools at its disposal to maintain stability in its backyard and help restore peace when conflict does break out.

The institutional collapse in Mali's capital, Bamako, and the military debacle in the north of the country are the products of local, national, and international factors that are inexorably intertwined. The "wicked" problems of worsening state fragility,[1] compounded by the devastating shock of the Libyan war, directly led to the explosion of festering historical grievances in the north and the subsequent political vacuum in the south. After the coup, the military restored civilian rule and an interim civilian government, but the new administration is still struggling to regain popular trust and assert itself over the military junta. In the north, Islamist militant groups have consolidated their control.

The crisis in Mali has exposed the country's tectonic fault lines, casting a shadow over efforts to reintegrate the north into the rest of the country. Diplomatic attempts to solve the crisis faltered. The core states that could influence the key stakeholders in the conflict were unable or unwilling to reconcile their interests and harmonize their actions. Accusations and counteraccusations of free riding and self-serving posturing remained the norm until France intervened on January 11, 2013, to stop the advance of insurgents from northern Mali further into the country.

The bottom line is that a sustained, cooperative, and sincere engagement by Algeria is critical to the success of conflict resolution in Mali. The country's economic and political power as well as its efforts to position itself as a leader in its neighborhood place it in a unique position to influence events. Of course, its potential should not be exaggerated. The time when Algeria exemplified "revolutionary third-world nationalism" and held the "moral edge of leadership" is long gone.[2] The country is eerily out of step with the historic political changes sweeping the Middle East and North Africa; its demeanor remains dour and its stances opaque.[3] Yet, these issues do not negate Algeria's assets as a critical player in the Malian conflict. Western powers should engage in the conflict in Mali in a way that is complementary rather than competitive to Algeria's security and diplomatic initiatives.

Things Fall Apart

Keen observers of Mali have long considered the country the weakest link in the Sahel and the most prone to radical Islamist destabilization.[4] Some have warned about the Malian public's simmering discontent with their seemingly democratic but deeply dysfunctional state. They predicted a resumption of ethnic militancy in the north—which has troubled the capital with secessionist rebellions off and on since 1962—even before the conflict in Libya erupted in February 2011. But none imagined the dramatic sequence of events that saw Tuareg rebels conquer the north and the government collapse in the south. The Tuareg are Berber nomadic pastoralists that had long pushed for autonomy from a central government they accuse of misrule and marginalization but never before succeeded in so fully destabilizing the state. The disintegration of Mali is attributed to the fragility of the Malian political structure, weak governance and neglect of the hinterlands, and the simmering insurgency in the north, trans- formed by the Libyan war into a full-fledged armed rebellion.

Before it backfired on him, Amadou Toumani Touré, the president of Mali from 2002 to 2012, found it economically and politically convenient to rely on a loose network of questionable actors to keep control of the north rather than pay the price necessary to extend the state's authority to the recalcitrant region. His strategy of preventing the thinly populated and expansive peripheral northern zones of Kidal, Gao, and Timbuktu (which comprise two-thirds of the country but only 10 percent of the popula- tion) from slipping into armed insurgency was based on outsourcing state functions to opportunist local elites and manageable armed factions and militias. The Touré administration was also widely suspected of having relations with political patrons and criminal entrepreneurs with ties to al-Qaeda in the Islamic Maghreb (AQIM), a hybrid transnational terrorist-criminal organization that emerged from the Islamist insurgency that ravaged Algeria from 1992 to 1998.[5]

The collaboration among these actors was seen as mutually beneficial. Touré's sponsors and allies benefited handsomely from corruption and revenues from transnational criminal activity while allowing him to maintain Bamako's juridical authority in inhospitable spaces and to neutralize hostile armed groups.

This strategy of governance was ultimately unsustainable. It exacerbated ethnic and tribal tensions and left the structural problems of underdevelopment and poverty that produced the rebellions of 1963, the 1990s, and 2006–2009 unattended. Worse, it was built upon shaky and unreliable alliances.

When the Touré government launched the €50 million (around $64 million in today's dollars) Special Program for Peace, Security and Development in August 2011 to try and make up lost ground in the north, it was too little, too late. The plan was ill-conceived and badly implemented, and it inflamed tensions between north and south. Funded by the European Union (EU) and other international donors, the program was designed to quell rising discontent and roll back the gains that AQIM and criminal entrepreneurs made at the expense of the state, but it ended up further alienating local populations, strengthening anti-Bamako sentiment, and paving the way for renewed militancy.

The Tuareg, who make up about a third of the population in the north, strongly opposed the investments the government made in reconstituting a military presence of its troops in the north. Bamako considered the force essential to reassert its lost authority and protect the Development and Governance Centers it had established for infrastructure development.[6] It was seen as a violation of the 2006 Algiers accords, which laid out a ceasefire between north and south after a Tuareg insurrection and stipulated a reduction of southern state security forces in the northern part of the country.[7] This episode underlined the depth of the historical mistrust between south and north that began with Mali's independence in 1960 and was aggravated by economic deprivations in the north.

Several Tuareg organizations tried to harness this anger at the central authority in Bamako. The most prominent was the National Movement of Azawad (MNA); the Azawad is the name the Tuareg use to refer to Mali's northern region. Created in 2010, it endeavored to build a local network of dissent and mobilize international support for its project of northern independence from Mali. The MNA's case for secession revolved around grievances that had long existed. The capital was often accused of intentionally neglecting the north economically. Officials, the MNA said, siphoned off international aid for their own purposes, did not fully implement previous peace accords signed between north and south, and colluded with organized crime and AQIM.

Ultimately, an outside force was necessary to spur definitive action. The Libyan war that ousted Muammar Qaddafi in 2011 became the catalyst that "precipitated the [MNA] network's transformation into a rebellion."[8] Hundreds of Tuareg who served in Qaddafi's pan-African force, established in 1972, and who fought against Libyan revolutionaries returned to their homes in northern Mali. Some of these fighters are the offspring of Tuareg who had migrated to Libya during the 1984 drought or fled the Malian government's repression during the 1963 rebellion. They ignited the simmering insurgency.

The armed revolt against Malian forces began on January 17, 2012, exactly six months after the Tuareg returned home from Libya. It was led by the National Movement for the Liberation of Azawad (MNLA), an offshoot of the MNA established in October 2011 and composed of a mosaic of armed groups bound by loose loyalties and conditional alliances.

Since its inception, the MNLA was built on shaky foundations, vulnerable to micropolitical, ideological, and tribal tensions. The fight, however, united the disparate groups and quieted their differences. The swiftness and decisiveness of the military campaign stunned the south, causing popular dismay and anger at Touré's handling of the war as well as a revolt within the military hierarchy. Capitalizing on the sour mood in the capital, a junta led by Captain Amadou Haya Sanogo overthrew the president on March 22, just six weeks before Touré's term ended. Sanogo defended his coup on the basis that Touré failed "to provide adequate equipment to the defence and security forces fulfilling their mission to defend the country's territorial integrity."[9]

The overthrow was a direct result of the Tuareg rebels' humiliating rout of Malian forces. But discontent within the lower ranks of the armed forces was simmering before the onset of the rebellion. Collusion and corruption were primary concerns. Junior officers fumed at the siphoning off of foreign military aid, unmeritorious military promotions, the corruption of the military elite, and their suspected ties to criminal traffickers. Anger was also directed at the president's inner circle, which many viewed as deeply venal.

The coup illustrated the creeping decay of electoral democracy and degradation of military institutions. As Aminata Dramane Traoré, former minister of culture and tourism, aptly put it, "Sanogo is not the problem, Sanogo is a symptom."[10] Mali, once a promising example of democracy in western Africa, was caught in a web of regional terrorism, drug trafficking, and organized crime. Its leadership unfortunately succumbed to these pressures with devastating consequences for state and society.

After the overthrow of Amadou Toumani Touré, the Economic Community of West African States (ECOWAS), which was initially seen as the appropriate consortium to mediate the conflict, pressured Sanogo to cede power to an interim government led by Dioncounda Traoré. The new administration, reshuffled recently, is still unable to assert itself politically. Political parties are also numerous and fragmented, hampering the creation of a much-needed united national front.

In the north, confusion still reigns about how convergent or overlapping the armed groups are. The MNLA, which declared the independence of Azawad on April 5, 2012, after chasing government forces from Kidal, Gao, and Timbuktu, was forced to cede ground to armed Islamist forces— led by the group Ansar Dine (the supporters of religion)—that is cash rich and better armed than it is. As the revolutionary forces advanced south, armed groups in Timbuktu and Gao came to a provisional arrangement and began to reconfigure the power dynamics in northern Mali—a process that continues to spread and develop. The leading force of Ansar Dine has so far benefited the most from these realignments.

Mali's Battle Lines

The power struggle in both the south and north has exposed the underlying fragility of Malian society and the various entrenched powers at play. As soon as their common enemy melted away, Mali's disparate forces redrew battle lines. The military junta that toppled the government in an effort to ostensibly save the integrity of the state only expedited the dissolution of the country and threw the army into disarray. And the secular MNLA had its revolution "stolen" by the Islamist Ansar Dine, which is backed by al-Qaeda in the Islamic Maghreb, initially called the Salafist Group for Preaching and Combat (GSPC) before becoming an affiliate of al-Qaeda in 2007.

Before the French intervention on January 11, 2013, the groups associated with criminal and terrorist organizations were the dominant actors in northern Mali. The actions of these groups, and AQIM in particular, disrupted the status quo and created new vested interests, buttressed by criminal associations and tactical alliances, contributing to the eruption of the conflict in the first place. Those developments also have complicated the search for a peaceful resolution to the crisis, as different and rival groups jostle to carve out a prominent role in any power-sharing agreement with Bamako.[11] These internal dynamics mean that any outside intervention could further inflame local tensions, spark new and more dangerous alliances, and, given these groups' links to other countries, potentially have spillover effects on the wider region.

The GSPC's transformation into AQIM was driven by the major setbacks it suffered in Algeria. By 2003, the group was plagued by internal divisions and was running low on money and fighters. Several militants put down their arms as part of two amnesty initiatives launched by President Abdelaziz Bouteflika while the rest were successfully hunted down by Algerian security forces or forced to flee Algerian territory into northern Mali. The GSPC also saw some of its fighters leave for Iraq to join the insurgency against U.S. forces. "The point to be underscored," as a USAID report put it, "is the extent to which events inside Algeria dictated the regional refocusing of the group's operations, embroiling Mali in dynamics with which it had little to do, and over which it had no control."[12] These "exogenous dynamics" necessitate a regional response to the crisis in Mali.

Since the GSPC set up shop in northern Mali in 2003, AQIM has become deeply ingrained in society, patiently building and expanding a network structure of family ties, social support, political relations, and economic exchange. Over the years, the group has become the "best-funded, wealthiest" terrorist and criminal organization[13] thanks to the toll it imposed on transborder smuggling of drugs and the large number of ransoms it extorted from Western governments to save the lives of their kidnapped countrymen.

Occasionally, AQIM has used its Arab roots to ingratiate itself with Arab communities. Timbuktu, for example, is a stronghold of AQIM and is where the group first built its network of social and political alliances, "including with Arab militias tolerated and even maintained by [Touré]."[14] At other times, it used the distrust and competition between Songhai and Peuhl on the one hand and Arabs and Tuareg on the other to its advantage. But the most critical factor in the success of AQIM has been "more economic than cultural."[15] AQIM has managed to use its financial prowess to tap into the deep cultural divide in northern Mali. A few influential tribal leaders, for example, "received payments and gifts from GSPC operatives (including, reportedly, four-wheel-drive vehicles) in exchange for safe passage or sanctuary." Other Malian Arabs enriched themselves through active participation in the smuggling networks controlled or connected to AQIM.[16] This has worsened the deep-rooted contentions and competitions between personalities and communities, upsetting the traditional sociopolitical patterns and the balance of power between and among communities.

The dominant role of criminal and terrorist organizations in the conflict dynamics is best illustrated by the alliance between Ansar Dine and AQIM. Ansar Dine and its leader Iyad Ag Ghali, a Machiavellian fixture of Tuareg insurrections, gradually outwitted and eventually outgunned the MNLA for control of the uprising. The secular MNLA rebels thought Ag Ghali had been marginalized during the preparatory stages of the rebellion. Ag Ghali, who comes from the Ifoghas clan, the noblest tribe in the Tuareg caste system, and had been a key force in the Tuareg rebellion of the 1990s, was present in the discussions that the MNLA held by the Algerian border to mobilize support for their armed rebellion. He wanted to be the movement's secretary general but was rebuffed in November

2011, reportedly because of his links to AQIM, ties to Algeria, and past deals with the Malian presidency.

Ag Ghali has always been "inscrutable" with "a kaleidoscopic career as a diplomat, separatist rebel chief, and government mediator with Al-Qaeda hostagetakers."[17] Hardliners in the MNLA accuse him of selling out the Tuareg cause in the Tamanrasset Accord of 1991, which established a ceasefire between north and south after months of fighting. Besides compromising too much, he is seen as tilting the accords in favor of his region, Kidal, and directly contributing to the fragmentation of the Tuareg movement. His closeness to organized crime and a range of local armed militant groups is also troubling. But this time, "the lion of the desert," as members of his Ifoghas tribe endearingly call him, is causing a major scare because of his reinvention as a firebrand radical intent on imposing an extreme form of Islamic law.

Ag Ghali's support for war in the north was predicated upon his desire to install sharia all over Mali. A convert to Salafism in the late 1990s, he knows that a number of Malians have become more conservative over the years and were influenced by the Tablighi ideas and preaching that has pervaded northern Malian society. Indeed, as the MNLA marched on Gao and Timbuktu during the uprising, it could not find adherents to its secular separatist project. The rebellion entered hostile "sociological, political and religious terrain" that was much more conservative, Islamist, and unsupportive of the MNLA's cause.[18] So there is in fact some "social legitimacy to the project to impose Sharia law embodied by Iyad Ag Ghali."[19]

Ag Ghali has certainly made headway. Once the military campaign began, he mobilized Ansar Dine and solicited logistical and personnel support from his purported cousin, Abdelkrim Targui, the emir of the militant unit Katiba al-Ansar, "The Battalion of the Victors." Soon after, his forces had the upper hand on the battlefield, conquering the town of Kidal one week after the coup in Bamako and expelling the MNLA from Timbuktu shortly thereafter. By April, the charismatic Ag Ghali emerged as the master of the desert, absorbing "MNLA leaders and fighters into his movement."[20] Nevertheless, his recent religious excesses are strongly rejected by the Tuareg.

Alongside Ansar Dine and AQIM, the Movement for Tawhid and Jihad in West Africa (MUJAO)—a splinter offshoot of AQIM—has gradually established itself as a major actor in Gao, but very little is known about the group.[21] It first burst onto the scene after the spectacular abduction of three European tourists from the heavily fortified camps of Tindouf in Algeria in October 2011. Besides a preference for Algerian targets and a sociological makeup distinct from that of AQIM (its core membership is from the Lamhar tribe, supplemented by Sahrawis and, increasingly, Songhai recruits), MUJAO has behaved like its extremist counterparts, combining criminal and radical religious activity. MUJAO, and Ansar Dine as well, has benefited from kidnappings of Westerners for ransom, and the bonanza of the Libyan arms bazaar. The proceeds from these activities have enabled the group to broaden its recruitment base, despite popular opposition to its fundamentalist project. In the very ethnically diverse city of Gao, for instance, MUJAO has solidified its presence and ties, particularly with the city's Arab communities. Residents of Gao have protested against the group but welcomed "the modicum of security that came with MUJAO and view the MNLA's departure as the first step in a broader process of 'getting things back to normal.'"[22]

These groups' association with AQIM—if only potentially fleeting given how notoriously volatile and fluctuating alliances are—portends ominous consequences for Mali and its neighbors. AQIM's Algerian guru in North Africa, Abu Musab Abdul Wadud, also known as Abdelmalek Droukdel, confirmed such fears when he instructed his fighters to discreetly facilitate Ansar Dine's project of (gradually) implementing sharia in the Azawad and to "keep the cover of (AQIM) limited to our activities in the global jihad."[23] In other words, Droukdel prefers to leave the management of Mali's north to local Islamist forces like Ansar Dine and MUJAO while al-Qaeda's North African wing pursues its wider goals of dominating the region.

How successful AQIM's project is turning out to be in a complex social environment where loyalties change constantly is hard to tell. Careful observers of the Sahel believe that despite a long-standing trend toward religious conservatism at the grassroots level, it is highly unlikely that any force will be able to impose its extremist Islamist project on the region. Even though Salafi ideology has been making inroads for the last two decades, radical Islam in general lacks significant popular support in northern Mali.[24] And even though AQIM has developed impressive networks in northern Mali, the group's presence rests on unstable foundations. The vicissitudes of tribal allegiances, clan loyalties, and nomadic alliances make for an ephemeral existence, as does the unstable equilibrium within and between the different communities that populate the north.[25] Even Droukdel warned of zealous overreach, cautioning his allies not to seek immediate imposition of sharia in Mali's north. "Know that it is a mistake to impose all the rules of Islam at once on people overnight," he said.[26]

AQIM, because of its cash war chest, acquisition of weapons from Libya, and ability to operate unhindered in northern Mali, remains a key factor in provoking instability across the region. With "increased freedom to maneuver, terrorists are seeking to extend their reach and their networks in multiple directions," then U.S. Secretary of State Hillary Clinton warned recently.[27] U.S. officials suspect that AQIM fighters were involved in the September 11 attacks on the U.S. consulate in Benghazi. How to get a handle on this force must be a central concern for any policy aimed at quieting the situation in northern Mali.

Meanwhile, Iyad Ag Ghali must also be aware of the pitfalls of over-reaching. Too close association with AQIM endangers his cherished status as the main power broker in Mali, as was evident in the lead-up to the rebellion. Ag Ghali is concerned with maintaining his extensive ties to a variety of actors. As Rolan Marchal aptly put it, "Iyad ag Ghali is a good illustration of the type of people often needed by Algiers and Bamako to interact with AQIM or the Tuareg to maintain channels of communication."[28] Ag Ghali boasts a formidable array of contacts in Bamako and the most influential regional capital (Algiers), and he is believed to have significant weight with armed (militant) groups. He has used this web of influence—especially in Algiers—in earlier conflicts to great success.

Algeria's Man in the Azawad

The dominant role of Ag Ghali in the current crisis in Mali and his connections to Algeria have placed enormous pressure on the Algerians to use their influence with him and his armed group. More broadly, based on decades of experience, Algeria knows the conflict dynamics in Mali and has the potential to pressure and influence the decision calculus of the main armed actors in the country.[29] Indeed, since 1990 the international community has come to rely on its good offices and diplomatic intervention to help mediate or avert conflicts in Mali.

But since the onset of the hostilities in January 2012, Algeria's role has been opaque to many in the international community.[30] In the early months of the Malian conflict, Algeria adopted a more passive "wait and see" approach than it took in 2006, when it helped broker the Algiers accords. It appeared to hedge its bets carefully to protect its strategic interests.[31] This attitude was interpreted in the region as "malignant neglect," intended to punish Mali for the "sins" of its soon-to-be-deposed president Touré, whom the Algerians accused of "willful complicity" with AQIM.[32] Malians in the south felt betrayed, especially when Algeria withdrew its military advisers and cut off the delivery of military equipment during the decisive battle of Tessalit in early March 2012, in which Malian forces were besieged. The Algerians justified their inactivity on the basis that their commitment to Mali was driven by counterterrorism goals and not by counterinsurgency warfare.[33]

The MNLA is suspicious of Algeria's intent and harbors resentment over the country's past mediation strategy and choice of interlocutors, which limited Algeria's influence over the MNLA. The group's most influential wing is represented by those who were disenchanted by the 2006 accords. And the marginalization of Iyad Ag Ghali during the formation of the MNLA was in many ways an indirect jab at the architects of those accords: Algeria and Ag Ghali.[34] Some of the malcontents are convinced that Ag Ghali in particular is an agent of the feared DRS, Algeria's military intelligence service.[35] Some observers go so far as to believe that Algeria is deliberately allowing Ansar Dine to gain full control of the north, as that would weaken the MNLA and its separatist project as well as slow the recruitment base of AQIM.

Ag Ghali in particular is a threat to the MNLA's desire to be the representative of the north. He has political, tribal, and ideological connections that make his movement more effective at establishing a modicum of order in its territory and, most importantly, reining in AQIM and its offshoots. He has also pushed for the release of Western hostages to show himself as a pragmatist and prudent leader.[36] It is therefore no accident that the MNLA turned down Algeria's invitation to attend peace talks in early February.

Of course, Algeria distrusts the MNLA as well, mainly because of the MNLA's links to the country's own separatist groups in France. For instance, the MNLA's association with Algerian Berber nationalists irritates Algiers. Kabyle activists in France who agitate for Berber self-determination in Algeria provide significant logistical assistance to the separatist activism of the MNLA. The group must also view as disingenuous Algeria's support of the Polisario's three-decade-long quest for the independence of Western Sahara from Morocco while it denies the Tuareg people their shot at self-determination.[37]

Each of these factors makes it all the more difficult to take action to stabilize northern Mali—even when outside forces, Algeria especially, have the capacity to act.

Algeria's Geopolitical Posture

Algeria is a regional military power and has the potential to put pressure on armed actors in northern Mali. It could indeed be a key actor in the evolution of the current crisis. Algeria boasts the largest defense budget ($10.3 billion in 2012) on the African continent, strong military power projection capabilities (thanks to its large fleet of aircraft), and recognized counterterrorism expertise. It also serves as a founding member and leader in several regional and global counterterrorism forums. Algeria hosts the Joint Staff Operations Committee (CEMOC) and the Fusion and Liaison Unit (FLU), institutional mechanisms that were the forums of choice for Algeria to shape the regional fight against terrorism while fending off foreign intrusion.

Algeria also plays a significant role in the counterterrorism structure the United States set up in the Sahel. From the 2002 Pan Sahel Initiative, expanded into the Trans-Sahara Counterterrorism Partnership in 2005, to the 2007 Africa Command (AFRICOM) based in Stuttgart, Germany, the United States has focused on getting Algeria to use its experience in counterterrorism and counterintelligence in the fight against terrorism and organized crime. The country's DRS "is arguably the world's most effective intelligence service when it comes to fighting Al Qaeda," writes John R. Schindler, a former counterintelligence officer with the National Security Agency. "It is also probably the most cold-blooded."[38] The DRS developed its skills during the 1990s civil war when Algeria was a living laboratory of counterterrorism policy and practice. It led a brutal and unrelenting campaign against violent Islamist insurgents that significantly reduced the militant groups' capabilities. The number of radical insurgents dwindled from a high of 27,000 fighters in the mid-1990s to no more than a few hundred in 1998.

The conduct of Algerian security forces in the peak period of horrific violence (1993–1997) put the country in the spotlight, and it became isolated internationally. After the September 11 terrorist attacks in the United States, Algeria was brought back into the fold. President Bouteflika skillfully used these tragic incidents to realign Algeria's security and foreign policy needs with those of America, selling Algiers as a valuable partner in the war on terrorism. Algeria was finally given the "kind of warrior's legitimacy" it long coveted, "similar to the revolutionary legitimacy it enjoyed among the Non-Allied countries during the 1960s and 1970s as a result of its war of independence against France."[39]

In discussions in Algiers, most interlocutors pointed out that the Algerians fought an existential war against Islamist extremists without any help from the outside world. For Algerian officials, the terrorist attacks in the United States proved that the Algerian regime was prescient in its warnings throughout the 1990s about the dangers of radical Islam. Since September 11, this narrative "has been subsumed into the West's counterterrorism,"[40] allowing the Algerian regime to move beyond international scrutiny of the gross violations of human rights committed in the 1990s. It also opened the way for the establishment of strategic relations with the United States.

The security partnership between the United States and Algeria was strengthened in 2010 with the signing of a customs mutual assistance agreement and a mutual legal assistance treaty. In February 2011, the two countries created a bilateral contact group on counterterrorism and security cooperation, and Algeria's importance in the security realm is enhanced by a set of defense partnerships with several European countries, including Great Britain and Germany. (Its relations, however, with the EU and especially France remain strained for historical and geopolitical reasons. Algeria sees France and its regional allies, namely Morocco, as the biggest hurdles in its quest for regional dominance.) It is also anchored in a set of multilateral institutions, including the African Union, where Algerian Ramtane Lamamra heads the Peace and Security Council, and the United Nations, where Saïd Djinnit is the special representative of the UN secretary general for West Africa.

With all these power attributes, Algeria is naturally seen as an indispensable actor in the Sahel. Its leadership might be "a prickly, paranoid group to work with," as former U.S. ambassador to Algeria Robert Ford wrote in a diplomatic cable in 2008, but its importance in the fight against AQIM is essential.[41] Still, deep-seated suspicion of Algeria's motives as a regional power—whose security policies in the Sahel reverberate across regional boundaries—were clearly evident in the several extensive interviews conducted with a range of specialists in Algiers, Berlin, Brussels, Nouakchott, Rabat, and Washington, DC.

Most interlocutors highlight Algeria's core strengths and strategic importance to the fate of a critical region, but they are frustrated by how brittle, paranoid, and opaque a partner the country can be. Most of these frustrations revolve around the spread of AQIM. Algiers has refused to direct its attack capabilities against AQIM outside its borders. It justifies those decisions with its long-established doctrine of state sovereignty and nonintervention.[42] But that fails to convince others, especially in France and the European External Action Service. To its European critics, Algeria has the material and military capabilities to weaken AQIM, especially if it coordinates with Western powers, but the resources it has applied have been disproportionate to its capabilities, enabling the group to establish footholds in unstable places like northern Mali.

Even American security officials, clearly the most patient and in favor of Algeria assuming the mantle of regional leadership, are not certain the country is willing to manage its backyard. In an interview with the author, a senior officer at AFRICOM portrayed Algeria as an ambivalent regional power whose expectations and actions are difficult to discern because they vary according to the issue area. The country can at times be very helpful in support of U.S. intelligence and surveillance operations in the Sahel but uncooperative at others, withholding some critical intelligence on AQIM activities and doing little to monitor and control the logistical supply lines to extremist armed groups in the Sahel. Similar complaints were advanced by a senior U.S. diplomat who expressed his frustration with Algerian officials' unwillingness to share the information they have on the main actors in the conflict in Mali.[43]

Algerian officials react defensively and angrily to these accusations. In interviews in Algiers and Brussels, Algerian officials bemoan the prevalent misreading of their country's role and functions in the Sahel. Algeria, they say, has done more than any other country to support the objective of security and peace in the region—and to contribute actively to conflict resolution in Mali. All the previous accords were signed in Algiers, and in the current conflict, Algeria hosts over 30,000 refugees and has donated tons of food and medicine to other camps in Mauritania and Niger. Algeria also pressured the MNLA to release dozens of Malian soldiers. Still, the Algerian regime is extremely worried about being dragged into a Saharan quagmire, which could have catastrophic effects on its domestic stability.

Algeria's Reticence

The Algerian regime's hesitancy is rooted in a number of factors, ranging from its norm of nonintervention to its wariness about outsider meddling and the spillover of the extremist threat into its territory. Several interlocutors in Algiers believe that an Algerian intervention in Mali would embroil the country in a disastrous adventure. Some claimed that such an eventuality is exactly the intention of ECOWAS and its foreign supporters, namely France and Morocco.

A former senior administrator in the influential African Center for Studies and Research on Terrorism in Algiers compared an Algerian intervention in Mali to that of the blunder of Argentina's military junta in the 1982 Falklands War. The British humiliatingly routed the Argentines who had occupied the islands; that defeat had repercussions in Buenos Aires, ending military rule of Argentina and ushering in a democratic transition.

The analogy of the Soviets' imbroglio in Afghanistan was also amply cited in discussions in Algiers. In the words of one journalist, the Algerian regime is not foolish enough to take the lead in fighting radical Islamists beyond its borders because such action brings along with it the potential to unite disparate armed groups behind the banner of AQIM and against Algeria. "This is exactly what the Americans did to Pakistan," said

Abdelaziz Rahabi, former Algerian diplomat and minister of communications. Pakistan, which was made to take on extremist groups, ended up being those groups' target of choice. Rahabi fears that subcontracting the war against terrorist and criminal groups in Mali to Algeria would make his country the main target of AQIM and its associates.[44] It would also "push tens of thousands of refugees to our southern borders, and more of the weapons' flow."[45]

The Algerian regime is also worried that an intervention in Mali would threaten the balance it has laboriously built between its foreign and domestic priorities.[46] The primary drivers of Algerian foreign policy are regime preservation and its legitimization by the international community.[47] Despite an inescapable divergence of interests within the ruling circle, there is a general shared consensus on the necessity to create favorable external conditions for securing the regime's hold on power and the country's privileged geopolitical position. Specifically, this means that the regime must control the instabilities in its southern Sahelian hinterland, protect against Western intrusion and interference, and neutralize its regional rivals. With the Islamist ascent to power in its neighborhood and Western intervention in Libya, the regime is "concerned that one of the main planks of the past decade's strategic balance struck with the U.S. and Europe has been weakened."[48]

Algeria is broadly suspicious that a French-led bloc is being established with the main goal of containing Algerian power. The country is distrustful of its neighbors, especially the so-called pro-French axis, led by Morocco and the weaker states of the Sahel. And the feeling of unease and insecurity has only grown with the momentous political changes that have engulfed neighboring Tunisia and especially Egypt, where Islamists swept away the old-guard generals without triggering any public protests or military coups. Very few observers anticipated a scenario in which a democratically elected Islamist president outmaneuvered his generals within a month of his election. It took Turkey's Islamists decades to finally jettison military rule. In contrast, in Algeria, twenty years ago, the generals cancelled the whole electoral process to prevent the Islamists from coming to power, plunging the country into a horrific civil war. The increasing closeness of post-Qaddafi Libya with Morocco only adds to Algeria's fears.

The dramatic purge of the senior Egyptian military command by President Mohamed Morsi, helped by disaffected younger officers, is no doubt troublesome to the aging generals in Algeria, including DRS's all-powerful and long-serving chief, General Mohamed Mediene, and eighty-one-year-old Army Chief of Staff Giad Salah. (A number of generals have already died or were forcibly retired.) To be sure, the security establishment in Algeria is entrenched and secretive, making it hard to know whether there is any disgruntlement in the ranks. But the status quo might soon become unsustainable as the old generation of military leaders is replaced by the new.[49]

The response of the international community to the stunning developments in Egypt equally worries the Algerians. Despite serious concerns about an Islamist power grab, the United States has not voiced (public) alarm nor has it threatened to cut off military and financial aid. This prudent and measured reaction feeds suspicion that the United States is cozying up to the Islamists. Since the onset of the Arab revolt, the Algerians have been perturbed by the positive engagement of Islamists and Washington's (gentle) prodding of military leaders in Egypt to refrain from monopolizing legislative and executive power.

The prospect of Islamists surging to power in Algeria remains remote (Islamist parties performed far below expectations in the country's May 2012 legislative elections),[50] but the acceleration of events domestically and regionally heralds a period of flux. So far, Algeria has successfully weathered the popular upheavals. Importantly, Algerians' appetite for revolutionary change remains subdued, as memories of the 1990s civil war are still vivid. The political opposition also remains weak, and the regime has successfully used oil and gas money and limited reforms to placate social dissenters. It has skillfully used the tragic developments in Syria, the turbulent transition in Libya, and the chaos in Mali to warn Algerians about the dangers of brusque radical change. The regime portrayed the Western-induced regime change in Libya as a sinister plot by Western forces, rekindling Algerian nationalist sentiment.

In the face of incessant calls for an intervention in Mali, the Algerian leadership has called for national unity. Last May, President Bouteflika urged Algerian youth to mobilize against the "instigators of *fitna* (chaos) and division" and guard against foreign meddling and interference. A few weeks later, it was the turn of the newly appointed prime minister to call for the establishment of a "strong internal front" to protect the country from "malicious hands" desiring to do harm to Algeria and its territorial integrity. Some Algerians believe that these calls for patriotism stem from genuine fears of external destabilization. According to a source close to the Algerian presidency, the historical precedent to these fears goes back to General De Gaulle's proposal in 1961 to rob Algeria of its Sahara.[51] Most analysts, however, believe that the regime is playing the nationalist card to temper Algerians' disgruntlement with their social conditions during a difficult leadership transition.

The country's leadership seems deadlocked over the succession to president Abdelaziz Bouteflika, who may or may not retire when his third term ends in 2014. It took four months after parliamentary elections were held for a new government to be appointed (key ministers kept their portfolios), exposing a rift in the ruling clans over who should be nominated for key ministerial posts and who to anoint as the next leader. This uncertainty over succession is a cause of concern as it creates a political vacuum and amplifies popular disaffection. "The main challenge for the leadership that has ruled Algeria since 1962," argued Algerian journalist Lamine Chikhi in an interview with the author, "is whether they can avoid a messy succession battle." The outcome would have ramifications for the pace of institutional change and the direction of economic reforms.

Securing Borders

The conflict in Mali is a test case of whether Algeria can reconcile its domestic priorities with its foreign goals. The threat that the conflict in northern Mali will spill over into Algeria is real, as is the prospect of a long-term French military presence in Mali. Both of these eventualities might affect the dynamics of the power struggle within Algeria's leadership and threaten the country's dominant position in its neighborhood. Kamel Daoud, an Algerian columnist, nicely summed up Algeria's perceived vulnerability when he stated that a Western military presence on the country's southern flank is detrimental to an Algeria already besieged by unfriendly neighbors and instabilities. The country is wary of its Moroccan rival in the West, concerned about rising discontent and instability in the southwestern Polisario camps of Tindouf, and threatened from the east by turmoil in Libya.[52]

Since the turmoil in Mali began, Algeria has taken actions to protect itself against the repercussions of these scenarios. It has significantly beefed up its troop presence on its southern flank and increased the number of checkpoints and surveillance flights to track the movement of drug dealers, arm traders, and terrorists that could carry the conflict across a range of territories. Border crossings were also tightened and transport of goods controlled and monitored.[53] In January 2013, the prime ministers of Algeria, Libya, and Tunisia met in the western Libyan border town of Ghadames, where they agreed to form joint teams to better coordinate security along their porous borders and stem the flow of drugs, arms, and fuel. The interdiction of the latter is critical as it allows militants mobility. These are the kinds of measures that the United States and the EU have been pushing Algeria to take for years now.

Algiers has also stepped up its monitoring of the massive refugee camps near Tindouf in southwest Algeria. On a number of past occasions, these camps were infiltrated by extremist groups and gangs intent on kidnapping Westerners for ransom.[54] Trouble seems to be brewing once again. On July 29, 2012, Spain sent a military plane to evacuate its aid workers from the camps in Algerian territory due to "well-founded evidence of a serious increase in insecurity in the region."[55] The evacuation represents a political embarrassment to Algeria, which has long maintained that the refugee camps are impervious to the advances of extremist and criminal groups.

As armed militias proliferate in northern Mali and the swelling number of vulnerable refugees and displaced Malians overwhelms aid efforts and strains neighboring countries that are already facing severe food shortages, Algeria has also recently stepped up its efforts to find a diplomatic solution to the conflict. So far, however, international action has lacked coordination, and Algeria's actions have simply not been enough.

The Intervention Calculus

Until the sudden French military intervention in Mali in January 2013, the mediation process led by the Economic Community of West African States had been ineffective. ECOWAS struggled to win the backing of the United

States, the United Nations Security Council, and Algeria, casting serious doubt on its plan to help Mali restore its authority in the north.

ECOWAS sought to implement a phased military deployment process in Mali. Phase one entailed securing the political transition and revamping Mali's (military) institutions to lay groundwork for military action. In phase two, a military intervention in the north was supposed to take place. But that strategy seemed unlikely to work. Despite being members of ECOWAS, Senegal and Ghana declared that they would not participate in military deployment to Mali. Other members of the bloc, especially Niger, were itching for war in the north even if the political conditions in the south were not propitious for such escalation.[56] The Malian army, meanwhile, was in disarray and it had refused to allow the deployment of West African soldiers in Bamako, rejecting any direct intervention of ECOWAS.

International Reactions

Before the French incursion, most United Nations Security Council members had serious concerns about the mandate and fighting capacity of the standby force of 3,000 troops that ECOWAS claimed to have mobilized. The plan was "too imprecise and too drawn out in its timetable," complained a diplomat on the Security Council.[57] On October 12, the UN Security Council passed a unanimous resolution giving ECOWAS, the African Union, and the United Nations forty-five days to present a credible plan for military action in the north.

The United States insisted on bolstering the political transition in Bamako first before contemplating an assault on armed forces in the north. Otherwise, "an ECOWAS mission to militarily retake the north is ill-advised and not feasible," said Assistant Secretary of State for African Affairs Johnnie Carson in testimony before Congress.[58]

But as the crisis persisted, the United States grew more concerned about the ability of AQIM to use northern Mali as a staging ground to destabilize its Sahelian neighbors and the new fragile democracies of North Africa. Washington increased its counterterrorism training and military aid to the countries most threatened by the chaos in Mali. For example, in July Mauritania was awarded military equipment (trucks, uniforms, and communications gear) worth nearly $7 million while Niger received two military transport airplanes to conduct surveillance that amounted to $11.6 million. In conjunction with France, the United States also led military exercises with its West African allies (Senegal, Burkina Faso, Guinea, and Gambia).[59]

Even now that the war to reconquer the north of Mali has started, there is still a debate within the American administration about the extent to which the United States should be involved in northern Mali. Washington is already conducting "a series of clandestine-intelligence missions, including the use of civilian aircraft to conduct surveillance flights and monitor communications over the Sahara Desert and the arid region to the south, known as the Sahel."[60] Those in favor of conducting unilateral strikes against AQIM strongholds in northern Mali believe the terrorist group represents a global menace rather than simply a regional one. They warn that "Al-Qaida in the Arabian Peninsula, as the Yemen-based affiliate is known, was similarly discounted as a regional menace until it was linked to the attempted bombing of a Detroit-bound plane on Christmas in 2009."[61] The alleged involvement of AQIM fighters in the killing of the U.S. ambassador in Libya, coupled with the January 2013 militant attack on the In Amenas natural gas field in Algeria, which was hatched in northern Mali and executed by a multinational group of militants who crossed through Niger and Libya, has fueled the drone advocates' calls.

Skeptics, however, warn of potential blowback. The "doings of obscure Malian Islamists" should not be a matter "of more than local concern," warns former CIA station chief Robert Grenier.[62] This is the same agonizing question that the United States confronted in Yemen in early 2011 with the emergence of the local militant group of Ansar al-Sharia, "Partisans of Islamic Law," that is related to but separate from al-Qaeda.[63]

This fear of a blowback is not far-fetched, as the Somali case illustrates. In 2006, the United States backed an imprudent Ethiopian invasion of Somalia that drove the country closer to al-Qaeda. The military campaign was designed to remove the Union of Islamic Courts from power but ended up empowering its radical fringe, the Shabab. The latter was thus transformed from a "marginal" force into "the backbone of the resistance," mobilizing significant swathes of the population to repel an attack by Somalia's archenemy.[64]

Intervention and Mali's Neighborhood

Military intervention needs the support of the so-called pays du champ, the core countries of the region—Algeria, Mali, Mauritania, and Niger. Mauritania, for example, has been extremely wary about "any military action that may lead to the 'Afghanisation' of northern Mali and the resulting 'Pakistanisation' of Mauritania."[65]

Algeria resisted calls for military intervention, urging patience and support for Mali's government in the south and warning about the fallout from an ill-conceived external adventure in the north. Algerians like to remind their neighbors and their Western supporters that had the international community heeded their warnings about an intervention in Libya, the chaos in Mali would not have occurred in the first place. The Algerian regime (rightly) faults NATO for failing to control the weapons within Libya and halting their flow into neighboring countries. It also believes that the humanitarian calculus behind the Libya intervention was bogus and fears the dangerous precedent that the enforcement of the doctrine of the "responsibility to protect" against the depredations of authoritarian regimes sets. Despite the success of the mission in stopping a bloodbath in Benghazi and ridding Libya of a nasty regime, the Algerians maintain that NATO's lack of foresight has opened a Pandora's box of far-reaching consequences. To Algiers, international supporters of ECOWAS, especially France, therefore need to accept that their quick resort to military intervention only worsened the risks of terrorism in the region.

Some ECOWAS members, especially Niger and Burkina Faso, interpret this prudent attitude toward military intervention as overcautious and self-serving. They are concerned that Algeria's insistence on diplomacy is a ploy to avoid sharing in the burdens and risks of restoring order in Mali. Some complain that Algeria's lack of engagement with ECOWAS stems from its desire to dominate the negotiation process. In their view, the Algerians do not tolerate the leadership of others. The country emphasizes sovereign equality and consensus building but insists on shaping the rules of engagement and influencing multilateral norms. In other words, Algeria seeks to establish itself as the supporter of a regional order rooted in institutions where it is the dominant agenda setter and the lead mediator of conflicts.

Algeria sees ECOWAS as a tool utilized by France to advance its interests in its former colonies in West Africa, which discredits the organization in Algerians' eyes. To make matters worse, Morocco has injected itself into the Malian conflict and has thrown its support behind ECOWAS. As in the Libya intervention, Morocco is expected to play a discreet but active role in any military campaign in Mali. The Moroccans have good relations within the organization, and they see it as a useful forum to cultivate soft power, compensate for their absence from the African Union, and thwart Algeria's determination to marginalize them from Sahelian affairs.

The Algerians of course see Morocco's foray into the Malian crisis as a ploy to entangle Algeria in an intractable war in the Sahara. Algeria's suspicion of Morocco's motives reached a fever pitch in the months preceding the French intervention, with Algerian press openly accusing Morocco of manipulating MUJAO for its own purposes (that is, undermining Algeria's support for the Polisario and delegitimizing the movement's quest for independence). Similar accusations were advanced in early September 2012 by a retired military officer.[66] The logic behind these allegations might be "bizarre," to use the word of an American scholar teaching in Algeria, but the fact that MUJAO has primarily targeted Algeria and its protégé, the Polisario, is apparently enough incriminating evidence against Morocco.

Algeria's Broader Regional Initiatives

For Algeria's critics within ECOWAS, the country seems more interested in isolating its regional competitors and limiting the influence of external powers than in coordinating the region's power assets to organize an effective regional defense against AQIM on its southern flank. Nigerien officials in particular have publicly criticized Algerian-led security initiatives.

The Tamanrasset-based Joint Staff Operations Committee (CEMOC) has been in hibernation since it was set up in April 2010, noted the foreign minister of Niger in June 2012.[67] The CEMOC's primary function is to bolster military and security cooperation, and intelligence and logistical coordination, between its members (Algeria, Mauritania, Mali, and Niger) and build support for a 75,000-strong joint force. Its future aim is to expand its operations to the "second ring" countries of the

Sahel (Burkina Faso, Nigeria, Chad, and Senegal).[68] But the troops and the communication infrastructure have yet to be built or made available, and the last meeting of the CEMOC's Joint Military Staff Committee of the Sahel Region in Nouakchott in July 2012 did not yield any concrete measures to help Mali.

The Fusion and Liaison Unit, which provides a mechanism for consultation between the core countries' intelligence services,[69] also lacks a coordinated strategy, not to mention the requisite mutual trust among participants, for intelligence sharing. The other members of these counterterrorism forums complain that Algeria hoards intelligence and monopolizes information while Algiers suspects Mali of intelligence leaks, according to interviews conducted in Rabat and Nouakchott.[70]

A series of interviews in Brussels revealed the same frustration with these Algerian initiatives. Several EU officials dismissed the CEMOC and the FLU as empty shells designed to ward off regional competitors (Morocco), undermine EU efforts in the Sahel (West Africa Police Information System, Sahel Security College, EUCAP Sahel), and frustrate any other attempt to fight insecurity in the region. Meanwhile, the Algerians are suspicious of EU initiatives because they suspect they are shaped and driven by their former colonial rulers, the French.[71]

The United States is the most amenable to and supportive of Algerian-led regional efforts. Despite the occasional frustrations of dealing with Algerian officials, Washington sees value in the Algerian-dominated framework of the CEMOC and FLU. In the words of one American official interviewed in Algiers, Algeria can certainly do more in counterterrorism and multilateral coordination, but its leadership in the region is essential. This explains why the U.S. position regarding the use of force in northern Mali seemed closer to that of Algiers—it was hesitant about the ECOWAS military strategy and wary of military entanglement in northern Mali.

A Shaky Foundation

Even with French intervention, the foundations for success are still missing. Bamako remains in a state of political and military flux, and the ECOWAS strategy for restoring order in the north, where ethnic tensions are rising dangerously, remains unconvincing.

An ill-conceived intervention in such a dangerously explosive mix of civil-military tensions, divergent communitarian identities, and conflicting ideologies might have devastating effects on Mali and neighboring countries that already suffer from the same institutional fragility, disgruntled military, and societal cleavages that bedevil Bamako. The overlapping ethnic communities and armed groups in West Africa seriously increase the possibility of such deleterious spillover into countries that can ill afford to relapse into ethnic conflict (Niger) or see an escalation of militancy (Nigeria) or terrorist attacks. A long and messy war also increases the risk of exacerbating disgruntlement in the military ranks of those countries that have promised to contribute troops (Niger, Nigeria, and Ivory Coast).[72]

Now What?

After he was informed of the French incursion into Mali, General Carter Ham, the head of U.S. Africa Command, asked, "Now what?" The real test, of course, is preventing a reenactment of the errors that followed NATO's operation in Libya, as well as the invasions of Afghanistan in 2001 and Iraq in 2003. But military responses alone will not defeat terrorist groups or eradicate violent ideologies. Armed militant groups might resemble each other, but the local circumstances (political, economic, and security) that drive their actions differ and need to be examined meticulously.

The French intervention will likely drive radical Islamist combatants out of Mali's main cities and urban centers and into the massive desert mountains near the Algerian border. Algeria's cooperation is crucial here, as border interdiction and sanctuary denial is essential to the success of the French mission in Mali.

The incursion might also exacerbate intercommunal tensions and inflame ethnic relations. There is a risk that the Malian army or vigilante militias will exact revenge on Tuareg and other light-skinned Arabs who participated in the rebellion that chased Malian troops out of the north. Clashes between the army and Tuareg in three prior rebellions resulted in horrific abuse of civilians. To mitigate the risks, the intervention must be accompanied by a sound political strategy that manages disparate group interests and integrates a coalition of key elites from all communities of northern Mali, including Tuareg and Arabs.

It is urgent that Malian authorities and their Western allies analyze carefully who supports militant organizations and why. Several analysts have drawn a clear-cut demarcation of the battle lines without serious regard for the mutation of interests and "political posturing" of the different actors involved. There are many collaborations in northern Mali—not just Islamist ones. Most are driven by complex sociopolitical dynamics, ideology, ethnicity, personality conflicts, criminal networks, and historical grievances.[73] Without an understanding of the human terrain, it would be difficult to dry up the militants' base of support. Even if AQIM is severely weakened, clan- or ethnicity-based militancy will continue.

The political and human elements of the war effort in northern Mali are critical to the stabilization of the north. That will not happen, however, unless the Malian state resolves its crisis of legitimacy and opens sincere dialogue with the disenchanted populations in the north. So far, the ruling class in Bamako seems more interested in recapturing the north and restoring an intolerable status quo ante than in facilitating national reconciliation, recovery, and reconstruction. That has to change. Only a legitimate government can tackle the festering grievances in the north. The political leaders in Mali must rebuild a new sociopolitical order that grants real autonomy to the north and strike a proper balance between religion and state.

But Mali cannot do this alone—it will need help from the international community and its neighbors to tackle its socioeconomic and security problems. And Algeria in particular no longer has the luxury of staying out of what's unfolding in Mali, nor can it afford to ignore the links between its domestic radical Islamists and those roaming the desert wastelands of the Sahel. After all, AQIM is an Algerian phenomenon.

Until the sudden French military intervention in Mali, Algeria was attempting to negotiate a political solution to the conflict by nudging the armed actors with whom it has connections. Algeria was especially focused on Ansar Dine. But the latter withdrew from the negotiation process with Bamako, putting a stop to Algeria's efforts to secure a diplomatic solution to the conflict in Mali.

There have been encouraging signs that Algeria is progressively becoming more practical and pragmatic in its approach to the conflict in Mali. Algeria opened its airspace to French military jet fighters and closed its southern border with Mali when the French intervention began. Controlling this border is necessary to weaken AQIM's capabilities and disrupt its logistics operations. If AQIM and its allies are cut off from the amenities they get from Algeria, they will have difficulty prolonging their fight. There is also hope that after the attack on the In Amenas gas field, the country will put its secretive and insular tendencies to the side and work with other states to help Mali tackle the political and security problems it faces.

Only time will tell, however, if the country's shift toward a more pragmatic foreign policy will lead to a permanent change in approach.

Notes

1 See Kenneth Menkhaus, "State Fragility as a Wicked Problem," *Prism 1*, no 2, www.ndu.edu/press/lib/images/prism1-2/6_Prism_85-100_Menkhaus.pdf.

2 William B. Quandt, "Algeria: How Pivotal Is It: And Why?" University of Virginia, August 1997, http://people.virginia.edu/~wbq8f/pivotal.html.

3 Francis Ghilès, "Algeria 1962–2012: More Questions Than Answers," CIDOB, no. 154, July 3, 2012, www.cidob.org/en/publications/opinion/mediterraneo_y_oriente_medio/algeria_1962_2012_more_questions_than_answers.

4 International Crisis Group, *Islamist Terrorism in the Sahel: Fact or Fiction?* Africa Report no. 92, March 31, 2005.

5 Wolfram Lacher, "Organized Crime and Conflict in the Sahel-Sahara Region," Carnegie Paper, Carnegie Endowment for International Peace, September 2012; Judith Scheele, "Circulations marchandes au Sahara: Entre Licite et Illicite," *Hérodote* 142 (3/2011): 143–62; "The Dynamics of North African Terrorism," CSIS Conference Report, March 2010, http://csis.org/files/attachments/100216_NorthAfricaConferenceReport.pdf.

6 "Paix et sécurité," Coopération Union Européenne-Mali, www.eeas.europa.eu/delegations/mali/documents/projects/paix_et_securite_fr.pdf.

7 Gregory Mann, "Africanistan? Not Exactly," *Foreign Policy*, July 24, 2012.

8 International Crisis Group, *Mali: Avoiding Escalation*, Africa Report no. 189, July 18, 2012, www.crisisgroup.org/~/media/Files/africa/west-africa/mali/189-mali-avoiding-escalation-english, 8.

9 As quoted in International Crisis Group, *Mali: Avoiding Escalation*.

10 Quoted in Jacques Delcroze, "The Malian Model Falls Apart," *Le Monde Diplomatique*, September 3, 2012, http://mondediplo.com/2012/09/03mali.

11 Wolfram Lacher, "Northern Mali: Key Is Strengthening Bamako; ECOWAS Plan Harbors Risks," Global Observatory, September 14, 2012, www.theglobalobservatory.org/analysis/349-northern-mali-key-is-strengthening-bamako-ecowas-plan-harbors-risks.html.

12 United States Agency for International Development, "Counter Extremism and Development in Mali," October 2009.

13 During a trip to Senegal in July, Army General Carter Ham, chief of U.S. Africa Command, called AQIM the best-funded, wealthiest affiliate of al-Qaeda in the world. See Greg Miller and Craig Whitlock, "White House Secret Meetings Examine al-Qaeda Threat in North Africa," *Washington Post*, October 1, 2012, www.washingtonpost.com/world/national-security/white-house-secret-meetings-examine-al-qaeda-threat-in-north-africa/2012/10/01/f485b9d2-0bdc-11e2-bd1a-b868e65d57eb_story.html.

14 Ibid.

15 USAID, "Counter Extremism and Development in Mali."

16 Ibid., 10.

17 Serge Daniel, "Mali Rebel Iyad Ag Ghaly: Inscrutable Master of the Desert," Agence France-Presse, April 5, 2012, www.google.com/hostednews/afp/article/ALeqM5j2E5T3FzSZKJ-OhCp fHOdsoA0idA?docId=CNG.479d25a6bbe0d8ec222921f745502da0.1f1.

18 ICG, *Mali: Avoiding Escalation*," 17.

19 Ibid.

20 Ibid.

21 See Andrew Lebovich, "Trying to Understand MUJWA," *Jadaliyya*, August 24, 2012, www.jadaliyya.com/pages/index/7031/trying-to-understand-mujwa.

22 Peter Tinti, "Mali: Understanding Northern Mali—Local Context Is Everything," Think Africa Press, http://allafrica.com/stories/201208290418.html.

23 David Lewis, "Qaeda Leader Tells Fighters to Support Mali Rebels," Reuters, May 24, 2012, www.reuters.com/article/2012/05/24/us-mali-qaeda-idUSBRE84N1BI20120524.

24 See USAID, "Counter Extremism and Development in Mali."

25 Ali Bensaâd, "La région saharo-sahélienne est contrôlée par les populations locales," *Le Monde*, January 19, 2011.

26 Lewis, "Qaeda Leader Tells Fighters to Support Mali Rebels."

27 Miller and Whitlock, "White House Secret Meetings Examine al-Qaeda Threat in North Africa."

28 Roland Marchal, "The Coup in Mali: The Result of a Long-Term Crisis or Spillover From the Libyan Civil War?" Norwegian Peace Building Resource Center, May 2012, http://reliefweb.int/sites/reliefweb.int/files/resources/3a582f1883e8809a0e18cd2d58a09a81.pdf.

29 See Souleymane Faye, "Q&A: Military Action in Mali Would Be a 'Huge Risk,'" Inter Press Service, August 14, 2012, www.ipsnews.net/2012/08/qa-military-action-in-mali-would-be-a-huge-risk.

30 See Peter Tinti, "Algeria's Stance on Northern Mali Remains Ambiguous," Voice of America, September 17, 2012, www.voanews.com/content/algerias_stance_on_northern_mali_remains_ambigious/1509747.html.

31 See Alexis Arieff, *Algeria and the Crisis in Mali*, Institut Français des Relations Internationales (IFRI), July 2012.

32 See U.S. Embassy, Bamako, New Algerian Ambassador to Meet With Ambassador," cable from February 19, 2010, as released by WikiLeaks, http://wikileaks.org/cable/2010/02/10BAMAKO99.html.

33 "Le Mali est le banc d'essai de la stratégie à long terme d'AQMI," *El Watan*, August 29, 2012, www.elwatan.com/international/le-mali-est-le-banc-d-essai-de-la-strategie-a-long-terme-d-aqmi-29-08-2012-183497_112.php.

34 ICG, *Mali: Avoiding Escalation.*

35 See Catherine Gouëset, "Mali: pourquoi l'Algérie parie sur les islamistes d'Ansar Eddine," *L'Express*, July 4, 2012, www.lexpress.fr/actualite/monde/afrique/mali-pourquoi-l-algerie-parie-sur-les-islamistes-d-ansar-eddine_1134319.html.

36 Ibid.

37 Interview with Algerian journalist, Algiers, June 18, 2012.

38 John Schindler, "The Ugly Truth About Algeria," *National Interest*, July 10, 2012, http://nationalinterest.org/commentary/the-ugly-truth-about-algeria-7146.

39 Thomas Serres, "The Malian Crisis Seen From Algeria," *Jadaliyya*, April 19, 2012, www.jadaliyya.com/pages/index/5330/another-take-on-the-malian-crisis-as-seen-from-alg.

40 Schindler, "The Ugly Truth About Algeria."

41 Ian Black, "WikiLeaks Cables: Algeria Goes From Security Joke to U.S. Ally in Maghreb," *Guardian*, December 6, 2010, www.guardian.co.uk/world/2010/dec/06/wikileaks-cables-algeria-security-maghreb.

42 The Algerian military has never intervened outside its borders (except in the desert/border wars against Morocco in October 1963 and 1976), nor has it ever participated in UN peacekeeping operations.

43 Interview with U.S. diplomat, October 15, 2012.

44 Quoted in Melanie Matarese, "Coup d'Etat au Mali: les conséquences pour l'Algérie," *Le Figaro*, March 23, 2012.

45 Dalila Henache, "Diplomat Abdelaziz Rehabi to Echorouk: 'Military Intervention Scary Because the Northern Mali Is the Southern Algeria," Echorouk Online, www.echoroukonline.com/ara/articles/134167.html.

46 Claire Spencer, "Strategic Posture Review: Algeria," *World Politics Review*, July 25, 2012.

47 See Salim Chena, "Portée et limites de l'hégémonie algérienne dans l'aire sahélo-maghrébine," *Hérodote*, 142 (3) 2011: 108–124

48 Ibid.

49 The year 2012 already saw the death of two former presidents: ninety-six-year-old Ahmed Ben Bella, the country's first president, and Chadli Benjedid (82) who was deposed in a bloodless military coup in 1992. Death, as Lamine Chikhi aptly put it, is "catching up" fast with the old generation of Algerian leaders who ruled the country since independence. See Lamine Chikhi, "Algeria Awaits Change After 50 Years Under Ruling Party," Reuters, October 16, 2012.

50 See Robert Parks, "Algeria's 10 May 2012 Elections: Preliminary Analysis," *Jadaliyya*, May 14, 2012, www.jadaliyya.com/pages/index/5517/algerias-10-may-2012-elections_preliminary-analysi.

51 Mélanie Matarese, "Face à l'ennemi, Alger mise sur l'unité nationale," *El Watan*, September 29, 2012, www.elwatan.com//actualite/face-a-l-ennemi-alger-mise-sur-l-unite-nationale-28-09-2012-186862_109.php.

52 Kamel Daoud, "Pourquoi l'Algérie ne veut pas intervenir au Sahel," *Slate Afrique*, September 28, 2012, www.slateafrique.com/95291/algerie-mali-guerre-au-sahel-le-complexe-cachee-de-l-armee-algerienne.

53 On August 22, "Security forces arrested smugglers in four SUVs carrying 2.3 tonnes of drugs and heavy weapons, machine guns, Kalashnikovs, ammunition, and night-military goggles." See Walid Ramzi, "Algeria Fears 'Afghanization' of Mali," *Magharebia*, August 28, 2012, www.magharebia.com/cocoon/awi/xhtml1/en_GB/features/awi/features/2012/08/28/feature-01.

54 "Three Qaeda Hostages Seized Last Week Alive: Mediator," Agence France-Presse, October 30, 2011.

55 "Spain Evacuates Aid Workers From Western Algeria," BBC, July 28, 2012.

56 ICG, *Mali: Avoiding Escalation*, 28.

57 Adam Nossiter, "Islamists Struggle to Run North Mali," *New York Times*, September 1, 2012, www.nytimes.com/2012/09/02/world/africa/holding-northern-mali-by-force-islamists-struggle-to-run-it.html?_r=1&pagewanted=all.

58 Testimony of U.S. Assistant Secretary of State for African Affairs Johnnie Carson before the House Foreign Affairs Committee, Subcommittee on African Affairs, Global Health, and Human Rights, June 29, 2012.

59 Miller and Whitlock, "White House Secret Meetings Examine al-Qaeda Threat in North Africa."

60 Ibid.

61 Ibid.

62 Robert Grenier, "Mali Counter-Terrorism and the Benefits of Doing Nothing," Al-Jazeera English, July 11, 2012.

63 "Understanding Yemen's Al Qaeda Threat," PBS *Frontline*, May 29, 2012, www.pbs.org/wgbh/pages/frontline/foreign-affairs-defense/al-qaeda-in-yemen/understanding-yemens-al-qaeda-threat.

64 Conn Hallinan, "The War in Mali," *Counterpunch*, August 28, 2012, www.counterpunch.org/2012/08/28/the-war-in-mali.

65 Jemal Oumar, "EU Counter-Terror Official Visits Nouakchott," *Magharebia*, September 4, 2012.

66 Wolfram Lacher, "Options et défis des acteurs extérieurs face à la crise au Nord-Mali," presentation in Rabat, September 10, 2012.

67 Cherif Ouazzani and Philippe Perdrix, "Crise malienne: Alger se fait attendre," *Jeune Afrique*, June 21, 2012.

68 See Luis Simon, Alexander Mattelaer, Amelia Hadfield, "A Coherent EU Strategy for the Sahel," European Parliament, May 2011, www.europarl.europa.eu/committees/fr/studiesdownload.htm l?languageDocument=EN&file=73859.

69 Bérangère Rouppert, "The European Strategy for the Sahel," GRIP, January 16, 2012, www.grip.org/sites/grip.org/files/NOTES_ANALYSE/2012/NA_2012-01-16_FR_B-ROUPPERT.pdf.

70 ATT's overthrow potentially "represents an opportunity to put regional relations on a new footing," as the northern Malian state security-organized crime-AQIM nexus has disintegrated.

71 See "A Coherent EU Strategy for the Sahel," 32.

72 ICG, *Mali: Avoiding Escalation*, 29.

73 Peter Tinti, "Understanding Northern Mali: Local Context is Everything," Think Africa Press, August 28, 2012.

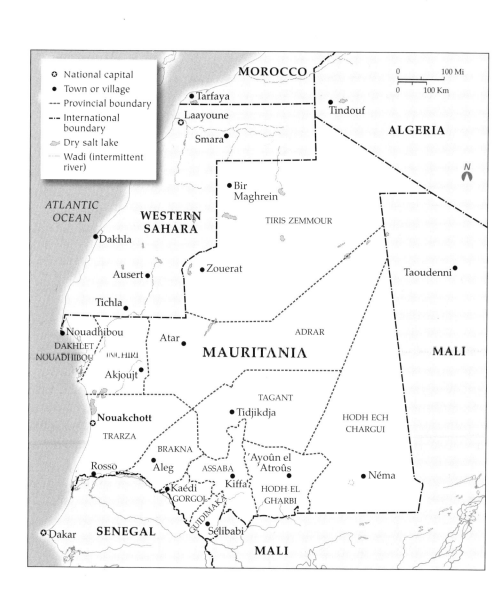

National capital
Town or village
Provincial boundary
International boundary
Dry salt lake
Wadi (intermittent river)

MOROCCO

0   100 Mi
0   100 Km

Tarfaya
Tindouf
Laayoune
ALGERIA
Smara

Bir Maghrein

ATLANTIC OCEAN
WESTERN SAHARA
TIRIS ZEMMOUR

N

Dakhla

Ausert
Zouerat
Taoudenni

Tichla

Nouadhibou
Atar
ADRAR
MALI

DAKHLET NOUADHIBOU
INCHIRI
MAURITANIA
Akjoujt

Nouakchott
TAGANT

TRARZA
Tidjikdja
HODH ECH CHARGUI

BRAKNA
Rosso
Aleg
ASSABA
'Ayoûn el 'Atroûs
Néma

Kaédi
Kiffa
GORGOL
HODH EL GHARBI

Dakar
SENEGAL
GUIDIMAKA
Sélibabi

MALI

05

The Drivers of Insecurity in Mauritania

Anouar Boukhars

Introduction

Mauritania is an increasingly fragile state, with rising levels of insecurity conducive to homegrown violent extremism and cross-border criminal and terrorist activity. Internal stresses combine with external spoiler factors to sap the capacity of an already weak state to respond.

This fragility is not only a concern for Mauritania's citizens and those seeking to promote development in the country, but it is also a threat to broader efforts to stabilize the Sahel region by preventing conflict and promoting recovery. Specifically, it undermines the counterterrorism efforts that have been a high priority for Western governments and international donors.

Mauritania is unfortunately not the only Sahelian country at risk of descending into Hobbesian anarchy—with serious consequences for the region's stability and world security. UN Secretary-General Ban Ki-moon raised such a specter when he most recently warned the Security Council that the region might soon be faced with "a crisis of the magnitude of the one in the Horn of Africa." The increasing reach and influence of organized crime in both state apparatuses and broader societies, a looming food crisis, and the suspected links between terrorist organizations, criminal networks, and insurgent ethnic groups threaten to reverse fragile democratic gains and hard-won peace-building progress in countries like Mali, Niger, and Mauritania. These forces could undermine social hierarchies and the very fabric of social cohesion.

These societies are among the poorest in the world, with absolute poverty rates exceeding 50 percent. Governments are chronically weak and indicators of state fragility are rife. States' penetration of society is limited—political institutions are feeble, essential services and public goods are lacking, tax bases are narrow due to the size of informal economies and endemic corruption, and there is cultural and ethnic resistance to state authority and territorial control. These governments also exhibit a limited capacity to monitor their borders and maintain a monopoly on the legitimate use of force.

In many ways, this precariousness dates to the birth of the modern Sahelian nation-state. Born dirt poor and with a weak sense of common identity, these states were soon confronted with daunting developmental challenges—worsened and at times induced by severe and recurring droughts and political and institutional instability, all of which negatively affected the ability of governments to provide for the political and economic needs of their people. These states are, of course, all varied in their capability to confront the stresses they face, but none so far has managed to overcome its fragility.

Mauritania is a useful case study in analyzing the nature and causes of state fragility and how they relate to the risks of internal instability. It is also a good place to evaluate the capacity of a fragile state to maintain itself in the face of significant stresses and limited resources. The conclusions reached here are in part based on interviews I conducted with clerics, journalists, civil society actors, and government representatives during a field visit to Mauritania in January 2012.

Internal Stresses

Three stresses emerged as critical in my interviews with a range of actors in Mauritania: the weakness and corruption of state institutions; sociopolitical tensions rooted in old tribal structures and historical ethno-racial divisions; and the growing radicalization of Mauritanian youth. These three factors reinforce each other, creating a vicious circle that must be broken in order to restore some stability.

Institutional Weakness and Corruption

All of my interviewees identified pervasive corruption and weak governance as critical sources of popular dissatisfaction, leading to social friction, tension, and potential instability. A number of these interlocutors also affirmed that a link seems to exist between corruption, state fragility, and illicit activity. The roots of these trends run deep. The state has faced a precarious confluence of forces since its independence in 1960 that has given rise to the contemporary insecurity the country confronts. Unable to establish a modern system of governance, the state found itself undermined by the traditional ethno-racial tensions, tribal identities, and other forms of societal divisions that some leaders and local power brokers—sometimes with regional connections to smugglers or insurgents—inflamed and exploited in the scramble for control over the channels that distribute public resources (such as land attribution) or at least a share of the lucrative informal sectors of the economy (such as trafficking and contraband).

The trajectory that Mauritania has followed since independence epitomizes that of other Sahelian countries that were hampered by a colonial legacy that institutionalized political privilege along ethnic lines and kept the country extremely underdeveloped. In 1960, the country had no paved roads, a tiny number of schools, and a dearth of professionals and qualified labor.[1] With the exception of the French-exploited minefield in the town of Zouerat and the small fishing port of Nouadhibou, small-scale agriculture and nomadic herding formed the backbone of the economy.

This system was not able to generate sufficient tax revenue to support the basic economic functions of the state. Worse, the state had neither the capacity nor the will to tax these two activities; it is, after all, hard to collect from nomads dispersed over large swaths of Mauritanian territory. It is also politically risky to try to impose taxes on agriculture, as the sector is controlled by powerful local notables with strong connections to state officials. And in a vicious circle, since it could not deliver social and economic development, the government lacked the popular legitimacy and the support of influential traditional elites necessary to enforce tax collection.[2]

The greatest weakness of the postcolonial government was this inability to raise enough tax revenue to begin the process of state building. Its reliance on foreign aid removed the incentive to invest in institutional development and enlarge the tax base, further impairing Mauritania's state-building efforts. These factors affected the overall governance capability of the state and created a permanent disconnect between the people and the authorities in the capital, Nouakchott.

Moreover, Mauritania lacks effective countervailing forces to check the misuse of power by influential power brokers within the military and tribal clans. After its liberalization in 1991, the party system became more fractured and factionalized than ever. With the exception of the few ideologically driven parties, mainly Islamists, the political system remains dominated by interest groups loosely linked by tribe, sect, ethnicity, or region. As described in the 2012 Bertelsmann Transformation Index (BTI) country report for Mauritania, "These channels and networks are very fluid, multifaceted and often changing, but they constitute the principal way by which the political system is structured below the formal level of institutions."[3]

Wherever the state's presence is minimal—especially in the peripheral parts of the country—the opportunities for different stakeholders to pursue self-interested goals increase. The powerful governors, for example, "are often involved in local political, tribal or factional intrigues without proper monitoring from the center," as the 2010 BTI country report for Mauritania put it.[4]

At the center itself, political infighting and factional rivalries among senior military officers undermine the institutional capacity of the government and make coordination of policies between ministries and departments very difficult. The brief tenure of President Ould Cheikh Abdellahi (seventeen months in office), who in 2007 won the first democratic election since independence, was partially undermined by political factions supporting the former regime. Senior military officers and powerful political and tribal supporters of the former regime were suspected of instigating clashes between the executive and the legislature to undermine the authority of the civilian leadership. By helping create disorder and political paralysis, the military found the right pretext to intervene and stage a coup in August 2008. Factional struggles within the military at times led to personnel shake-ups in top command positions, as was seen following the coups of 2005 and 2008, but the oligopolistic order itself has not changed much.

In this clientelistic system, democratic and opposition forces are at a serious disadvantage. The dominant individuals and groups in parliament always belong to the ruling party and enjoy the support of the military. The same patterns and antidemocratic leanings exist in the bureaucracy and the civil service, as was evidenced by their endorsement of the 2008 coup.

This situation extends to the economic realm as well. Only a few individuals, families, and clans with ties to factions within the military dominate the most important sectors of the economy (for instance, imports and exports, banks, and agribusiness). Several reports, including those produced by the World Bank and the International Monetary Fund (IMF), have highlighted the hurdles that enterprises face in operating in the Mauritanian market. As the BTI 2012 report for Mauritania explains, the hurdles stem from "the power of the oligopolistic conglomerates which dominate all lucrative markets (banking, fishery, public infrastructure and construction, the import and export of consumer goods and foodstuffs, telecommunications, insurance, and so on)."[5]

The judiciary, which in theory is tasked with delivering justice, is also politicized and hampered by customary mechanisms and an informal system dominated by influential groups. Furthermore, the judicial and regulatory arms of the state are underfinanced. Wherever these institutions have an actual physical presence, they are inept and more often than not compromised. In some instances, the government has abdicated its duty to govern, as in the case of health care and education—programs that would collapse without funding from international donors.[6]

This failure to provide basic social services and enforce the rule of law naturally affects the credibility of the state. This credibility problem is further compounded by human rights abuses, the military's dominance of power, and gross levels of endemic corruption. Mauritania ranks 143 out of 178 countries on Transparency International's 2010 Corruption

Perceptions Index. That corruption undermines poverty reduction, exacerbates existing shortfalls in economic opportunities, and facilitates the rise of illegal economic flows.

The state's loss of legitimacy engenders all forms of negative consequences on stability, foremost among them the risk of seeing citizens shift their allegiance to malevolent nonstate actors such as drug traffickers and violent extremists. In other words, capacity and legitimacy can be mutually reinforcing, contributing to either a virtuous or a vicious circle whereby weak state capacity weakens legitimacy, and vice versa, exacerbating state fragility.[7] As Mauritanian ambassador Ould Dedach rightly stated, "The contraction of [the] nation-state and its failure to realize economic development and real social harmony, and its alienation from citizens have aggravated the problem in Sahel, especially as the region's peoples haven't known the national state throughout their long history."[8]

Mauritania's new president, Mohamed Ould Abdel Aziz, has vowed to restore trust in the country's public institutions and address the structural challenges that have heightened the state's vulnerability to destabilization. A new code of ethics for public servants was introduced with the desired goal of moralizing the activities of the administration, and the Investigations Unit of the Office of the Inspector General, created in 2005, launched several criminal investigations of agencies suspected of waste, fraud, and misappropriation of state funds. The result was the prosecution (the chairs of the National Human Rights Commission and of the national anti-AIDS agency were charged with corrupt practices) or dismissal of senior civil servants and government officials, including the governors of Nouakchott and Nouadhibou, and the heads of major state agencies, such as the Central Commission of Public Contracts and the public microcredit agency, Procapec.[9]

While applauded by the public, this campaign to minimize corruption and safeguard public finances still falls short of delivering improved economic governance. A number of companies or state agencies directed by allies of the president and his supporters (especially military officers) have so far escaped the scrutiny of the inspector general.[10] Indeed, many of my interviewees doubt that the president has the political will to take on the vested interests of a small but powerful coalition of dominant status quo stakeholders and interest groups. The cynics, and there are many of them, believe that the investigations and judicial pursuits are politically motivated and target only the political enemies of the ruling faction in power. As his predecessors did, this president will also foster his allies' special interests and thus perpetuate the clientelistic system on which political survival is ultimately based.

Sociopolitical Tensions

The second source of insecurity resides in the stratified nature of Mauritanian society. Since it was established, the country has been divided along ethno-racial lines, which has increased the salience of identity-based conflict. The failure of the postcolonial state to create a unifying national identity based on inclusion, participation, and respect for diversity is a distinct cause of protracted tension and conflict in the country.

In particular, confrontations in Mauritania between Arab and black Africans (the non–Arabic-speaking minorities originally from the tribes found on both shores of the Senegal River, which separates Senegal from Mauritania) have deep roots. In the 1960s, the new regime began Arabicizing the education system and reducing the numerical dominance of black Africans in the administration to their proportion in the population.[11] The French colonial powers had privileged black Africans in administrative and other governmental posts, though they accounted for only one-third of the population. This Arabicization program led to serious conflicts that degenerated into unrest, as happened in 1966 when riots broke out in response to the government's decision to make Arabic compulsory in secondary schools.

In the 1980s tensions reemerged when the regime introduced land reforms to deal with the problem of desertification, moving Arab herders closer toward the banks of the Senegal River and the black African farmers living there.[12] Black Africans perceived the government's move as yet another attempt to advance the interests of one ethnic and linguistic group at their expense, by depriving them of their land and the important resources of the river basin. Most controversially, the 1983 Law on Land Reform gave the state the right to expropriate private land (with due compensation) deemed necessary for "economic and social development needs." Local power brokers, especially the regional governors entrusted with "attribution of property rights," abused those powers.[13]

The bloody events of 1989 are but a manifestation of the difficulty that Mauritania—and indeed most societies in the Sahel with multiple ethnicities, tribes, and sects—has faced in establishing the conditions for intergroup coexistence. That year a border dispute between Mauritania and Senegal over herdsmen's grazing rights quickly degenerated into mutual ethnicity-based repatriations and at times expulsions. The event exposed the historic cultural tension between Arab and black Africans and competition over power and resources.[14] Radical forces took advantage of domestic power struggles to mobilize ethnic interest groups and majority opinion against fears of the "other," exacerbating ethnic and racial rivalries. Some of the worst killings and violent expulsions were the work of these officials and other elements in society.

In Mauritania, zealous government officials whipped up fears of black power and portrayed the border dispute as part of the struggle to correct the demographic imbalances and limit the losses inflicted by French colonialism. Black Africans were uprooted and expelled from their villages.[15] The Mauritanian army was "cleansed" too of some 500 soldiers suspected of weak loyalties to the established order. In total, between 40,000 and 60,000 black Africans (Mauritanian citizens from the Halpulaar, Wolof, Soninke, and Bamana ethnic groups) were expelled to Senegal and another 15,000 to 20,000 to Mali.

The economic situation of the black African communities is not worse than that of the *bidan* (white Moors) of Arab-Berber extraction who make up the dominant racial group in Mauritania, constituting about one-third of the population. There are many poor white Mauritanians in urban shantytowns and villages.[16] But the problem for the non-Arabic-speaking minorities is that "their situation is structurally precarious," according to the 2010 BTI country report. Suspected by the "*bidan* power-holders," they "have always run the risk of being targeted by political and economic forms of punishment."[17]

The Haratin, the so-called black Moors who are Arabic-speaking, dark-skinned descendants of slaves, were not subjected to this systematic campaign of ethnic expulsion.[18] Making up at least 40 percent of

Mauritania's 3.1 million inhabitants, the Haratin came in great numbers to Nouakchott during the 1973–1990 droughts.[19] They have assimilated into Arab culture and tend to side with the *bidan*, which does not mean, however, that the Haratin are well off. They rank at the bottom of the pyramid. Most Haratin are illiterate, are considered second-class citizens, and face severe socioeconomic conditions. They are denied basic rights and suffer from discrimination in various aspects of life.

A number of organizations have tried to raise domestic and international awareness of the severe plight of the Haratin as well as mobilize this community to pressure the government to address their status. The government's efforts have thus far been wanting. Corrupt implementation by local political leaders derailed a well-meaning policy to eradicate squatter settlements (*gazra*) in large cities, especially in and around Nouakchott. As a result, political scientist Cédric Jourde writes, "thousands of poor families, most of whom are from the low-caste Haratin, are being ejected from the 'gazra'. Their land, the value of which is very high around Nouakchott, is then bought by connected people who can buy members of the survey commission."[20] Additionally, the government recently established a "program for the prevention of conflicts and the consolidation of social cohesion," but its impact has been very limited so far.[21] The integration of the Haratin remains one of the major challenges facing Mauritania.

Ethnic-based tensions over access to economic resources are symptomatic of the asymmetric power dynamics that cripple culturally plural states and complicate efforts at intercommunal coexistence and democratization. In any country where significant minority groups are discriminated against and poor governance prevails, it becomes hard to transcend identity cleavages and foster a sense of belonging to the nation. In Mauritania, the pervasiveness of ethnic identity-based politics leads to perpetual ethnic agitation.

In 2008, these tensions once again surfaced in the form of conflict over land. Clashes broke out "between local communities and local state authorities which had authorized the purchase of land titles by business persons in the Senegal River Valley," as described in the 2010 BTI.[22] The same problem occurred in 2010 when reports emerged that speculators were selling property rights on the black market designed to benefit the dwellers of Nouakchott's biggest shantytowns.

Protracted identity conflicts erupted in violence in March 2010 between black Africans and Arabic-speaking students after a statement made by the prime minister and the minister of culture referred to Arabic as a dominant language. And in late 2011, riots broke out in protest against a controversial civil census that the government said was designed to "give the country a modern and accurate biometric census as a step on the way to reforms."[23] Black Africans, especially in the south, believed the census to be "racist" and "discriminatory." Some genuinely feared that if they failed to provide documents (such as the death certificates of great-grandparents) proving their nationality, they might be deported, as happened in 1989. "How can you understand other than the fact that we are being targeted by this census when the commission of inquiry for instance asks a Negro-Mauritanian to prove his 'Mauritanian-ness' by talking in Hassanya [a Moorish dialect] or reciting part of the Koran?" said Dia Gando, an activist with Don't Touch My Nationality.[24]

In the last few years, however, there has been a growing emphasis on conflict prevention and ethnic reconciliation. In 2007, the government took the unprecedented step of calling on the black African citizens who were expelled from the country in 1989 to return home from their exile in Senegal and Mali. Since the beginning of this process of voluntary repatriation, over 20,000 refugees have returned. Granted, all of those returns did not take place after 2007—refugees began returning to Mauritania in 1993 when diplomatic relations between Senegal and Mauritania improved.

In another attempt to redress past wrongs and come to terms with the state's legacy, in 2010 the current president publicly acknowledged the legitimacy of the deep-seated grievances felt by black Africans. Then in March 2012, parliament passed a number of constitutional amendments, affirming the multiethnic character of the state, criminalizing slavery (as already stated in a 2007 law), and prohibiting military coups. By recognizing the cultural and linguistic character of the black African polity and criminalizing extra-constitutional takeovers of the state, President Aziz wanted to contain the mobilization of black Africans, manage rising popular discontent with his rule, and send a strong signal that he wants a clean break with a past often marred by regular military interventions (out of seven leaders to rule Mauritania since independence, seven were military men) and ethno-racial conflict. Still, the state has many challenges to overcome before it can address its ethnic security dilemma and resolve the much broader issues of democratic governance, rights, and citizenship.

Internal Radicalization

The third internal stress in Mauritania emanates from violent extremism. The country initially seemed resistant to al-Qaeda in the Islamic Maghreb's (AQIM's) strategic ambition of tapping into the anger of the legions of young Mauritanians frustrated by poor job prospects, injustice, corruption, and more. Before his ouster in 2005, President Maaouya Ould Sid Ahmed Taya repeatedly warned of the presence of dormant terrorist cells in the country, but very few Mauritanians took him seriously, as he was notorious for instrumentalizing threats from within and without to delegitimize his political opponents, especially moderate Islamists whom he suppressed and excluded from the political system. Several incidents since June 2005—when a deadly attack perpetrated by AQIM against the Lemgheity barracks in the northeastern part of the country killed fifteen Mauritanian soldiers and wounded 39 others—have brought home the uncomfortable realization that Mauritania is a target of extremist armed groups and that disaffected youth might be at risk of falling prey to the lure of violent extremism.[25]

Initially, Mauritanians blamed a spike in abductions and killings of foreigners and the country's own soldiers on foreign AQIM actors. That reluctance to acknowledge the risk of youths' participation in violent extremism largely disappeared when evidence emerged that since late 2005 a few dozen Mauritanians have become important players in AQIM or have gone through military and ideological training in the militant camps of northern Mali and Algeria. Numerous arrests in Nouakchott in 2008 demonstrated the extent of the links between Mauritanian youths and AQIM.

The threat should not be overstated. The number of youths recruited into AQIM remains very small and the attacks perpetrated or foiled on Mauritanian soil lack sophistication. AQIM's capabilities are extremely limited in the country and its affiliated networks are disorganized and weak. The government's aggressive pursuit and imprisonment of suspected violent extremists has temporarily disrupted the growth of a nascent militant movement from taking root in Mauritania. And several other elements have helped to stem the rise of extremism in the country, including tribalism and a pluralistic society that generally practices an open and moderate form of Islam.

But the penetration of imported Salafi ideas into Mauritanian society has affected Mauritanians' culture of tolerance and particularistic Islamic identity. That influence is clearly visible in an ever-more-public display of austere piety and in rising social pressures for conformity to ritual purity and rigid religious commandments. More perniciously, some of the Salafi ideas have contributed to the radicalization of religious discourse, fueling the contemporary wave of extremism in Mauritania.

Ironically, it was the state that encouraged the spread of Salafi ideas without seeming to appreciate that such a policy risked diluting its own monopoly on Islamic interpretation. The Arabicization of education, for example, necessitated the importation of teachers from Egypt and the Near East. Those scholars exercised considerable influence over the introduction, reform, and interpretation of Islamic laws, and they provided the needed ideological depth for the upsurge in the Arabist/Islamist trend in Mauritania. Islamism also thrived thanks to financial donations and incentives coming from the Persian Gulf, particularly from Saudi Arabia, which funded mosques, Islamic study centers, and *mahadras* (religious schools) to propagate its own rigid version of Islam. The influence of Mauritanians coming back from the Gulf also contributed to the spread of Wahhabism.

Several of my interlocutors singled out these institutions as conduits for material and ideological support to radical Islamists. Some Saudi-influenced *mahadras*, particularly in the Trarza region, were especially cited as liable to produce fundamentalists and militant recruits. According to journalist Mohamed Mahmoud Abul Maali, the *mahadras* and mosques can become important social networks that bind together students that are already alienated and isolated from their surroundings. In this instance, strong bonds of brotherhood are forged and predate radicalization of thought and commitment to violence. Charismatic preachers play a crucial role in ideological formation and in reinforcing group solidarity and norms.

The *mahadra* network more often than not expands beyond its space, developing and spreading its reach through mechanisms like the Internet.[26] It is for this and other reasons that there is a widespread assumption that a connection exists between the important role that *mahadra* schooling generally occupies in the educational landscape and rising militancy in the country.

The majority of *mahadras*, however, do not propagate violent ideologies, and they cater to a sizable population that is left behind by a failing educational system. It would therefore be a mistake to stigmatize their graduates—graduates who often have a hard time finding employment opportunities. Mauritania's biggest problem is not *mahadras* but the lack of access to education and the underperformance of the educational system.

The level of education a person attains appears to be an indicator of the risk that he will turn to violent extremism.[27] The Mauritanians who have been arrested for terrorism offenses are young—aged sixteen to twenty-four—poor, speak only Arabic, and possess little education. Indeed, only a few completed high school while most failed to complete secondary school. Unlike many leading figures in terrorist organizations who are well-educated, no Mauritanian violent extremists who have been arrested thus far hold higher degrees, said one interviewee, professor Moctar Mohamed Cheikhouna.[28] The question of how low levels of education—often the result of poor performance in school, which leads to dropping out or expulsion—and its logical consequence, a lack of integration into the job market, contributes to extremism in Mauritania is therefore an obvious topic that merits further attention.

That risk is heightened when combined with other driving factors, such as the fragmentation of social structures and widespread feelings of unfairness. Indeed, all my interviewees in Nouakchott identified a connection between feelings of injustice and violent extremism. These pervasive feelings of injustice are generated by anger about the treatment of Muslims in Palestine and other theaters of conflict and outrage at the obscene levels of corruption of the Mauritanian political elite. Journalist Mohamed Mahmoud Abul Maali said that in his opinion, injustice breeds conflict and invariably fuels the flames of revenge and reciprocal violence. At each instance, he said, the main driving force behind the emergence of violent extremist movements was foreign military occupation or brutal repression of Islamists. This pattern was noticeable in the 1980s in Lebanon and Afghanistan and confirmed in the decades that followed in Iraq. Throughout the 1990s, Algerian terrorists could not recruit regionally or in

Mauritania specifically, but that changed after the invasion of Iraq. Other interlocutors, mostly imams and religious scholars, noted that the first extremists in Islam's history were Khawarij, who revolted against what they considered political oppression of the Umayyad dynasty.[29]

All of my interviewees painted the same profile of violent extremists in the country—young males, living on the periphery of Nouakchott, where social fragmentation permeates poor neighborhoods, as evidenced by high divorce rates and delinquency.[30] This leads to a decline in social cohesion at the community level and exacerbation of social exclusion, said professor Yahya Ould El Bara.[31] Most of those who have been arrested on charges of extremism were stuck in a vicious cycle of social fragmentation, social exclusion, and human insecurity. Most followed the same trajectory: After failing at school, they were drawn into extremism through radical preaching. All blame their plight on the corruption of the state and its serious deficiencies of governance. Violent extremist groups in Internet forums, mosques, and prisons have taken full advantage of the dissolution of these societal controls and the pervasive marginality of significant numbers of youths to lure them into extremism. The groups not only magnify the youths' grievances and whip up their frustrations and anger at an unjust domestic system and unfair international order, they also provide them with a way to rectify those injustices through violence. The extremist organizations help empower those marginalized by society.[32]

So far, most of the recruits into the extremist networks have been white Moors, but there is growing concern that other racial groups, especially the Haratin, might be vulnerable to radicalization as well.[33] Having suffered structural injustices and subjugation, members of Mauritania's large Haratin population have been lured by the egalitarian and anti-traditionalist rhetoric of the Islamists. By contrast, the Islam of the Qadiriya and the Tijaniyya Sufi brotherhoods is tainted in the eyes of these oppressed Mauritanians due to those brotherhoods' close association with a rigid caste system.

The Tablighi movement, a transnational Islamist group that preaches re-Islamization of society through nonviolent means and opposes ethnic divisions, has made inroads among the Haratin population. More worrisome for Mauritanian authorities is the fear that some Haratin might be tempted by the message of violent extremist movements who also denounce the stratification of society. Many terrorists do not act out of religious zealotry alone but instead act in reaction to a system they perceive as unjust and oppressive. Al-Qaeda thrives on manipulating people who are hungry for social justice—and that might be one of the reasons why the only two Mauritanian suicide bombers (so far) have been Haratins. A U.S. National Counter Terrorism Center terrorism bulletin reported in 2009 that AQIM leader Mokhtar Belmokhtar "wanted to attract black African recruits because they would agree more readily than Arabs to becoming suicide bombers and because poor economic and social conditions made them ripe for recruitment."[34]

Interestingly, AQIM has failed to attract any recruits among the Halpulaar, Soninke, and Wolof. In the past, similar struggles for social justice based on ethno-racial identity have typically pushed these groups further toward the fringes of society. It is only natural that there is a high level of distrust between black Africans and AQIM, a movement led and dominated by Arabs. The non-Arabic-speaking black African minorities are also not particularly drawn to Islamism more broadly. The Halpulaar, Wolof, Soninke, and Bamana "conceive of Islamism as a reincarnation of an older 'Arab nationalist' ideology that favors the 'Arabness' of Mauritania to the detriment of its non-Arab communities," as Cédric Jourde rightly points out.[35]

The Mauritanian government has undertaken several steps and initiatives to combat extremism. In addition to improving its fighting capability and modernizing its military equipment through the acquisition of high-performance aircraft and other matériel, the government has bolstered its legal system. New antiterrorism legislation tries to balance security and the rule of law, as establishing the legitimacy of counterterrorism laws is essential to gaining popular support for prosecuting the country's war on extremism and terrorism.

The government has also tried to delegitimize the ideological justifications for radicalism by hiring hundreds of new imams to preach in the country's mosques as well as engage extremist prisoners through a dialogue with state-sponsored Islamist scholars and clerics.[36] The goal is to rehabilitate violent extremists as well as to demobilize and deradicalize potential recruits. According to Mohamed Mahmoud Abul Maali, the program has been very effective, leading to the repentance of dozens of former radicals.

There has been only one case of recidivism out of the 40 to 50 people who have been released from prison, he said.

External Stresses: Drug Traffickers, AQIM, and Arms Dealers

The problem of homegrown radicalization in Mauritania is further compounded by its interconnectedness with transnational factors like illicit trafficking and regional terrorist networks. The country has traditionally played a central part in trans-Saharan trade as well as cross-cultural and religious exchanges and influences. Due to its location and vast and porous borders, Mauritania has been especially vulnerable to all kinds of trafficking, including arms. That has also put the country at risk of becoming a major transit route for global cocaine trafficking. Leaked confidential documents from the U.S. embassy in Nouakchott reveal such concern and raise the specter of Mauritania becoming a new drug-trafficking hub.[37]

Such a development would be troubling in any country, but that is particularly true for Mauritania, which suffers from serious deficits in governance and an easy availability of arms. The insecurity is even more pronounced in the north of the country given its proximity to the Western Sahara, a conflict-ridden territory. Crossborder traffic of illicit products with the Western Sahara has been a booming industry, with the Polisario Front, which is fighting for the Western Sahara's independence from Morocco, dominating the supply side of arms to Mauritania.[38] A 2008 report by the Mauritanian Department of National Security estimates that the number of uncontrolled weapons in Mauritania stands at 70,000. This "has led to a wave of criminality due to the fact that it is easier and easier to procure arms of different types and calibres, including weapons of war," according to a study by the Small Arms Survey.[39]

The recent influx of more weapons from Libya as a result of the conflict there and the continuing inflow of refugees from Mali fleeing the armed clashes between ethnic Tuareg rebels and the army add to the combustible mix of a looming food crisis, cross-border criminals, and regional armed militants linked to banditry. "The entry of al-Qaeda, trafficking networks, training camps and [their] involvement in traditional conflicts have turned [the] Sahel from a grey zone to a powder keg ready to go off," said Mauritanian ambassador and former housing minister Mohammed Val Ould Belal. "This puts us in the face of interrelated and overlapping wars between Tuareg and the Malian army, al-Qaeda and Mali, Arabs and al-Qaeda and Tuareg and Arabs."[40]

If the illicit drug industry intensifies, the consequences for state and society could be severe. The funds generated by drug trafficking can destabilize a weak political system through the financing of electoral campaigns, further erosion of the rule of law, and corruption of the elite. Already, public suspicion of the complicity of top-ranking officials in the drug trade is rampant, with several of my interlocutors pointing out such involvement. The involvement began during the tenure of President Ould Taya, who was known to control the major trafficking and contraband hub in the north of the country thanks to the alliances he forged between the Rgueibat tribe, which also controls the Polisario independence movement, and his own tribe, the Smacid. Such suspicions deepened in 2007 after the arrest and sentencing of a former Interpol agent and cousin of President Ould Taya as well as the son of former Mauritanian president Mohamed Khouna Ould Haidalla. These strategic alliances were sustained by commercial, political, and military patronage networks.

The government's control of the northern zone, however, weakened as new forces emerged on the scene, namely illegal immigration networks, drug smugglers, weapons traffickers, and Tuareg.[41] These networks have transformed Mauritania's already fluid and constantly shifting tribal-ethnic-caste-state relations. Rivalries between and among these actors have intensified the fight for control of the rents generated from lucrative criminal activities.

In the words of Ghanaian economist George Ayittey, in this "mafia-like bazaar" where those with the ability to capture rent "pillage at will," the distinction between state actors and criminal ones becomes blurred.[42] Indeed, in many instances, state officials hail from the same tribe, clan, or even family as the insurgents or drug traffickers.[43] "The result is a seemingly irreconcilable tension," as Cédric Jourde aptly put it. "The state as an abstract entity is threatened by this illicit business, yet simultaneously many state agents are deeply involved in these activities."[44]

Another major danger posed by drug trafficking is the insidious effect it can have on the local population. The significant value generated from drug sales can distort the economy and affect social stability and cohesion through increased levels of domestic consumption (cocaine is expensive but can easily be transformed into crack), violence (kidnapping, extortion, gang crimes), and delinquency.[45] Such criminality has also been linked to violent extremism in Mauritania. In February 2012, ten people in Nouadhibou, the economic capital of the country, were indicted for possession of two tons of Indian hemp drugs, or *chanvre indien*.[46] Security officials said that "the drugs were used to finance al-Qaeda in the Islamic Maghreb (AQIM) operations."[47]

In Mauritania, there seems to be a connection between criminality and violent extremism, with the former acting as a stepping-stone to the latter. According to interviews I had with state officials and journalists who consulted police reports, a significant number of those apprehended for terrorism offenses had a criminal past. Of them, 50 to 70 percent were delinquents, said journalist Issselmou Oud Moustapha of *Tahalil Hebdo*.[48] Most were implicated in petty crime (car theft, drug peddling). Some were radicalized in prison through their interaction with radical preachers. All were believers, but before their radicalization, none was particularly pious. Many were devoid of any hope, as they faced a bleak future and the prospect of a lifetime of unemployment and disenfranchisement.[49]

In some cases, the transition from petty criminality into violent extremism can be regarded as a sort of atonement for sinful misconduct. Radical Salafi preachers in Mauritania encourage such pursuit of religious redemption whereby "reformed" criminals make amends for their guilty soul and that of their community by joining the violent struggle against the forces of injustice. Only by purifying Mauritanian society of its corrupt elite and the pervasive influence of imperialist powers can Mauritanian youths put an end to the indefinite perpetuation of failed governance and dysfunctional statehood. In the eyes of the new converts, disorder and corrupt governance cannot be but the consequence of the state's deviance from the right path and purposeful ignorance of divine guidance. Indeed, it is not difficult to see how these moralizing arguments can be appealing to a generation that is increasingly socially isolated and whose desire for basic dignity and equal recognition is trampled on in a rigid and suffocating social structure perpetuated by a corrupt state and a religious establishment co-opted by the dominating elite.

To be sure, the elder generation suffered from the same patterns of state dysfunctions and neglect yet did not turn to criminality or extremism. The major difference is the emergence of new structural forces that disrupted the operational links between traditional society and its social support networks and familiar contexts. Rapid urbanization has weakened the traditional nomadic and rural mechanisms of social regulation. It has contributed to the breakdown of the traditional family. The high rate of divorce has led to higher rates of dropping out of school and higher levels of delinquency. With the state's failure to create "alternative sources of incentives and sanctions," writes USAID, "too many have slipped through the cracks of modern society, felt abandoned by it, and in some cases, turned against it."[50]

When it suits their ambitions, extremist networks have condoned and profited from drug trafficking. They have also provided moral legitimacy and religious validation for involvement in illicit activities as long as the profits generated are used to bolster the militant cause. In some jihadi circles, the recruitment of hardened criminals is justified on historic grounds, as well. The story of Umar bin al Khattab, the second caliph of Islam, is often cited as the best example of how one of the most ardent enemies of Islam—he worshipped idols, drank heavily, and wanted to destroy the tiny but growing number of converts to Islam—was transformed into one of its best-known fervent defenders and formidable warriors.[51] Such validation and justification from independent religious figures can carry important weight with youths who are angry, disaffected, and disoriented.

The connections between illicit activities and militancy are also driven purely by self-interest. Drug barons and violent ideologues both have a common interest in weakening the state's structures, bypassing its territorial control, and circumventing its interdiction—generally undermining its authority. The delegitimization of the state remains one the key goals of violent extremists in a country where the traditional mechanisms of social regulation have already been weakened by a host of forces.

Most traffickers do not seek the overthrow of the state and do not share ideological affinities with violent extremists. One, of course, cannot assume that will always be the case, since what starts as an alliance of convenience for logistical and pragmatic reasons might develop into ideological unity. For now at least, such ideological affinities have not emerged.

In fact, there are instances where relationships between criminals and violent extremists have deteriorated and led to conflict. "In a game that involves three actors—criminals, state officials, and violent extremists," however, "any two of them may be reluctant to forge an alliance when doing so might lead one of those two actors to expose himself to the costs involved in antagonizing the third one."[52] In other words, collusion with the state may be more beneficial to criminals than cooperation with violent extremists, who are often at war with the state.

Conclusion

The confluence of the revolts in North Africa and growing regional and Western trepidation about the proliferation of weapons, transnational trafficking of illicit goods, and terrorist activity led by AQIM are generating acute interest in the trans-Saharan region. Like most of its neighbors, Mauritania has been plagued by poverty, ethno-political tensions, and corrupt governance—indeed Mauritania, Chad, Niger, and Burkina Faso, as well as Mali until a recent military coup overthrew the president, are currently led by former military men. In the dozens of interviews I conducted in Mauritania, a range of actors stress the clear correlation between insecurity and institutional weakness, as measured by misgovernance and the state's limited penetration of society. The evidence I garnered all points to institutional instability, corrupt governance, economic deprivation, and weakness of social trust as major risk factors contributing to insecurity.

Due to its strategic location between the Maghreb and sub-Saharan Africa, and the pervasive and multifaceted insecurity problems confronting it, Mauritania has naturally become a focus of international development agencies and European Union and U.S. counterterrorism programming. For international development–oriented donors, of the many interlocking causal factors of conflict, the connection between the lack of broad-based economic development and insecurity in Mauritania is the most obvious and frequently cited driver of instability. International nongovernmental organizations operating in Mauritania stress that there can be no economic development without security.

For defense officials and military strategists, Mauritania epitomizes the risks that states with weak capabilities pose to regional and international security. It is a case that illustrates how the internal drivers of insecurity intersect with external factors, reinforcing in the process the vulnerability of the state to destabilization. Besides impoverishing their populations, weak governments are usually corrupt and easily infiltrated by organized crime groups, undermining their efforts at building workable governance structures. This creates a debilitating service gap amid already-weak state capacity. "Ungoverned, undergoverned, misgoverned and contested areas" are breeding grounds for organized crime groups and terrorists, says the Pentagon's National Defense Strategy. The European Union's security strategy also advances the fragile state–organized crime–terrorism nexus: "Neighbours who are engaged in violent conflict, weak states where organised crime flourishes, dysfunctional societies or exploding population growth on its borders all pose problems for Europe."[53]

Combating transnational criminal syndicates becomes a futile endeavor as long their main enablers (namely corruption) are not tackled. Stemming the tide of youth radicalization would also be unsuccessful unless the sources of disillusionment and frustration are addressed. The greater the chasm between youth expectations and the capability or willingness of the state to meet them, the greater the risk that angry youths might look to nonstate actors for essential goods.

The analysis here supports the contention that the risk of societal conflict and insecurity increases where the state and its social institutions are unwilling to meet, or incapable of meeting, the basic needs of its citizens. Promoting good governance and reinforcing the state's capacity is therefore critical to improving economic conditions and building people's trust in national institutions. For Mauritania to move away from its state of fragility, the government needs to bolster its anticorruption initiatives, strengthen the reforms of its education sector, professionalize its security apparatus, and promote social justice.

The urgent steps that need to be taken are as follows: First, anticorruption commissions already exist and need to be empowered to fulfill their auditing functions (by being given bigger budgets as well as competent and nonpartisan staff, for example). Second, effective controls must be established to protect against fraud, expropriation of land, and abuse by provincial governors and other regional agencies that provide services and programs for rural areas. Mismanagement of land titling projects in urban areas is a major problem and source of societal conflict.

Third, the level of political inclusion and cultural rights needs be enhanced. The 2007 legalization of the moderate Islamist party, Tawassoul, was an important step toward promoting engagement and broadening the system of participation. Similar political efforts are needed to increase the representation of black Africans and Haratin in state institutions. These steps are necessary to bridge the cultural and ethnic divide and move toward a more inclusive and egalitarian society.

Fourth, immediate steps are required to improve the economic plight of the Haratin. The government has established programs to address their marginalization, but the resources allocated so far are insufficient. It is here that international donors can play a significant role. Investing in such development programs can help promote peace and stability in the country.

International donors should support the government's (timid) efforts to address the education supply gap in the country. Lack of access to education disproportionately affects citizens who are already poor and marginalized, further exacerbating their feelings of anger at the system. Low levels of education, when combined with other drivers of extremism, can become an important factor in the radicalization of Mauritanian youth. There is enough empirical evidence to show that equitable (quality) education provision reduces the risk of societal conflict.

Transforming the state-society compact will not be easy or quick. Such institutional transformation requires responsible national leadership as well as determined international donors willing to link economic assistance to improvement in human security. Economic aid, as the new European Neighborhood Policy states, must be linked to the idea of "more for more" with "precise benchmarks and a clearer sequencing of actions." President Mohamed Ould Abdel Aziz has declared his commitment to improving public administration and deepening democratization. It is only fair that the United States and Europe hold him to his promises.

The stakes are considerable. There are powerful constituents who will resist any substantive reforms to rationalize public-expenditure management, and to strengthen rules for procurement procedures and those governing conflicts of interest. For reforms to be successful, national reformers within the government need to establish broad-based and inclusive coalitions with influential sectors in society as well as international donors and investors. Those forces will have a better chance of withstanding the pressures that are bound to emanate from groups standing to lose out in the reform process.

Notes

1   Interview with sociologist Cheikh Saad Bouh Kamara, January 21, 2012, Nouakchott.
2   See Alain Antil and Sylvain Touati, "Mali et Mauritanie: pays sahéliens fragiles et États résilients," *Politique Etrangère*, 76(1), (Spring 2011): 59–69.
3   *BTI 2012—Mauritania Country Report* (Gütersloh: Bertelsmann Stiftung, 2012), 12, www.bti-project.org/fileadmin/Inhalte/reports/2012/pdf/BTI%202012%20Mauritania.pdf.
4   Ibid., 6.
5   Ibid., 16.
6   Mauritania was ranked 150 out of 169 countries on health and on education by the UNDP's Human Development Index.
7   "The State's Legitimacy in Fragile Situations: Unpacking Complexity," OECD 2010, 20, www.oecd.org/dataoecd/45/6/44794487.pdf.
8   Jemal Oumar, "Sahel Instability Impacts Mauritania," *Magharebia*, March 19, 2012, www.magharebia.com/cocoon/awi/xhtml1/en_GB/features/awi/features/2012/03/19/feature-02.
9   *BTI 2012—Mauritania Country Report*, 10.
10 Ibid.
11 Ron Parker, "The Senegal-Mauritania Conflict of 1989: A Fragile Equilibrium," *Journal of Modern African Studies*, vol. 29, no. 1 (March 1991): 155–71.
12 Ibid.
13 In this tense ethno-racial climate, in 1983 three underground parties created the African Liberation Forces of Mauritania (Flam). In 1986, the state started cracking down on dissent, especially after the appearance of the "Oppressed Black African Manifesto," a document accusing the regime of pursuing an apartheid policy that purposefully marginalized black Africans. The authors of the pamphlet were arrested and tortured. Others were fired from their jobs in the public service. In 1987, the authorities targeted several Halpulaar army officers after a failed coup plot.
14 Stéphanie Pézard, with Anne-Kathrin Glatz, "Arms in and Around Mauritania: National and Regional Security Implications," *Small Arms Survey*, Graduate Institute of International and Development Studies, Geneva, 2010, 8, www.smallarmssurvey.org/fileadmin/docs/B-Occasional-papers/SAS-OP24-Mauritania-EN.pdf.
15 The Halpulaar community suffered the most, especially those in the Brakna region, southwest of Mauritania. See Antil and Touati, "Mali et Mauritanie : pays sahéliens fragiles et États résilients."
16 Ibid., 14.
17 Ibid.

18 Indeed, "[T]he Mauritanian government had allowed Haratin, some of whom had themselves just been expelled from Senegal, to settle on the land of Afro-Mauritanians who had been expelled to Senegal ... these new inhabitants, who organized militias for their own protection, received arms from the government with which they committed serious acts of violence against other villagers, with the consent of the security forces present." Pézard and Glatz, "Arms in and Around Mauritania: National and Regional Security Implications," 9.

19 International Crisis Group, *Islamism in North Africa IV: The Islamist Challenge in Mauritania: Threat or Scapegoat?* Middle East/North Africa Report no. 41, May 11, 2005, www.crisisgroup. org/en/regions/middle-east-north-africa/north-africa/mauritania/041-islamism-in-north-africa-4-the-islamist-challenge-in-mauritania.aspx.

20 Cédric Jourde, "Mauritania 2010: Between Individual Willpower and Institutional Inertia," IPRIS, *Maghreb Review*, March 2011, www.ipris.org/php/download.php?fid=475.

21 *BTI 2012—Mauritania Country Report*, 21.

22 Ibid., 17.

23 "Police Arrest 56 in Mauritania Over Census Protests," Agence France-Presse, September 30, 2011, www.google.com/hostednews/afp/article/ALeqM5hc_1JRl-_LWVW6JeHTY4W lSJ1JZQ?docId=CNG.d9df7a767e5cfba2d4b83b752fec7796.6e1.

24 Ibid.

25 The AQIM attack was in retaliation against Ould Taya's imprisonment of seven Mauritanians who attended training camps in Mali as well as his support for the Pan Sahel Initiative (PSI) and diplomatic relations with Israel. Indeed, the terrorist attack "took place only a short while after the visit of the Israeli foreign minister to Nouakchott and just before the beginning of the 'Flintlock' military exercise organized as part of the PSI." Pézard and Glatz, "Arms in and Around Mauritania," 23.

26 Interview with Mohamed Mahmoud Abul Maali from Nouakchott, January 16, 2012.

27 See Guilain Denoeux and Zeric Smith, "Mauritania Pilot–CT and Development," USAID, June 2008, 8; Rebecca Winthrop and Corinne Graff, "Beyond Madrasas: Assessing the Links between Education and Militancy in Pakistan," Working paper 2, Brookings Institution, June 2010, www.brookings.edu/~/media/Files/rc/papers/2010/06_pakistan_education_win-throp/06_pakistan_education_winthrop.pdf.

28 Interview with Professor Moctar Mohamed Cheikhouna, January 17, 2012.

29 Interviews on January 18, 2012, Nouakchott.

30 According to the USAID study, Boutilimit, Kiffa, and Néma were all "municipalities where radical preachers are active, where larger concentrations of extremists can be found, and/or as the locations from which extremists arrested in the past two years often originated." My interlocutors confirmed such findings, citing Boutilimit as a particular area of concern. According to Abul Maali, Boutilimit is a hub of Salafi preachers and an incubator of extremist thought. Children are particularly vulnerable to indoctrination, he said. Boutilimit is also the area where a number of Mauritanians who fought in Afghanistan originated.

31 Interview with Yahya Ould El Bara, January 19, 2012, Nouakchott.

32 Denoeux and Smith, "Mauritania Pilot–CT and Development," 12.

33 "Islamism in North Africa IV."

34 Jake Tapper, "Terrorism Bulletin Says Highlighting Al Qaeda Racism Could Deter African Recruits," ABC News blog, July 24, 2010, http://abcnews.go.com/blogs/politics/2010/07/terrorism-bulletin-says-highlighting-al-qaeda-racism-could-deter-african-recruits. The NCTC bulletin stated that some AQIM recruits claimed that the organization "was clearly racist against some black members from West Africa because they were only sent against lower-level targets."

35 Cédric Jourde, "Sifting Through the Layers of Insecurity in the Sahel: The Case of Mauritania," *Africa Security Brief*, no. 15, September 2011, 4, www.ndu.edu/press/lib/pdf/Africa-Security-Brief/ASB-15.pdf.

36 According to Moctar Mohamed Cheikhouna, the government doesn't control more than 10 percent of mosques.

37 See "Mauritania: A New Drug-Trafficking Hub in the Making?" WikiLeaks, June 9, 2011, http://wikileaks.org/cable/2009/06/09NOUAKCHOTT386.html.

38 See Pézard and Glatz, "Arms in and Around Mauritania," 47–48.

39 Ibid., 22.

40 Jemal Oumar, "Sahel Instability Impacts Mauritania," *Magharebia*, March 19, 2012, www.magharebia.com/cocoon/awi/xhtml1/en_GB/features/awi/features/2012/03/19/feature-02.

41 Laurence Aida Ammour, "La Mauritanie au carrefour des menaces régionales," Centre Français de Recherche sur le Renseignement, February 1, 2011, www.cf2r.org/fr/tribune-libre/la-mauritanie-au-carrefour-des-menaces-regionales.php.

42 George B. N. Ayittey, *Africa in Chaos* (New York: St. Martin's Griffin, 1999), 151.

43 This is the dilemma that the international community faces when helping build Mauritania's anti–organized crime units. The challenge is twofold: (1) making sure that better trained and better equipped anti-drug police and customs officers are not transformed into capable and potent drug smugglers and (2) convincing the ruling elites that the development of professional units would not pose a threat to the order of the state (that is, a coup).

44 Cédric Jourde, "Sifting through the Layers of Insecurity in the Sahel: The Case of Mauritania," *Africa Security Brief*, no. 15, September 2011, 3.

45 See "Mauritania: A New Drug-Trafficking Hub in the Making?"

46 According to the U.S. Cables released by WikiLeaks, "Chanvre indien, also known as Diomba, is mostly used by the Soninke and Pulaar. It is a cheap drug—a tea glass costs 1,000 Ouguiya (approximated $4 USD)—that comes from Ghana and enters Mauritania through Senegal."

47 Raby Ould Idoumou, "Mauritania Spreads Moderation Through Mosques," *Magharebia*, March 15, 2012, www.magharebia.com/cocoon/awi/xhtml1/en_GB/features/awi/features/2012/03/15/feature-04.

48 Interview with Isselmou Oud Moustapha, January 18, 2012, Nouackchott.

49 Antil and Touati, "Mali et Mauritanie: pays sahéliens fragiles et États résilients."

50 Denoeux and Smith, "Mauritania Pilot–CT and Development," 8.

51 Interviews with Mohamed Mahmoud Abul Maali, January 16, 2012, and Moctar Mohamed Cheikhouna, January 17, 2012.

52 Denoeux and Smith, "Mauritania Pilot–CT and Development," 12.

53 Ibid.

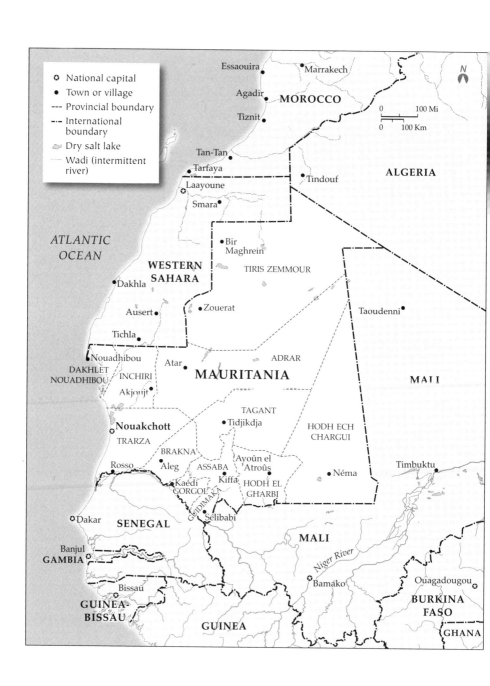

Legend

- ⊕ National capital
- • Town or village
- --- Provincial boundary
- -·- International boundary
- 🏝 Dry salt lake
- --- Wadi (intermittent river)

Essaouira
• Marrakech
Agadir •
MOROCCO
Tiznit •

N

0   100 Mi
0   100 Km

Tan-Tan •
Tarfaya •
Laayoune •
Smara •

• Tindouf

ALGERIA

**ATLANTIC
OCEAN**

• Bir
Maghrein

**WESTERN
SAHARA**

TIRIS ZEMMOUR

• Dakhla

Ausert •

• Zouerat

• Taoudenni

Tichla •

Nouadhibou •
**DAKHLET
NOUADHIBOU**   INCHIRI
Akjoujt •

Atar •

ADRAR

MAURITANIA

MALI

Nouakchott
TRARZA

TAGANT
• Tidjikdja

HODH ECH
CHARGUI

BRAKNA
Rosso •   • Aleg   ASSABA
Kaédi •   Kiffa •
GORGOL

Ayoûn el
• Atroûs
HODH EL
GHARBI

• Néma

Timbuktu •

• Dakar   **SENEGAL**
GUIDIMAKA
Sélibabi •

MALI

Banjul
GAMBIA ⊕

Bissau •

**GUINEA-
BISSAU**

Niger River

Bamako •

Ouagadougou ⊕

**BURKINA
FASO**

GUINEA

GHANA

06

Mauritania's Islamists

Alex Thurston

Mauritanian Islamism's Mixed Implications

Kidnappings of Westerners and embassy bombings have made
Mauritania, along with the broader Sahel region, a source of concern for
American and European governments worried about the potential spread
of transnational terrorist movements in Africa. Western policymakers
have different perspectives on Mauritania's problems. Some believe that
the army's willingness to hunt terrorists both domestically and in neighboring Mali makes the country a strong partner for U.S.-led counterterrorism efforts in the region. Others fear that Mauritania's turbulent
politics (the country has suffered two coups in the past decade) make it
unstable, and thus fertile ground for Muslim extremist recruitment.

The strength of Mauritanian Islamism contributes to such fears.
Legalized Islamist parties are on the rise, and their popular appeal is
evident in Islamist leaders' electoral victories, frequent media appear-
ances, and ability to organize mass anti-Israel demonstrations. Islamists'

political gains, moreover, have gone hand in hand with a broader Islamization of society, as seen in the spread of mosques and Islamic associations in the capital, Nouakchott, and elsewhere.

Nevertheless, Mauritanian Islamist organizations do not currently threaten the United States. The mainstream Islamist movement appears committed to democracy and is unlikely to capture power, whether violently or at the ballot box. Indeed, the Islamists' rising profile may even have some positive implications for the United States: Mainstream Islamist leaders publicly condemn the Muslim terrorist group al-Qaeda in the Islamic Maghreb (AQIM), which Mauritania's government has been combating since 2005. By taking part in government efforts to reform militants, Islamists have helped reduce AQIM's recruiting potential. Moderate Islamists also strengthen Mauritania's flawed democracy by channeling popular anger into participation in mainstream politics.

Washington should also be interested in Mauritanian Islamists for what they can reveal about anti-Western sentiments within an energetic and influential segment of society primarily composed of young, educated, urban activists. This constituency, for instance, opposed Mauritania's 1999 recognition of Israel and helped spur the government's decision to break ties with Jerusalem in 2009. And although it supports the objective of defeating AQIM, it has also criticized the government's acceptance of Western help in counterterrorism. The lesson for the United States is clear: Pressuring the Mauritanian regime to override this constituency's concerns could increase anti-Western sentiments among both Islamists and the population as a whole.

Islamists also participate in global religious networks, extending their relevance beyond Mauritania. Islamists sometimes mediate relations between the state and foreign Islamic groups, and as the fallout from the 2011 Arab uprisings alters North African politics, they will likely forge tighter bonds with Islamists in Algeria, Tunisia, and Libya. Noting which bonds they do strengthen will help policymakers understand and anticipate broader political changes in the Arab world.

Mauritanian Islamists See the State as a Vehicle for the Islamization of Society

The Islamic Republic of Mauritania has long worked to juggle its Arab identity, Islamic character, and Western ties. This juggling act has created opportunities for Islamists to pursue their defining goal: further integrating Islamic values into policymaking—especially in law, education, and foreign policy. Although nearly all Mauritanians are Muslims, they are not all Islamists. Islamists differ from other Muslims in that they make Islam the basis of a political ideology and urge the state—rather than just individual Muslims, scholars, or the community—to enact policies that will more deeply Islamize society. Islamists want more public piety, more mosques and Islamic associations, and a higher profile for Islamic scholars in media and public life. But they also want a government that enforces Islamic law and promotes Islamic beliefs, as well as a foreign policy that shuns reliance on non-Muslim states in favor of greater solidarity with the Muslim world.

Islamists in Mauritania are a broad group. They interpret Islamic principles differently, and they favor different means for Islamizing state and society:

- *Mainstream political Islamists* want to achieve power through elected office and use the state to enforce Islamic law, promote Islam in public life, and craft a more "Islamic" foreign policy.

- *Salafis*, on the other hand, hold the theological viewpoint that contemporary society should conform to the model of the early Muslim community in Medina. In Mauritania, Salafis and mainstream political Islamists have formed tactical alliances, with some Salafis supporting Islamists' electoral campaigns and political organizations. But other Salafis disdain Islamists' participation in formal politics as a corrupt, worldly pursuit. These Salafis prefer to reform society through sermons, instruction, and charitable work, not through electoral campaigns and political protests.

- *Jihadis* advocate the use of violence against political authorities in the name of Islam. Jihadism is a more extreme form of Islamism. Some jihadis embrace Salafi theology, but not all Salafis are jihadis; nor are all jihadis Salafis. Moderate Islamism, which seeks change through nonviolent activism, remains distinct from violent jihadism.

In addition to its interactions with Salafism and jihadism, mainstream Mauritanian Islamism has been shaped by frequently negative, but sometimes close, interactions with the state. At times, state repression has pushed Islamists underground; in other moments, Islamists have been able to broadcast their ideas to society by working together with political authorities. The idea that Mauritania is an "Islamic Republic," as its official name declares, has been particularly important to this relationship. Precisely what such a republic might be has been neither completely clear nor uncontested in the country's political life.

Rulers' attempts to define the place of Islam in society have at times competed with, and at other times borrowed from, Islamist visions of government. For example, the present administration's diplomatic breach with Israel helped bring Islamist positions into mainstream politics, but it also forced Islamists to distinguish themselves from their political rivals. In other words, repression has generally strengthened Islamism, while co-optation has sometimes weakened it.

Social Change and Foreign Influence Spurred Early Islamist Mobilization

Political and demographic changes dating back to the 1970s nurtured the growth of Islamism in Mauritania. Drought pushed nomads into cities, increasing the number of urban dwellers in Mauritania from 8 percent of the population in 1962 to 25 percent in 1975. Urbanization gave rise to new civic associations, including the country's first Islamist organization, the Jemaa Islamiyya (Islamic Association), a Nouakchott-based group sympathetic to the Muslim Brotherhood.

A 1978 military coup against President Moktar Ould Daddah, who had ruled Mauritania since its independence from France in 1960, brought further opportunities for Islamists. Daddah had fostered Islamic values in government and education, and military leaders continued and strengthened this commitment. Colonel Mohamed Haidalla, who ruled from 1980 to 1984, introduced sharia (Islamic law) provisions with the assistance of the Jemaa Islamiyya. Colonel Maaouya Ould Taya, president from 1984 to 2005, rolled back elements of sharia but continued to stress the Islamic character of the state. State efforts to promote Islamic values—for example, the state-run Institut Supérieur d'Études et de Recherche Islamiques (High Institute of Islamic Study and Research, ISERI), founded in 1979—helped create a new generation of Islamist leaders.

Islamists' early experiences in politics divided the newly emerging class of Islamist leaders in Jemaa Islamiyya and in the growing network of Salafi mosques and organizations in the capital. Dissatisfied with Jemaa Islamiyya's closeness to the state, a group of teachers and imams (Islamic clergy) formed Hasim (Harakat al Siyasiyya al Islamiyya fi Muritaniyya, the Islamic Political Movement in Mauritania) in the mid-1980s. Hasim advocated nonviolent democratic engagement to eliminate corruption and promote social justice as outlined in the Qu'ran, especially by giving charity to the poor. Hasim became the forerunner of today's Islamist parties.

Foreign influences also boosted Salafi networks, which nurtured the growth of Islamists' political base. In the 1980s and 1990s, Salafi activists, some of whom received funding or training from Saudi Arabia or other Arab Gulf states, preached in poor urban areas and distributed sermons on cassettes. The boom of international Islamic NGOs in Mauritania in the 1980s,[1] along with increased activism by Egypt's Muslim Brotherhood and other foreign groups, aided Salafis' efforts. In general, Gulf Arab money and manpower have contributed to the increasing visibility of Islam in Mauritanian society, evident in the construction of hundreds of mosques and the founding of dozens of Islamic schools for children and adults. These developments created religious spaces that lie outside of state control and empowered new scholars, trained in Mauritania or abroad, to promote Salafism as a blueprint for social reform. The growth of Salafism has in turn fed the growth of Islamism as a political ideology, as Islamist activists seek to apply Salafi ideals to the state.

Mauritania's complex racial politics have also affected the terrain in which Islamists operate. Mauritania has three main racial groups: the *bidan,* or "white Moors," who speak Arabic; the Haratin or "black Moors," who also speak Arabic; and non-Arabic-speaking black populations, including ethnicities like the Wolof and the Soninke. White Moors, descendants of slave-owning groups, have long sat atop the political and social hierarchy in Mauritania, and slavery of non-whites has persisted to the present despite repeated laws banning the practice.

Since the late 1970s, non-white Mauritanians have become increasingly vocal in fighting slavery and demanding a share of political power. Islamist leaders and activists have primarily been white Moors. Yet as the Haratin in particular become more influential and take on leadership roles not only in politics but also as imams and Muslim scholars, Islamists, who appear to be interested in using Islam as a platform for pan-racial political mobilization, may be able to tap into new constituencies.

Geopolitical Pressures on Mauritania Inadvertently Strengthened Islamism

Beginning in the 1980s, changes in Mauritania's political relations with the outside world damaged the state's popularity and supplied Islamists with rhetorical ammunition to use against the government. Economic liberalization, pushed by the World Bank and the International Monetary Fund, increased social inequality, which in turn made some groups, particularly unemployed youth, sympathetic to declarations that Islamization would solve the country's problems. In the early 1990s, Mauritania's poor human rights record and support for Saddam Hussein during the Gulf War added international isolation to its list of problems. The government made dramatic policy changes to win back U.S. aid and international support. Ironically, these changes boosted the popularity of the Islamist movement.

First, President Ould Taya launched a multiparty system in 1991. In Mauritania's first multiparty municipal elections in 1994, the ruling party swept 172 of 208 districts, but the main opposition party, which included Islamist candidates, took 17 districts. Following the elections, the government cracked down on journalists, opposition figures, and Islamists, apparently out of a desire to reaffirm control. Authorities arrested dozens of Islamists, banned several Islamist groups, and forbade political preaching. This crackdown did not slow the growth of Islamism, but it did fragment its leadership, prompting some activists to flee to the Gulf and others to reconcile with the state and accept government posts. As an older generation of Islamists retired, new leaders emerged, such as Jamil Mansour, the leading Islamist politician in Mauritania today, and Mokhtar el Hacen Ould Dedew, the country's leading Salafi preacher.

Second, Mauritania recognized Israel in 1999, in response to U.S. pressure. This decision proved deeply unpopular at home. Many Mauritanians, increasingly connected to the wider Arab world through Al Jazeera and the Internet, continue to sympathize with the Palestinian cause. The widespread anger over the government's perceived capitulation to the West gave Islamists a political opening. In the religious domain, Dedew issued a fatwa (Islamic edict) against relations with Israel that circulated widely and gained substantial support. In the political domain, Mansour formed Ribat ("League"), an organization that contests Mauritania's relations with Israel. Ribat and other Islamist groups organized a series of mass demonstrations against Israel in the early 2000s that further raised the profile of the Islamist movement. Framing the issue as an Arab and Islamic cause, Islamists effectively positioned themselves as defenders of both Mauritanians and Palestinians against the machinations of corrupt local elites and powerful foreign actors.

Third, following the attacks of September 11, 2001, Mauritanian leaders began participating in U.S.-led counterterrorism efforts like the Pan-Sahel Initiative and its successor program, the Trans-Saharan Counterterrorism Partnership. Islamists agree with the objective of fighting terrorism, but they have insisted that Mauritania and its allies can solve their problems without help from Washington or Paris. At a forum on extremism held in Nouakchott in October 2010, Mansour implied that French involvement in strikes against AQIM might lead to a form of neocolonialism. He advocated regional cooperation as an alternative. Such denunciations of Western involvement in Mauritanian security affairs offer another avenue for Islamists to position themselves as champions of national autonomy.

Profiles of Islamist Leaders

All these factors contributed to the growth of a broad and extremely diverse Islamist movement whose leadership includes educated intellectuals, experienced politicians, and veteran activists. Five figures, in particular, are emblematic of different aspects of the Islamist movement: Mansour; Dedew; Mohamed Ghoulam Ould El Haj, a respected figure and a link between Tawassoul and international Islamist activism; Dr. Yaye Ndaw Coulibaly, a well-known woman and non-Arab within Tawassoul; and Outhmane Ould Abi El Maali, leader of the Fadila ("Virtue") party.

Jamil Mansour (born 1967) currently serves as president of the National Rally for Reform and Development, or Tawassoul, and as a member of parliament. He attended ISERI, as well as Mohamed Ben Abdellah University in Fes, Morocco. He was a student leader in the 1980s and a member of the Islamist opposition in the 1990s. From 2001 to his ouster in the crackdown of 2003, he served as mayor of Arafat, an impoverished neighborhood in Nouakchott. After weathering repression from 2003 to 2005, Mansour concentrated on building Tawassoul and speaking out on international issues.

In the National Assembly, Mansour serves on the Committee for Foreign Relations. He cultivates an aura of moderation and personal righteousness. When he ran for president in 2009, his website called him a "promoter of centrist Islamic thought" and "a symbol of uprightness and honesty."[2] Mansour's regional base (he was born in Beila, in the Trarza region in south central Mauritania) provides many of Tawassoul's supporters.

Mokhtar el Hacen Ould Dedew (born 1963) is the spiritual patron of Tawassoul. Dedew embodies the complex and sometimes ambivalent relationship between Salafism and Islamism: He is a public figure committed to religious reform but not a politician; he focuses more on preaching than on building a political movement. Dedew received Islamic training from scholars in his family and then attended ISERI. He has spent significant time in Saudi Arabia, where he worked as an imam in Riyadh and obtained a Master of Arts degree at Muhammad Ibn Sa'ud University. He has published works on sharia and pilgrimage, and is particularly known for his mastery of hadith (traditions of the Prophet Muhammad).

Dedew has taken leadership roles in several Islamic organizations in Nouakchott, such as the Center for Training Islamic Scholars, and he enjoys a large following among youth. His ties to Saudi Arabia and his exposure in Arab media have given him a global reputation that in turn enhances his status in Mauritania. One episode will help demonstrate his stature. In early 2010, Dedew helped mediate the release of several

Mauritanian businessmen whom the government had detained on corruption charges. The government reportedly sought Dedew's intervention on the advice of Sudanese President Omar al-Bashir. That al-Bashir had heard of him and saw fit to recommend him is evidence of Dedew's international prestige. Dedew has also led government-sponsored dialogues with imprisoned jihadists.

Mohamed Ghoulam Ould El Haj Cheikh (likely in his 40s or 50s) is vice president of Tawassoul and secretary-general of Ribat. He has played a leading role in Islamist anti-Israel activities. He was a prominent passenger on the Gaza Freedom Flotilla, which was boarded by the Israeli navy in May 2010, and his return to Mauritania was marked by an Islamist anti-Israel rally in Nouakchott. He acts as one of the party's faces for international media and outreach to foreign countries, appearing frequently on networks like Al Jazeera and leading delegations to countries like Algeria.

Dr. Yaye Ndaw Coulibaly (age unknown) is one of the most prominent female politicians in Tawassoul (women play a significant role in the organization and public persona of the party). She was mayor of the Tevragh Zeina district of Nouakchott from 2007 until political opponents forced her out in April 2008. Coulibaly served as president of the Campagne des Femmes (Women's Campaign) for Mansour's 2009 presidential campaign. Her party leadership role helped Tawassoul present itself as a vehicle for political and social progress for women in an Islamic framework. Coulibaly, an ethnic Soninke, is also a prominent non-Arab representative of a party whose leaders, including the other figures profiled in this section, are primarily white Moors. She currently serves in the Senate.

Outhmane Ould Ebi El Maali (born 1948) is head of the Fadila party. From a family of Islamic scholars and educated at ISERI, he has had a decades-long career in diplomacy and politics. Between 1979 and 1992, he served as consul general in Libya, Niger, and Saudi Arabia before becoming ambassador to Qatar and later Kuwait. He ran as an independent in the 2006 parliamentary elections and the 2007 presidential elections, losing in the former and scoring less than 2 percent of the vote in the latter. Fadila, legalized in 2007 along with Tawassoul, is seen as basically powerless.

Ebi El Maali's importance lies in his connections to North Africa, Egypt, and the Arab Gulf. For example, the world-famous Egyptian theologian Yusuf al-Qaradawi paid a visit to Ebi El Maali (accompanied by Dedew) during a trip to Mauritania in 2010. Ebi El Maali has also served as president of "La coordination de l'action nationaliste et islamique" (Coordinating Group for Nationalist and Islamic Action), a group of small parties and organizations that speak out on politics and Islamic affairs.

These figures exemplify several trends among the country's Islamist leaders: they tend to have university education, strong ties to foreign countries, and a keen sense of political symbolism. They are comfortable using mass media, and they reject the use of violence in the service of Islamic values. Yet the leadership class is not entirely homogeneous. Women and non-Arabs have attained prominence within the Islamist movement, and prominent leaders have pursued different forms of political activism, as indicated by the difference between Mansour's focus on electoral success and Dedew's career in preaching and mediation.

The Tawassoul Party: Years of Underground Organizing Taught Islamists Political Sophistication

The most important Islamist organization in Mauritania today is Tawassoul, a large, legally recognized, and openly Islamist party associated with the Mauritanian branch of the Muslim Brotherhood. The formation of Tawassoul testifies to the political skills Islamist leaders acquired during their time underground and honed as independent candidates in parliamentary elections and supporters of opposition candidates in the 2003 and 2007 presidential elections.

Tawassoul is not the only Islamist party in Mauritania. In addition to the already mentioned Fadila, there are other small parties, previously sympathetic to the late Libyan leader Muammar Qaddafi, which espouse some Islamist values. But since 2007, Tawassoul's modest electoral gains and its ability to win media attention and drive the political conversation have made it the most important Islamist group in the country and a player in Mauritanian politics.

Tawassoul's legal recognition in 2007 followed a period of turbulence during which the government severely repressed Islamists. As popular discontent increased in the early 2000s, President Ould Taya cracked down on Islamists but won only pyrrhic victories against them. Arresting Islamist leaders only raised their domestic and international profiles, evoking sympathy demonstrations and strikes in Nouakchott and elsewhere.

After a coup toppled Ould Taya in 2005, the military sponsored a transition to civilian rule. During this transition, the junta banned Islamist parties from running in the 2006 local and parliamentary elections, but five Islamists running as independents were elected as representatives and two as senators, and Islamists won several mayoral elections. Islamists did not run a major candidate in the 2007 presidential elections, but when the two main candidates largely avoided discussing the Israel issue, Islamists jumped into the breach, allowing them to maintain a high political profile in the media and in the streets.

Following the elections, civilian President Sidi Mohamed Abdellahi's government legalized Tawassoul. Islamists participated in national government for the first time, joining the cabinet in May 2008. Habib Ould Hemdeit, one of Tawassoul's founders, headed the Ministry of Employment, Access, and Professional Formation, and Mohamed Mahmoud Ould Sidi, a former professor and one of Tawassoul's publicists, led the Ministry of Higher Education. This cabinet lasted less than three months, however. When parliament threatened a no confidence vote, partly to protest Abdellahi's inclusion of Islamists, the cabinet was dissolved and replaced with one composed solely of members of the president's party.

In August 2008, as confidence in Abdellahi collapsed, General Mohamed Abdel Aziz led a new coup d'état. Tawassoul objected strongly, joining a multiparty coalition that demanded the restoration of democracy. This commitment to democracy was to some extent self-serving, in that Islamists believed they would fare better under civilian governance, but many Islamists genuinely objected to the overthrow of Mauritania's fragile democracy. During the period of greatest uncertainty, mainstream Islamists did not, notably, demand the imposition of an Islamic state, but only the restoration of civilian democratic rule.

After the coup, Tawassoul struggled to adjust to the new political landscape. The party's survival depended on the regime's toleration, but Tawassoul also had to compete with the regime rhetorically in order to remain politically relevant. In early 2009, Abdel Aziz undercut the party's relevance by adopting some of its anti-Israel and anticorruption rhetoric and, ultimately, recalling Mauritania's ambassador from Israel.

The party is making some headway. Tawassoul attempted to distinguish itself by conducting its first official presidential campaign, nominating Mansour for the July 2009 elections. Abdel Aziz won with 52.5 percent of the vote, and was followed by major opposition leaders like racial justice activist Messaoud Boulkheir (16 percent), and opposition veteran Ahmed Daddah (14 percent). Yet Islamists outperformed the other minor parties and candidates, including former military ruler Colonel Ely Vall. Mansour placed fourth out of ten total candidates, earning nearly 37,000 votes (5 percent). Even if the official results were rigged, as some have alleged, the elections elevated Mansour's political status and increased Tawassoul's public profile.

As Abdel Aziz consolidated power after the elections, Tawassoul's leaders decided that working with the president would enhance their political survival, and so joined the ruling coalition in November 2009. This shows that Tawassoul's leaders are pragmatists: Islamist ideology has not prevented Tawassoul from sometimes acting like other Mauritanian opposition parties, moving between pro- and anti-regime stances depending on the political imperatives of the moment. Tawassoul's major political initiatives since 2010 have included continued anti-Israel activism (such as participation in the Gaza Flotilla), support for increasing the use of Arabic in higher education, and cautious, unofficial participation in youth protests against Abdel Aziz.

With Abdel Aziz's popularity declining and protests spreading throughout the Arab world in 2011, Tawassoul resumed an anti-regime stance. In June 2011, Tawassoul joined a group of opposition parties calling for national dialogue on issues like security sector reform and media freedom. This call partly aimed to capitalize on the country's youth ferment. Mansour stepped up his attacks on the regime, decrying its alleged corruption, the mismanagement of a national census, and other issues.

Tawassoul remains a potential partner for the president, particularly if Abdel Aziz decides that he needs its connections to the Gulf and North Africa. Yet the government has not stopped imprisoning Islamists, and dozens remain incarcerated today—both activists and suspected terrorists. Moreover, some Tawassoul supporters were disillusioned when the party failed to make headway on Israel and other policy objectives. Islamists remain vulnerable despite their political successes.

In terms of party structure, Tawassoul is a sophisticated organization that boasts a youth wing and a women's group. The party holds five of the National Assembly's 81 seats and two of the Senate's 56, but it enjoys disproportionate strength due to its supporters' intense commitment and the leadership's skillful use of mass media. It maintains a frequently updated and well-organized website, www.tewassoul.org, available in both Arabic and French, and has a Facebook profile, a YouTube channel, and a Twitter account. The party organizes many press conferences and rallies, and its leaders appear regularly in pan-Arab media, especially Al Jazeera, as well as in the local press. Ideologically, the party continues to emphasize its commitment to Islamic values and political moderation, though at times Islam appears to be a set of guiding values rather than a set of specific policy prescriptions.

The party's social base remains primarily urban, middle class, and young. Tawassoul draws many female supporters, and in some ways the party functions as a social movement in which young people can meet potential spouses and deepen their piety. Most members are white Moors, though the party enjoys some support from the Haratin and from non-Arabic-speaking black populations. The leadership includes many businessmen, augmenting the party's economic power, and though the leaders are not necessarily elites, they have been able to mobilize human and financial resources to grow the party.

Tawassoul has not yet achieved major-party status in Mauritania, and its electoral gains remain modest. But when compared with Islamists' political position in the 1990s, Tawassoul, as a legalized and well-organized political party with a sophisticated internal structure, represents a major advance. Islamists' future success will depend partly on whether they can continue to carve out their own rhetorical niche in the larger political scene and partly on whether they can reach new constituencies, particularly non-white Moors and rural populations.

Mauritania's Islamists Have Close Ties With Other Arab Islamists

Mauritanian Islamists have cultivated close ties with other Islamist movements, especially in the Arab Gulf and Algeria, which could give the movement a higher profile in Arab media and attract external political and financial support for its activities in Mauritania. Tawassoul has a National Secretary for External Relations, and since the 2009 elections, it has signed an accord with a major Algerian Islamist party, the Mouvement de la société pour la paix (Movement of Society for Peace). The party's foreign connections have made it a significant broker in the Mauritanian state's external relations with the Islamic world. For example, in addition to the afore-mentioned connection between Dedew and Sudan's al-Bashir, Mansour was invited to a meeting between a Hezbollah delegation and Abdel Aziz in January 2011. Tawassoul has also developed strong relations with some non-Islamist parties, including the Baath Party of Syria. It considers itself part of the broader Arab political landscape, and is interested in forming political alliances that will boost its domestic and international strength.

In the context of the "Arab Spring" and Libya's civil war, Tawassoul became a vehicle for anti-Qaddafi sentiment among many Mauritanians. In an appearance on Al Jazeera in February 2011, Dedew condemned government-sponsored violence within Libya, and Mansour tore apart Qaddafi's Green Book in a meeting of the Mauritanian parliament. Islamists' role in domestic opposition to Qaddafi added to the pressure on Abdel Aziz, who broke with the Libyan ruler in June 2011. More recently, Tawassoul has declared its support for anti-regime protesters in Syria.

Islamists will have small but significant influence over Mauritania's relations with its neighbors in the new North Africa. Their ties to Algeria could mean that Libya's weakness is Algeria's gain, but Islamists will also likely strengthen ties with their Libyan counterparts in post-Qaddafi Libya. Political Islam's fortunes could improve generally in the new North Africa; Mauritanian Islamists will be in a position to help shape this trend.

The Gulf remains an important destination for Mauritanian Islamists. Leaders like Mansour and Dedew have spent time in Saudi Arabia, the United Arab Emirates, and other Gulf countries. Numerous Mauritanian preachers and activists, including well-known Salafis like Sheikh Abdullah Bin Bayyah, reside in the Gulf but return home regularly, acting as personal links to the global Islamist web. The UAE is home to several thousand Mauritanians, dozens of whom work as imams, preachers, judges, and professors.

Beyond the Gulf, Mauritanian Islamists' support for the Palestinian cause continues to shape the movement. And Tawassoul's affiliations with the Muslim Brotherhood make it part of a loose network of Islamist parties throughout the Arab world. These links constitute pathways of political and cultural exchange but are unlikely to fuel Islamic extremism.

Jihadism Is a Radical Fringe That Mainstream Islamists Oppose

Since a June 2005 attack by militants on a military base in northern Mauritania, the Mauritanian state has steadfastly battled jihadists, with Abdel Aziz taking a particularly hard line on the issue. The 2005 attack was carried out by the Salafist Group for Preaching and Combat, an Algerian jihadist splinter group that renamed itself al-Qaeda in the Islamic Maghreb (AQIM) in 2007. AQIM operates throughout Algeria, Mali, Niger, and Mauritania, and has claimed responsibility for about a dozen kidnappings and attempted kidnappings of Westerners in recent years. AQIM has attacked symbols of Western power in Mauritania, opening fire on the Israeli embassy in 2008 and carrying out a suicide bombing near the French embassy in 2009. In early 2011, Mauritanian soldiers intercepted an AQIM convoy carrying explosives to Nouakchott as part of an assassination plot against Abdel Aziz, a bomb plot against the French embassy, or both.

Abdel Aziz sees AQIM as the country's greatest security challenge, although some believe he has incentives to exaggerate the threat in order to increase the financial support he receives from the West. He has attempted to destroy the group's camps in Mauritania and neighboring Mali. This operation has driven militants out of some areas and has won cooperation from Mali, which has an enduring reputation as the Sahelian country least committed to armed counterterrorism.

AQIM's attacks in Mauritania form part of its broader political and criminal strategy in the Sahel. They are also a response to Mauritania's domestic political tensions over the state's geopolitical stances. The overwhelming majority of Mauritanians reject AQIM's brand of Islam. But AQIM's uncompromising stances on Israel and the war in Afghanistan appeal to some Mauritanian youth, and the jihadist group's online propaganda and rural preaching tours have allowed it to recruit a number of Mauritanians.

A few Mauritanians have been accused of involvement with al-Qaeda Central. One example is Mohamedou Ould Slahi, who spent time with the mujahideen in Afghanistan, reportedly aided several of the 9/11 pilots, and is currently being held in Guantánamo Bay. Some Mauritanian nationals have also joined extremist cells in Saudi Arabia. Most of the concern around jihadism in Mauritania, however, has centered on AQIM.

Moderate Islamism is distinct from jihadism, but Mauritanian regimes have sometimes conflated the two tendencies. In the past, authorities regularly accused Islamist politicians of spurring radicalization and plotting violence. The military still harbors suspicions of Islamists; the 2008 coup sprang in part from officers' perceptions that Abdellahi was weak on terrorism and too tolerant of Islamism.

Since 2008, however, Abdel Aziz has worked to co-opt the Islamist movement, partnering with Islamists like Dedew to rehabilitate jihadists. Terrorism has topped the agenda at meetings between Abdel Aziz and Mansour. The president will likely continue to seek Islamists' help in this domain.

Mainstream Islamists have stridently rejected violence in general and AQIM in particular. The existence of legalized Islamist parties and moderate Islamist and Salafi organizations has likely reduced the spread of jihadism by providing young Mauritanians with nonviolent avenues for expressing a politicized Muslim identity. Denunciations of jihadism, moreover, likely carry weight among Mauritanian youth when they come from preachers and politicians whose piety is taken seriously and whose credentials as opposition figures have been demonstrated through years of activism and long stints in government prisons.

One reason for Islamists' objections to jihadism is that it directly competes with Tawassoul for recruits. For example, residents of Arafat, one of Tawassoul's strongholds in Nouakchott, have expressed fears that jihadist websites are radicalizing youth. This trend threatens to undermine Tawassoul among its own constituents and in the eyes of the government. It could pressure Tawassoul to sharpen its Islamic rhetoric while more effectively presenting a nonviolent alternative to jihadism.

Moderate Islamists' reaction to jihadism, however, involves a balancing act. Islamists face pressure to criticize jihadists without overly antagonizing their sympathizers, and to cooperate with the regime without becoming too closely associated with it.

Islamists' enthusiasm for cooperation with the state is limited by their need to retain a distinct political identity. If Islamist politicians align too closely with the regime, they could lose their credibility as independent voices. Moderate Islamists support the fight against AQIM, but they want to carefully manage their contribution to the effort. The complexities of this balancing act mean that Islamists will denounce terrorism on their own terms, for example by calling for a fight against jihadism but also rejecting Western support in that fight.

Conclusion

Islamism in Mauritania gives voice to the religious convictions, political frustrations, and anti-Western sentiments of a significant segment of the population. Due to their increasing role in multiparty politics in the past six years, Islamists have influenced policymaking on issues like Israel and counterterrorism. Mauritanian Islamism is also a formidable presence on the global Islamist circuit.

Islamists face several challenges, including President Abdel Aziz's success in co-opting their rhetoric, the pitfalls of preserving Islamic principles while navigating electoral politics, and the need to respond to jihadism. But the trends that gave rise to Islamism continue: urbanization proceeds, social inequality remains, and mosques and Islamic schools still proliferate, allowing Islamists to expand their influence in urban spaces and reach new audiences, particularly among the youth. Tawassoul as well as politicians like Jamil Mansour are likely to lose support if they draw too close to Abdel Aziz or if they make no progress in implementing their agenda.

Western actions in Mauritania will affect the trajectory of Islamism going forward. An increased Western military presence in the Sahel, pressure from Washington on Nouakchott to restore full relations with Israel, and negative Western rhetoric surrounding Islamist electoral victories elsewhere in the region are all factors that could present Mauritanian Islamists with political opportunities. Islamists have often attracted popular support by casting themselves as champions of Muslims oppressed by Arab and Western governments. Islamists will likely denounce rhetoric and actions coming from Washington that they see as revealing ambitions to control and dominate Mauritania.

This does not mean that Washington and Mauritanian Islamists have no interests in common. Moderate Islamists' denunciations of jihadists should be encouraged, as should the regime's working relationship with parties like Tawassoul. Yet if relations between the regime and the Islamists deteriorate, or if Islamists are able to make campaign issues of Mauritania's war on terrorism and the regime's ties to the West, Islamists could begin to capture a larger share of the electorate and to mobilize larger protests against the regime and against foreign actors.

In this Islamic Republic, as tensions over what Islam means continue to shape political life, religious debates, and social activism, Mauritanian Islamism will remain a strong political force and an influential social movement, moderate on domestic issues and outspoken on international topics. Mauritania will continue to juggle its Islamic identity, its societal divisions, and its precarious geopolitical position.

Further Reading

Boucek, Christopher. "Saudi Extremism to Sahel and Back." *Jane's Islamic Affairs Analyst*, February 2009.

International Crisis Group. *Contestation Islamiste en Mauritanie: Menace ou Bouc Émissaire?* Brussels: International Crisis Group, 2005.

Ould Ahmed Salem, Zekeria. "Islam in Mauritania between Political Expansion and Globalization: Elites, Institutions, Knowledge, and Networks." In *Islam and Muslim Politics in Africa*, edited by Benjamin F. Soares and René Otayek, 27–46. New York: Palgrave Macmillan, 2007.

Ould-Mey, Mohameden. "Mauritania: Between the Hammer of Economic Globalization and the Anvil of Multiparty Factionalism." In *North Africa: Politics, Region, and the Limits of Transformation*, edited by Yahia H. Zoubir and Haizam Amirah-Fernández, 71–89. London and New York: Routledge, 2008.

Al-Tajammu' al-Watani li l-Islāh wa l-Tanmiya (Tawassoul). "Al-Ru'ya al-Fikriyya (The Intellectual Vision)." Mauritania: Tawassoul, date unknown.

Notes

1   These NGOs include the Saudi-run International Islamic Relief Organization, the Kuwaiti-directed Africa Muslim Agency, and Sudan's International African Relief Agency.

2   "Biographie du symbole de la droiture et de l'honnêteté: Mohamed Jemil Ould Brahim Ould Mansour," 2009, http://jemilmansour.net/francais/index.php?option=com_content&view=category&layout=blog&id=10&Itemid=13.

Canary Islands
(SPAIN)

MOROCCO

ALGERIA

Sidi Ifni

Guelmim

Tan Tan

Headquarters of
the Polisario Front

Tindouf

Tarfaya

Mahbés

N

Laayoune

Smara

ATLANTIC
OCEAN

Amgala

Tifariti

Bir
Lahlou

Bu Craa

Boujdour

Bir
Maghrein

WESTERN
SAHARA

Guelta
Zemmur

MAURITANIA

Oum
Dreyga

Baggari

Dakhla

National capital

Mijek

Town or village

Berm (barrier separating
Moroccan and Polisario-
controlled areas)

Ausert

Zouerate

International boundary

Dougaj

Dry salt lake

Guerguerat

Tichla

Wadi (intermittent river)

0   100 Mi

Bon Lanuar

0   100 Km

La Guera

MAURITANIA

07

Simmering Discontent in the Western Sahara

Anouar Boukhars

Introduction

In discussions of organized criminal activity in the Sahel and the growing reach of al-Qaeda in the Islamic Maghreb (AQIM), most regional and Western defense strategists agree that urgent efforts are needed to address the frozen conflict in the Western Sahara because it encourages the emergence of violent entrepreneurs, drug warlords, and other nefarious elements. A Spanish colony since 1884, the Western Sahara did not become independent when Spain withdrew. Instead, Spain ceded the territory to Morocco and Mauritania in 1975, with Mauritania relinquishing its acquisition in 1979.

Not all inhabitants of the territory accepted the deal, however. The Popular Front for the Liberation of Saguia al-Hamra and Rio de Oro (Polisario), formed in 1973, established a government-in-exile in 1976. The Polisario claims that under international law, as a former colony, the Western Sahara should have been granted independence. Based in and backed by Algeria, which is motivated both by principle and its rivalry with Morocco, the Polisario led a guerrilla war against Moroccan forces until a 1991 cease-fire.

The fighting has caused the displacement of thousands of people—most of whom fled to refugee camps located around Tindouf in southwest Algeria—and the killing of thousands of fighters. The territory was divided into a heavily fortified Moroccan zone, constituting 85 percent of the territory and protected by defensive walls (called "berms") built in the mid-1980s and manned by 150,000 soldiers. The Polisario controls the remainder of the area, deemed by Morocco as a buffer zone and of no strategic or economic value.

Besides inflicting these terrible human and economic costs, the conflict has also negatively impacted trans-Saharan security. The undergoverned areas abutting the Western Sahara, especially northern Mauritania and the Polisario-administered camps in southwest Algeria, are becoming major hubs for drug trafficking, the smuggling of contraband, and the circulation of weapons. There is growing evidence to suggest dangerous connections between criminal organizations, AQIM, and the Sahrawi refugees in Tindouf. Such links are bound to deepen should the social and political conditions in the camps deteriorate further or if civil unrest plagues the Moroccan-controlled Western Sahara.

Furthermore, young Sahrawis in the camps are becoming increasingly disenchanted by the failure of the nationalist agenda and upset by the perceived corruption and clientelism of the Polisario elites. The prospect that the Western Sahara can become integrated into the criminal and terrorist networks threatening North Africa and the Sahel is troubling to the United States and its European allies. Already, the Western Sahara conflict has undermined regional security cooperation and assistance. The hostility and distrust between Morocco and Algeria have been so destructive that the whole region has been dragged into a vicious circle of collective suspicion, counterproductive rivalries, and self-defeating policies.

This long-standing rift between the two North African countries is a source of great frustration to their weaker southern neighbors. Cooperation between Morocco and Algeria, with their credible intelligence services and military capabilities, would help the region avert a slide "into hell," to use the words of Chadian General Adoum Ngare Hassan.[1] Jean-Francois Daguzan of France's Foundation for Strategic Research echoed that sentiment when he recently told Reuters, "If there is no Algerian-Moroccan agreement on the security of the Sahel, there cannot be true security, simply because the terrorists will use this fundamental fault."

Resolving the Western Sahara conflict would help untangle the main existing deadlocks in North Africa and the Sahel: impediments toward regional reconciliation and coordination in the fight against violent extremism and organized criminal activity. Based on the author's multiple trips to the Moroccan Western Sahara and dozens of interviews, this paper examines the security risks of the persistence of the conflict by analyzing the destabilizing forces that heighten local tensions and regional instability.

Western Sahara in 2010: A Deceptive Calm

In the Moroccan-controlled Western Sahara, a semblance of stability and calm has returned since the deadly violence that rocked its biggest city, Laayoune, in November 2010. Despite intermittent protests and sporadic ethnic and tribal skirmishes, the major population centers have resisted the ongoing tide of insurrection and demonstrations that has altered the status quo in North Africa. The near absence of political agitation is quite notable given the underlying drivers of discontent and simmering ethnic frictions.

The region's inhabitants sat out pro-democracy protests by the February 20 Youth Movement that launched demonstrations elsewhere in Morocco. They also turned out in force to endorse the July 2011 constitution and vote peacefully in the November parliamentary elections. The Islamist Justice and Development Party, which won the plurality of votes in the November 2011 parliamentary elections, managed to make inroads into the Sahara by successfully tapping into its reputation of probity and growing understanding of the intricacies of local power politics. Given its ethnic and tribal configurations and notoriously patronage-ridden politics, the Islamists had never before managed to win a single seat in the Sahara.

Senior Moroccan officials enthusiastically point out how the region has withstood the "three evil forces" of separatist uprisings, widespread socioeconomic protests, and ethnic strife. The Polisario, the proclaimed defender of Sahrawis' rights to self-determination, failed to whip up ethno-separatist sentiments and drive political revolt against Moroccan rule, and its calls for the boycott of recently held elections also largely fell on deaf ears. The Sahrawis, an ethnic group that shares the same language and social customs, populate an area that encompasses swathes of northern Mauritania, western Algeria, southern Morocco, and the disputed Western Sahara. In the latter, one can find native Western Saharans as well as Sahrawis from the adjacent southern Moroccan provinces.

During my most recent trip to the region, locally elected representatives, tribal leaders, and senior political and security officials gleefully reminded me—just in case I failed to take notice—of the juxtaposed realities on the ground in the Moroccan-administered Western Sahara and in the Polisario-controlled Tindouf camps. The former remains relatively stable and secure while the latter is increasingly becoming infested with illegality, drug smuggling, and kidnapping. The most recent example of this state of affairs in the camps took place in October 2011. Three aid workers—an Italian and two Spaniards—were kidnapped from within the camps administered by the Polisario. That seems to confirm the long-held Moroccan belief that the deteriorating social and political conditions in the camps of Tindouf represent a tinderbox waiting to explode.

Populated by thousands of idle and frustrated fighters and networks of seasoned traffickers, the camps are naturally an appealing target for AQIM's military and smuggling wings. The slide of growing numbers of disenchanted Sahrawis toward banditry and militancy should therefore come as no surprise to the international community, though such a development carries enormous risks to the stability of North Africa and the Sahel.

AQIM and its criminal offshoots in the Sahel work relentlessly to expand their partnership with smugglers from the camps and enlist recruits among disenchanted Sahrawis. The terrorist group has already made small inroads into the Arab and Tuareg tribes in Niger, Mali, and Mauritania. If it can expand its alliances of convenience with the Polisario tribesmen of the Tindouf camps, the militant movement can become a formidable terrorist and criminal organization.

The involvement of Sahrawi youths in narcotrafficking is also becoming a disturbing reality. Sahrawis are increasingly socially isolated, lack direction, and have no prospects in sight. They feel abandoned by their aging and out of touch leadership, and turning to criminal networks becomes a way of turning against a regime that has failed them and an international community that pays lip service to their sufferings. It is in this context of increasing criminal activity and social tensions in the camps that AQIM's presence becomes threatening.

The partnerships between militant groups and some elements of the Polisario may not be based on ideological affinity and are not as widespread as is feared, but they do exist and constitute a major security threat to the Maghreb and the Sahel. The fear has always been that the frustration that leads to criminality might also lead to militancy and criminal terrorism. "Powerful terrorist organizations like AQIM are expert at detecting persons showing signs of vulnerability," said Michael Braun, a former director of operations of the Drug Enforcement Agency. "Thus, the camps of Tindouf represent a potential gold mine for recruiters from groups like AQIM."[2] With the significant amount of loose Libyan weapons and the proliferation of skilled and angry fighters, the potential for destabilization is real.

A Regional Concern

The destabilizing consequences of the potential spread of organized crime and militancy in the camps of Tindouf is of great concern to the countries of the region, including Mali, which shares a border with Algeria and Mauritania.[3] The last two years have seen a number of skirmishes between rival Malian and Sahrawi drug traffickers. Regularly, Sahrawi or Malian assailants take members of their respective communities hostage to guarantee that drug shipments will be delivered. This has led to some "dramatic reprisals" with civilians as collateral damage. As drug money increases, there will likely be more battles over trafficking routes and turf, with serious consequences for the state and society. The regular vendors, traders, and peddlers have the impression that they can no longer eke out a living or that what they bring in pales in comparison to the earnings from smuggling and drugs.

Mali accuses the Polisario of being a major player in the region's drug-trafficking industry. According to a document penned by the Malian security services and titled "Al-Qaeda in the camps of the Polisario," elements within the Polisario are engaged with AQIM in kidnapping operations and are using Malian territory for drug trafficking. The document implicated two young Sahrawis in the abduction of two French nationals in Hombori in northeast Mali at the end of November 2011.

The kidnappers were inspired by the "legend of Hakim Ould Mohamed M'barek, alias Houdheifa, a major figure in the Polisario AQIM." According to Oumar Diakité, a Malian security official, "AQIM is getting implanted everywhere, Algeria, Mauritania and Mali, and this has ramifications in the ranks of the Polisario. Middlemen have been recruited."[4]

In December 2011, Mali forcefully condemned the Polisario for using its territory for extortion, kidnapping, and drug smuggling. "Our country is not the Wild West where they can come to kill, and kidnap people," a Malian minister told Agence France-Presse. According to Amadou Diré, communal councilor of Timbuktu in northern Mali, "It is the second time in less than two years they come to leave us in shambles. The first time was for a story between drug traffickers [2010] in which they [Polisario elements] were involved."[5] In February 2013, the Malian foreign minister confirmed the presence of Sahrawi combatants from the Tindouf camps among the groups that fled the French-led intervention, which was launched to counter an advance of insurgents from northern Mali toward the capital.[6]

Algeria, the main patron of the Polisario, must also be concerned about this looming threat emerging from the camps within its territory. For years now, Polisario leaders and their Algerian backers have categorically denied that the Sahrawis, placed under their tight control, engage in any mercenary or militant activity. The Sahrawis are not, according to the Polisario and its supporters, part of the booming trans-Saharan drug-trafficking networks and kidnapping cells.

The evidence, however, runs counter to this official line. Indeed, a study conducted by Altadis (a European tobacco company) revealed that "Sahrawis are involved in a vast network of smuggling... using various routes, passing through the Western Sahara to Algeria via Tifariti and Bir Lahlou, oases controlled by the Polisario Front."[7] As proceeds increase, these Sahrawi criminal networks have expanded their operations and influence, undermining social structures and the checks on illegal behavior that the traditional tribal lifestyle used to provide.

Sahrawi smuggling networks have also used their influence in northern Mauritania, especially in the regions of Adrar and Tiris Zemmour, which border the Western Sahara, to expand their illegal trafficking and make the country a major hub of cigarette, drugs, arms, fuel, and human trafficking. To be sure, this illegal activity has existed for decades. It has been fueled by the conflict over the Western Sahara and has benefited from the ethnic kinship that relates the Sahrawis of northern Mauritania and those of the camps of Tindouf as well as from the complicity of the Algerian army, the Polisario, and senior Mauritanian officials. The problem today, however, is that these illicit activities occur in the context of the expansion of AQIM, growing interdependence of organized criminal networks and state officials, and rising social and ethnic conflict. The combination of these developments can be dangerously destabilizing not only for the fragile states of Mauritania and Mali, but also for the stronger ones, namely Algeria and Morocco.

In Morocco, political officials like to emphasize how their heavy military presence in the Western Sahara has kept stability in the area. Indeed, this is probably one of the last areas of the Saharan desert that Western tourists can visit without fear of being kidnapped. But despite the well-guarded border, the area is not impervious to smuggling activities and small-arms trafficking. On January 5, 2011, Moroccan security forces dismantled a twenty-seven-member AQIM cell around Amgala in the Western Sahara, discovering a cache of weapons.[8] This arsenal was smuggled through the Western Sahara's defensive wall. More unsettling was the subsequent arrest of five Moroccan soldiers accused of taking kickbacks from arms traffickers. The arrests demonstrate once again the links between AQIM and transnational smugglers of drugs and arms as well as the difficulty of monitoring the porous borders.

The Moroccan-controlled Western Sahara is also vulnerable to societal tensions and ethnic frictions that seriously threaten to destabilize the whole region. Despite the calm that reigns in the area, the challenges to stability and peace remain unchanged. The fact is that the underlying causes that set Laayoune on fire fifteen months ago still persist. Without immediate adjustments in policy, tensions are bound to escalate and mushroom into dangerous ethnic and tribal divides, worsening cultural prejudices and deepening a growing clash of identities.

Should ethnic tensions or social conflict escalate, the Moroccan Western Sahara could easily become caught in the turmoil that afflicts other parts of the Sahel. The threat is not so much terrorism as it is the combination of rising ethnic animosity and expanding transnational criminal networks. That animosity and the rise of criminal networks are deeply embedded in local ethnic conflict, which can seriously destabilize the Western Sahara, weakening social hierarchies, and further exacerbating conflict within groups and the broader communities.

Unrest in Hitherto Unexpected Places?

Twice in 2011, Dakhla, a small city situated at the heart of the Western Sahara long known for its ethnic harmony and calm, was rocked by ethnic unrest and violent rampages. In each instance, the immediate trigger was a trivial dispute among rowdy young men that quickly degenerated into all-out intercommunal violence. Behind the violence and underneath the rage is a mixture of ethnic animosity and resentments tied to long-standing socioeconomic grievances that continue to fuel radicalism and unrest.

Despite Moroccan authorities' claims to the contrary, this ethnic tension and enmity, tinged at times with racism, is real and was readily spilled out during the dozens of interviews I held with different communities in Dakhla and Laayoune. Some indigenous Western Saharans, now a minority of the population, speak contemptuously of migrant "interlopers" and opportunists from the north who reap the benefits of the region's resources at their expense. In Dakhla, the indigenous population dubbed a whole neighborhood "Al Wakkala" (the eaters).

That neighborhood is a residential area populated by tens of thousands of Sahrawis who lived outside the disputed territory before being transplanted into the Western Sahara in 1991 to vote in a referendum on self-determination for the territory that never took place. The state provided them with housing and still supplies them with food subsidies. The perception that government largesse disproportionately benefits nonindigenous Western Saharans has sowed the seeds of anger and hatred within this community. The bloody events that shook Dakhla in 2011 pitted the indigenous Sahrawi population against the inhabitants of "Al Wakkala" camps.

Relations between indigenous Western Saharans and Moroccans from the north are also tense. The latter are referred to as Dakhilis, a generic term that means people from the center of Morocco and designates anyone who is a non-Sahrawi. That includes military personnel and their families, civil servants, workers (carpenters, mechanics), shopkeepers, and traders. There is deep mistrust between the two communities. In the eyes of the indigenous population, Dakhilis are chauvinistic carpetbaggers who steal jobs. They are referred to in demeaning terms as "Ch'lihat" (little Berbers). Those Dakhilis who occupy menial jobs—work Sahrawis view as beneath them—are degradingly called "hammal" (porter). Dakhilis have their own denigrating designations for Sahrawis, who are usually referred to as lazy, untrustworthy, and ungrateful in spite of government preferential treatment.[9]

This ethnic disharmony and these mutual feelings of antagonism were laid bare in the November 2010 conflict in the streets of Laayoune. Insurgent Sahrawis deliberately burned properties owned by northerners; the latter responded in brutal kind. The violence and killings of that day put an end to any semblance of harmonious cohabitation between native Sahrawis and Dakhilis.

Despite the Moroccan state's efforts to promote peaceful coexistence, the Western Sahara remains a territory where ethnic cleavages, tribal tensions, and socioeconomic grievances intertwine inextricably. Such fissures have deepened in recent years, creating new divisive forces that threaten the stability of the region.

While ethnic nationalism was never a force to reckon with in the Moroccan-controlled Western Sahara, ethnic identity is becoming more pronounced. This does not translate into support for separatism, but it does enhance the forces of divisiveness, which erode the rule of law and undermine the existing social fabric.

The Roots of Conflict

The growing unrest in the Moroccan Western Sahara is the consequence of the far-reaching demographic and social changes the area has experienced since its annexation by Morocco in 1975. The area experienced four successive waves of migration, each introducing the cleavages that still affect the present state of the region.

The first phase began immediately after Spain turned over control of the Western Sahara to Morocco and Mauritania in 1975. The Polisario's propaganda portrayed Moroccan troops as monsters intent on killing and subjugating Sahrawis. Several native Sahrawi tribes, by some estimates nearly half the population, heeded the Polisario's call to flee the territory toward the camps of Tindouf in Algeria.

To govern the territory, the state had to rely on the remaining local elites and imported other Sahrawis from outside the contested zone, especially from the neighboring region of Oued Noun, north of the Western Sahara. The Moroccan southern Saharan cities of Tan Tan and Guelmim supplied many of the current elites that hold sway in the Western Sahara.

Though this policy was necessary to develop a vast territory that the Spaniards left extremely underdeveloped, it began to alter the societal balance of the region and foment the perception that the indigenous Sahrawis were deliberately deprived of positions of authority. In interviews with the original inhabitants of the region, the Sahrawi "transplants" are accused of deliberately marginalizing the indigenous population while enacting policies that favored their ethnic kin.

During the first phase of development, hundreds of political appointees, civil servants, skilled workers, and teachers from Morocco were dispatched to assist in governance and to staff lower, intermediate, and senior professional positions in the local administration (justice, health, interior) and schools. These professionals are often described by local Sahrawis as disconnected from local realities and unable to adjust to the local culture and its tribal specificities.

The mid-1980s saw a different wave of migrants enticed by the economic opportunities suddenly made available by the state's aggressive policy of developing the Sahara. The government provided generous subsidies, tax exemptions, and higher salaries than in other regions of Morocco. This period also coincided with severe droughts in the kingdom and serious spikes in unemployment. It didn't take much to convince thousands of skilled and unskilled workers to migrate to the dynamic economic centers of the Western Sahara.

This stream of migration increased linearly throughout the decade, creating new cleavages that proved difficult to mend. The new communities remained detached from the indigenous Western Saharans despite efforts by the state to encourage social contact and intermarriage. The consolidation of the communities never really materialized. It is important to note that though the migrants from the north of Morocco represent a majority of the population in the major cities of the Western Sahara, they are severely underrepresented in elected institutions. Indeed, until the late 1990s, they were barred from participating in local elections. Today, they are merely discouraged from organizing or leveraging their numerical superiority.

Another dramatic change in the size and demographic composition of the population in the Western Sahara came in 1991, when the United Nations brokered a cease-fire between Morocco and Polisario rebels. Both parties agreed to a peace plan that was supposed to lead to a referendum in January 1992 in which Western Saharans would choose between integration with Morocco and independence. It was at that time that the Moroccan government transported tens of thousands of Sahrawis, mainly from the southern towns of Sidi Ifni, Guelmim, and the region of Oued Noun, to the Western Sahara to be registered to vote in the promised referendum, which never came. They were housed in tent camps in Laayoune, Smara, Boujdour, and Dakhla. These improvised shelters, dubbed "Al Wahda" (Union), were designed to be temporary, but as the process of integration dragged and stalled, they became permanent. Worse, they were gradually transformed into squatter settlements, where tents were replaced by dilapidated shantytown homes, posing serious sanitary and security problems.

The state removed these settlements and provided most residents with newly built housing in the mid-2000s. But to this day, the state still supplies Al Wahda inhabitants with food subsidies and pays their electricity bills. This has created significant resentment and important fissures in society. The indigenous Western Saharans and non-Sahrawis still complain bitterly about this spoils system and culture of handouts, which allow some groups to scoop up most of the economic opportunities.

And a new category of people had been added to the swelling ranks of the welfare system in the mid-1990s. This new stream of arrivals was greatly prized, as it was made up of Sahrawis who fled the Tindouf camps in Algeria. Moroccan authorities saw vindication of their long-held belief that the misery of the Tindouf camps would ultimately prompt Sahrawis to desert the Polisario and its corrupt rule. Senior members of the Polisario were rewarded handsomely upon their return to the country with high-level government positions.

The most recent example is that of the current Moroccan ambassador to Spain, Ould Souilem. One of the founders of the Polisario Front, Souilem defected to Morocco in July 2009, denouncing a movement he had helped lead after growing increasingly disenchanted with the authoritarianism of

Polisario leader Mohamed Abdelaziz and his protectors in Algeria. "The Sahrawi Polisario is dead," he said in an interview with the French weekly *Jeune Afrique*. "Only the Algerian Polisario remains."[10] Revolutionary romanticism has given way to a militarized organization that has no place for discordant voices, lamented Ould Souilem. Similar discontent was voiced by then police inspector general of the Polisario, Mustapha Salma Ould Sidi Mouloud, who publicly endorsed Morocco's proposal to grant autonomy to Western Sahara in August 2010. That statement led to his imprisonment and then expulsion from the camps.

The rest of the returnees from the camps of Tindouf, numbering currently about 8,000 people, were supplied with free housing and a monthly salary. Whole neighborhoods, dubbed "Al Aouda" (Return) were built in the different cities of the Western Sahara to accommodate these new arrivals. Returnees were assigned their residence according to their cities of origin. This generosity of the state was not accompanied by any work requirements or job training. In some cases, the local authorities failed to take advantage of returnees' experience and skills. "Some of us were teachers, doctors, nurses, and so on in the camps of Tindouf," said two of my interviewees, "but the Moroccan government either deliberately or unintentionally did not hire us in professional positions that match our skills, preferring to condemn us to receiving a meager $160 monthly handout."

It is this frustration with relative deprivation that led many returnees to desert the Polisario in the first place and that is now pushing some to threaten (without ever following through) to go back to Tindouf in protest of the lack of equal opportunities they received upon their return to Morocco. Instead of helping move people from welfare to work, state policies contributed to the development of an entitlement mentality and a dangerous perception that government resources are endless. Worse, these preferential policies did not result in eliciting much goodwill from the beneficiaries of the state's largesse, as they naturally came to expect more benefits.

In talks with this community of former Polisario supporters one easily detects deep malaise and dissatisfaction. Several complained to me, especially among the youth, that they fled the misery and oppression of the camps only to be disappointed by the way the authorities treated them. "The leaders of the communist dictatorship in Tindouf are corrupt, but the collective provides the basic essentials for all," said one of them. Another added that "Life in Tindouf was very hard, but at least it was a shared misery. Here, we witness the unequal sharing of the richness of our territory." This inequality is especially bitter when one remembers that others, especially former top Polisario military and political leaders, have fared very well upon their return to Morocco. These are the same leaders who plotted and led a brutal guerilla war against Morocco for several years. Morocco, as one returnee sarcastically but tellingly put it, "compensates only those who betray it."

Former Polisario followers expected more material benefits and greater compensation for their years of displacement. They ended up, however, experiencing the same levels of economic and social hardship that their Moroccan counterparts have endured for several decades. The state's failure to help integrate them into the social and economic fabric of society is especially dangerous. Most of these returnees have been exposed to the Polisario's nationalism, which exalts militarism and revolutionary transformation in society. All now denounce the Polisario as a corrupt and authoritarian organization, but their views of Morocco cannot be reshaped easily. Their disenchantment with the traditional spoils system, in which local tribal leaders, notables, influential Sahrawi refugees who deserted the Polisario, and elected officials take most of the economic and political opportunities, can easily degenerate into open revolt against the system.

The New Conflict Dynamics

There is a growing fear that the state's clientelistic practices and economic mismanagement are contributing to a polarization of society and sharpening tension and competition between and within ethnic groups over the distribution of rent. Since 1975, the problem has always been that many of the resources were not efficiently used and that money was often quickly thrown at socioeconomic challenges in order to co-opt indigenous Sahrawis and silence dissent. The state has not tried to deal earnestly with the socioeconomic challenges of the region. Thus Morocco's significant investments have not moved the local economy into a productive stage nor have they fostered sustainable development practices.

Frustration with the state for promoting this patronage system was bound to explode, as it did in September 1999 when Laayoune descended into violence. Indigenous Western Saharans took to the streets to demand social justice (jobs, housing, and so on). The security services in turn violently repressed these demonstrations. In 2005, rioting again erupted in Laayoune, after a peaceful sit-in in front of the local prison was transformed into bloody confrontations with the police. Native Sahrawis wanted to benefit from free housing and monthly allowances too, and street protests became a sure means to get the authorities' attention.

After these occasional but deadly outbursts of violence, the state came to realize the mounting gravity of indigenous discontent. The grievances, as articulated in the protests and the dozens of interviews I had in the region, fall into two broad categories: resource distribution and self-governance. Separatist tendencies have always been negligible and the Polisario's credibility very low, as leaked U.S. State Department cables from Morocco revealed. "Extensive interviews and independent sources in the territory," wrote senior American official Robert P. Jackson in a confidential document in 2009, "suggest that the principal goal of most Sahrawis is more self-government than self-determination." Nevertheless, Sahrawis' frustration and disappointment with state policies in the Sahara are creating sympathies for the separatist cause. The young are especially susceptible to separatists' appeal and promises of a better and equitable distribution of resources and recognition of their worth and dignity.

To address the main drivers of discontent, the government first committed to tackling the housing shortage triggered by steady population growth and the continuing flow of new arrivals. The number of inhabitants went from 74,000 people, according to the Spanish census of 1974, to 507,160 today. In 2008, the authorities designated 18,000 plots of land for distribution to the indigenous Sahrawis. Instead, the land—after the municipal elections of 2009—was allocated based on tribal and electoral calculations. Senior elected officials grabbed public land and handed property deals to their allies and powerful constituencies.

The frustration engendered by this gaming of the state's policy to provide free housing for low-income Sahrawi families quickly turned into anger at the system. In September 2010, thousands of angry Sahrawis began setting up tents outside the city in the now-infamous camp of Agdim Izik on the outskirts of Laayoune to demand jobs and housing.

For three weeks, tensions mounted and protesters' demands hardened, as initial calls for jobs, free housing, and anticorruption measures made way for calls for the immediate resolution of all their socioeconomic grievances. In a predictable sequence, separatist forces and notorious traffickers quickly infiltrated the protesters' ranks, helping set up popular committees to administer the camp. Once legitimate social demands became contaminated by politicized and criminal elements, the security services decided to dismantle the camp on November 8, 2010. The whole city would then be set ablaze.

Video footage of the riots showed gruesome images of hysterical crowds lynching unarmed security officers. Such frightening carnage, prevalent at the height of the civil war in neighboring Algeria in the 1990s and a trademark of AQIM, has always been alien to the Western Sahara. Laayoune had seen violence and rioting before, but never had the city witnessed such militancy. The sight of masked insurgents marching in the streets of Laayoune—armed with knives, Molotov cocktails, and stones, setting fires to public buildings, schools, and private property—sent a chilling reminder of the region's vulnerability to destabilization.

The violence also demonstrated the deep enmity that has developed between indigenous Western Saharans and communities from the north of Morocco. Since 1975, important fissures have developed and this naturally created societal tensions, though at restricted levels. But it is only in the last two years that ethnic cleavages and cultural animosity have become dangerously more pronounced, threatening to fuel radicalism and more confrontations. The causes are various and profound, but most centrally they are political.

The government's preferential policies have exacerbated existing ethnic divides while its noncontingent welfare handouts have promoted a culture of entitlement that is difficult to sustain. The government has directed benefits according to people's tribal and ethnic status as well as strict political considerations. This has heightened ethnic and tribal consciousness instead of strengthening the development of a common identity based on citizenship and democratic rights. For over three decades, the Moroccan government's Saharan policy has failed to develop a system in which every citizen enjoys the same rights and is protected by the same laws.

Inhabitants who hail from northern Morocco complain bitterly that the government usually ignores their concerns, encourages them to maintain a low profile, and avoids disputes with indigenous Western Saharans. For its part, the native Sahrawi community feels that its views and interests are not represented by its elected political elites. Some have the impression that the local administration treats them with paternalistic condescension.

Finding a Way Past the Tensions

Counterterrorism analysts and Western diplomats must be increasingly worried that organized criminal networks and other violent entrepreneurs are expanding their influence and reach into North Africa and the Sahel by exploiting regional rivalries, growing lawlessness in the camps of Tindouf, and rising ethnic tensions in the Moroccan Western Sahara.

At a recent security conference in Morocco, several terrorism experts warned that insufficient cooperation between Morocco and Algeria hampers the development of a coherent and coordinated security architecture and "narrows the flows of information that are vital to disrupting an upsurge in smuggling and hostage-taking believed to be funding militants and racketeers with links to criminal syndicates in West Africa, Europe and Latin America."[11] The recent warming of relations between the two countries, however, has renewed hope that Morocco and Algeria are seriously working to alleviate their disagreements and jointly address the dangers emanating from their southern flank.

No one is under any illusion that the two rivals will soon resolve their differences over the Western Sahara. Any significant inroads toward peace and reconciliation would probably have to wait for the upcoming generational shift in the Algerian military and political leadership. The aging elite are still trapped in their Cold War mentality and wedded to their original uncompromising stance over the principle of self-determination.

This insistence on independence for Western Sahara has always been "an unrealistic option," to use the phrase of Peter van Walsum, the United Nations (UN) secretary-general's personal envoy for Western Sahara (2005–2008). Walsum correctly pointed out that Morocco will never cede its control over the territory unless the major world powers and the UN Security Council attempt to impose such a solution. This is highly unlikely to ever occur, as it would certainly destabilize the kingdom and threaten the monarchy's own survival.

The Western Sahara is probably the only issue in Morocco that enjoys near-universal and unwavering popular support. For many Moroccans, renouncing their historical right to the Western Sahara—where thousands of soldiers have died and billions of dollars have been spent defending a territory that represents almost half the size of Morocco—would be a national tragedy. This deep-rooted belief in the righteousness of their cause has unfortunately led to the negation of the legitimacy of the other point of view.

It has always been unrealistic to expect the Polisario to completely renounce its competing narrative and hence its raison d'être. The movement is indeed autocratic and unrepresentative of all Sahrawis, but its aggrieved nationalism rooted in real or imagined indignities committed by Morocco still resonates in the camps. It is therefore naive and indeed counterproductive to demand that the Sahrawis in the camps accept the Moroccan self-assured historical narrative.

Morocco has long resisted the idea of instituting an autonomous region in the Western Sahara lest it accentuate the Sahrawis' separate identity and boost their ethnopolitical mobilization. That might be the case if the regional autonomy that is sought links territorial control to one particular ethnicity. But in the Western Sahara, an autonomous state structure must make way for the equal representation of all ethnicities. As Javier Perez de Cuellar, former UN secretary-general, wrote in his memoirs, such a "reasonable solution under which the Western Sahara would be integrated as an autonomous region in the Moroccan state would have spared many lives and a great deal of money."[12]

The only possible solution is for the parties to negotiate a constitutional arrangement that focuses on the present and the future instead of the past. Morocco's proposal for autonomy for the Western Sahara is a good starting point. The July 2011 Moroccan constitution sets into motion a promising decentralization process, whereby effective power is devolved to elected regional councils. This process has great significance for the Western Sahara, as it has the potential to increase participatory development and government responsiveness. It will also meet one of the main demands of disgruntled Sahrawis: the ability to manage their own affairs. The new constitution provides for cultural inclusiveness as well, specifically guaranteeing Sahrawis their linguistic and cultural rights. And the new Moroccan political pact constitutionalizes the principles of individual rights (freedom of expression, freedom of association, and criminalization of torture and arbitrary detention) and equality for all citizens.

The kingdom's friends in the West, especially the United States and France, must pressure Rabat to expedite this significant devolution of power and consecrate the protection of civil liberties. In the Western Sahara, the authorities must do more to protect freedom of speech, including expressions of separatist tendencies. Suppressing opposing views does not gain Morocco the sympathy of Sahrawis. Only democracy can. One has only to look to Spain, whose democratic system has withstood the threats of strong separatist groups in Catalonia and the Basque region.

The disappointment of those Sahrawis who are disenchanted with Moroccan rule does not stem from ideological convictions but from political, social, and economic deprivations. As in the rest of Morocco, the region had its share of arbitrary repression, corruption, bad governance, and rigged elections. Things have started to change under the reign of King Mohammed VI, but more needs to be done to provide the inhabitants of the Western Sahara with the dignity they deserve.

Morocco has long believed that a solution to the Western Sahara conflict can only emanate from New York and Algiers. Now, there is finally a realization that the fate of the territory resides in how democratic it can become. The Polisario's political project lacks creativity and is still controlled by the same aging generation, directed by Algeria. A real and credible autonomy will give significant prerogatives to the people and might end up convincing the refugees in the Tindouf camps that Morocco is serious in its calls for granting self-governance to the Western Sahara.

Notes

1   William Maclean, "Analysis: Africa's Sahel Scrambles to Avert Slide 'Into Hell,'" Reuters, January 23, 2012, http://af.reuters.com/article/maliNews/idAFL5E8CN13M20120123?sp=true.
2   "Transnational Threats Updates," Center for Strategic and International Studies, vol. 8, no. 3, May 2010, http://csis.org/files/publication/ttu0803.pdf.
3   For a detailed examination of the connection of the Sahrawi refugees to armed and criminal groups in Mali, see François Soudan, "Mali: Polisario Connection," Jeune Afrique, November 8, 2012. See also, Abdul Hameed Bakier, "Al-Qaeda Infiltration of the Western Sahara's Polisario Movement," *Terrorism Monitor*, vol. 8, issue 19, 2010, www.jamestown.org/programs/gta/single/?tx_ttnews%5Btt_news%5D=36385&cHash=3f0c0a07e1; "Key Members of Sahara Drug Ring Captured Are From Polisario," Middle East Online, December 21, 2010, www.middle-east-online.com/english/?id=43149. Laurence Ammour, "New Security Challenges in North Africa After the 'Arab Spring'" Geneva Center for Security Policy, 2012, www.gcsp.ch/Regional-Capacity-Development/Middle-East-North-Africa/Publications/GCSP-Publications/Policy-Papers/New-Security-Challenges-in-North-Africa-after-the-Arab-Spring.
4   Ibid.
5   "Sahara occidental : divorce consommé entre le Mali et le Polisario?" *Jeune Afrique*, December 27, 2011, www.jeuneafrique.com/Article/ARTJAWEB20111227114811/maroc-mali-enlevement-terrorismesahara-occidental-divorce-consomme-entre-le-mali-et-le-polisario.html. See also, Serge Daniel, "Le Mali prend ses distances avec le Front Polisario," Agence France-Presse, December 27, 2011, www.google.com/hostednews/afp/article/ALeqM5i4CHA2HdwpcQJ_XrfCkoFfM4eHBQ?docId=CNG.09c4b8e975cfc23c8718b820ade10fec.161.
6   "Le Mali confirme la présence des combattants du Polisario dans les rangs des djhad-istes au Nord," Atlasinfo, February 6, 2013. See also Thierry Oberlé, "Mali: combattant d'Aqmi, il rapporte la mort d'Abou Zeid," *Le Figaro*, January 3, 2013, www.lefigaro.fr/international/2013/03/01/01003-20130301ARTFIG00354-mali-combattant-d-aqmi-il-rapporte-la-mort-d-abou-zeid.php.
7   Quoted in J. Peter Pham, "Not Another Failed State: Toward a Realistic Solution in the Western Sahara," *Journal of the Middle East and Africa*, vol. 1, no. 1 (2010): 1–24.
8   David Goodman and Souad Mekhennet, "Morocco Says It Foiled Terror Cell in Sahara," *New York Times*, January 5, 2011, www.nytimes.com/2011/01/06/world/africa/06morocco.html.
9   See Driss Bennani, "Sahara: La Bombe à retardement," Tel Quel, November 5, 2011.
10 François Soudan, "La longue marche d'Ahmedou Ould Souilem," *Jeune Afrique*, June 9, 2010, www.jeuneafrique.com/Articles/Dossier/ARTJAJA2577p022-030.xml1/algerie-maroc-ambas-sadeur-mohammed-vila-longue-marche-d-ahmedou-ould-souilem.html.
11 Maclean, "Analysis: Africa's Sahel Scrambles to Avert Slide 'Into Hell.'"
12 Javier Perez de Cuellar, *Pilgrimage for Peace: A Secretary-General's Memoirs* (New York: Palgrave Macmillan, 2006), 352.

Conclusion

Anouar Boukhars | Frederic Wehrey

F ragile and failing states pose real threats to international security. They can provide training bases and safe havens for al-Qaeda and its affiliates as well as offer violent extremists an environment suited for generating large profits from smuggling and illicit trafficking. They are ideal locations for radical, violent organizations to recruit disenfranchised and alienated youth. Problems in these states can exacerbate protracted regional crises and reignite violent conflicts. Refugee flows, arms, drugs, and insurgencies regularly spill over the borders of fragile states with devastating consequences for neighbors.

The fragile states and territories of the Sahara and Sahel—in this case, Mauritania, Mali, Niger, the Western Sahara, and Libya—present significant challenges not just for the United States and Europe but also for the states of sub-Saharan Africa and the broader Middle East. The roots of their instability and conflict are complex and run deep. Internal sources of insecurity include institutional weakness and corruption, endemic poverty, and sociopolitical tensions. Unaddressed identity-based grievances splinter these societies, while legacies of past abuses and religious radicalization stir up tensions further. External stresses range from transnational organized crime, terrorism, and weapons proliferation to foreign meddling and global economic shocks.

Compounding these pressures is the weak capacity of many Saharan states to deal with their problems—local governments have exacerbated conflict either through inept responses or, in some cases, active collusion with criminal networks, Islamist militants, or ethnic dissidents. This finding has important implications for framing effective policy responses in this troubled region.

Weak and Corrupt States
Fragile Institutions

The most critical source of insecurity in these states is institutional fragility, which is closely related to corruption and conflict. Misgovernance in a complex sociopolitical setting, as is present in all of these countries, is a strong predictor for persistent ethno-racial tensions.

In Mauritania, where old ethno-racial tensions and other forms of societal divisions linger, stability is directly affected by widespread corruption and money politics. The military dominates political affairs and clientelism is prevalent, which alienates a majority of Mauritanians who lack the right tribal or personal connections. Despite encouraging macroeconomic performance and improved economic growth, the country is still hampered by a lack of transparency and accountability. The fundamental challenge facing Mauritania was and still is the absence of legitimate institutions that elicit the trust of the population. If these structural constraints are not addressed, the challenges the country faces will only get worse.

In Libya, Qaddafi's highly personalized, authoritarian rule deprived the country of formal political institutions and civil society for forty-two years. A diffuse, bottom-up revolution toppled his government in October 2011. Although the country has made great strides in restarting the oil sector and holding parliamentary elections in July, the absence of a strong central government, army, and police force has handed authority and power to the country's plethora of revolutionary brigades. While some of these units enjoy a degree of legitimacy and support from the central government, others pursue more nefarious criminal aims, local agendas, or a militant Salafi posture. Similarly, Libya lacks formal judicial structures, and tribal justice has filled the vacuum.

Generally speaking, this weakness and corruption of state institutions has a corrosive effect on the sociocultural makeup of a country, which is also influenced by deep-seated tribal structures and historical ethno-racial divisions. The disintegration of Mali, for example, is attributed to the fragility of its political structure. Pervasive corruption and weak governance were critical sources of popular dissatisfaction, leading to social friction, tension, and a military mutiny that escalated to overthrow the government. The excesses, corruption, and mismanagement of the state as well as the political and military authorities' lack of control laid the groundwork for the state's collapse.

Mali is also a textbook case study of the failure of Western governments and international donors to correctly diagnose the sources of state fragility. Mali is a classic example of a fragile state with a leadership incapable of combating terrorist groups and unwilling to rectify its weaknesses. Top officials in Mali's government actively collude with organized crime. Building the security capacity of such a government only compounds state fragility. International stakeholders were all too eager to dispense economic and military aid to Mali while ignoring the state's links to criminal activity. In fact, the dispensing of foreign aid coincided with a dramatic increase in organized criminal activity. It is therefore crucial for the international community to assess state willingness and capacity.

The control of criminal activity requires more than just capable national institutions. The willingness of state actors to thwart the criminal marketplace and the financial flows of the proceeds of trafficking is critically important. Without such resolve, externally led efforts to empower the executive branch and prop up its coercive apparatus—namely, the military, police, and judiciary—are counterproductive.

A state that lacks capable institutional capacities but has leaders determined to fight terrorism and organized crime is the most suitable candidate for technical capacity building. Mauritania and Niger are good examples, even if the problems of organized crime and corrupt state officials are real in both countries. Western governments must therefore insist that state collusion with or toleration of organized crime will carry consequences for countries heavily dependent on foreign aid.

In the West, Mauritania is generally considered the least problematic state of the Sahel.[1] Its president, Mohamed Ould Abdel Aziz, has managed to portray himself as tough on national security. Nigerien President Mahamadou Issoufou is also appreciated for his firm stand against terrorism. His country is seriously threatened by several transnational terrorist actors originating in Libya and Nigeria. In this context, it makes sense that international donors have supported Issoufou's programs for security and development. In July 2012, the European Council launched the EUCAP Sahel Niger mission to strengthen the country's security forces. This support, however, must be conditional on democratic accountability and the implementation of verifiable and concrete anticorruption measures.

Limited Control of the Periphery

Another source of insecurity is the limited presence of the central state in the hinterlands. In certain areas, the state is completely absent. Failing to provide the most basic services to meet the needs of its citizens, the state is also often incapable or unwilling to guarantee people's personal security. These fragile states have a limited capacity to monitor their borders and maintain a monopoly on the legitimate use of force.

Periodic attempts to exercise control, often when the state feels threatened, is pressured to act by international donors, or discovers lucrative natural resources, are sometimes undertaken too late to have an impact. For instance, when international donors pressured the government in Mali to make up lost ground in the north in late 2011, its efforts ended up further alienating the local population.

Indeed, neglecting the periphery has caused a host of problems in Mali. It was a direct source of the successive rebellions in the north launched by members of the Tuareg ethnic group, and it has also facilitated criminal groups' and terrorist organizations' infiltration of the country. The government devised a plan to invest around $64 million for peace, security, and development, but it was ill-conceived and badly implemented and the Tuareg strongly opposed the investments in reconstituting a military presence of southern troops in the north. The deposed Malian leader

Amadou Toumani Touré also tried to control the north by outsourcing state functions to opportunist local elites and militias. This contributed to inter- and intra-communal violence, the latter of which is often the result of major transformations in society that upset political, social, and economic hierarchies.

In Libya, the eastern region has been wracked by militia violence, vendettas, and criminality as well as a vitriolic strand of Salafi militancy. Much of this is due to the legacy of neglect that afflicted the region under Qaddafi and the tenuous reach of the post-revolutionary government.

In the south and west, conflicts simmer between rival tribes, ethnic groups, and towns, some of which enjoyed Qaddafi's patronage. The weakness of the central state has enabled the proliferation of heavy weaponry, giving local feuds a new intensity and lethality. Added to this, a lack of border control along the southern periphery and the lack of a local economy have helped to entrench cross-border smuggling as a way of life.

Ethnic and Socioeconomic Divisions

In each of these fragile states, entrenched ethnic inequalities have contributed to conflict, ranging from criminality and insurgency in Mali to riots and bloody racial clashes in Mauritania and the Western Sahara.

In Mali, the main driver of the recurrence of insurgency is the Tuareg's perceived high levels of economic and social polarization. As a USAID report put it, "The perception held by many Tuareg is that their way of life, tradition and very survival are under threat; that the state in Bamako is both culturally foreign and politically and economically hostile to them; that, as a people, they are besieged and embattled."[2]

In the Moroccan-controlled Western Sahara, the perception that government largesse disproportionately benefits nonindigenous Western Saharans has sowed the seeds of anger and hatred. This ethnic disharmony and mutual feelings of antagonism were laid bare during the bloody street confrontations in Laayoune in November 2010. Ethnic grievances have fueled separatism in the Western Sahara, where some members of the indigenous Sahrawi ethnic group that have been economically and politically marginalized intermittently protest against the Moroccan state.

And in Mauritania, the pervasiveness of ethnic-identity-based politics leads to perpetual ethnic agitation, as in late 2011 when riots broke out in protest of a controversial biometric census that the government said was designed to facilitate broader reform, but that black Africans, especially in the south, believed to be racist and discriminatory.

Ethnically based tensions over access to economic resources are also common. In Libya, peripheral conflicts have arisen between Arab tribes that were favored by Qaddafi and marginalized, non-Arab groups such as the Tuareg and Tabu. Libya's federalist movement arose in the east, which stirred tension and violence in the run-up to the July 7 parliamentary elections. Although the movement petered out and enjoyed limited support, the underlying grievances in the east remain. Far to the south, in Kufra, ethnic, non-Arab Tabu have complained about continued discrimination and marginalization. Periodic fighting has raged there between aggrieved Tabu and local Arab tribes.

Radicalism

Then there is the interaction of radical elements with these underlying sources of instability. The region's tribalism and the existence of pluralistic societies that generally practice an open and moderate form of Islam have helped to stem the rise of extremism in the Sahel. But Salafi ideas have penetrated society, affecting this culture of tolerance.

In Mauritania and Mali, some Salafi ideas have contributed to the radicalization of religious discourse and fueled a contemporary wave of extremism that plagues both countries. In particular, Persian Gulf countries, especially Saudi Arabia, have funded mosques, Islamic study centers, and religious schools in the region to propagate their own rigid version of Islam. Some of these institutions have become conduits for material and ideological support going to radical Islamists. The influence of Mauritanians and Malians returning from the Gulf has also contributed to the spread of Wahhabism.

The problem of homegrown radicalization in the Sahel is further compounded by its interconnectedness with transnational factors like illicit trafficking and regional terrorist networks. Al-Qaeda in the Islamic Maghreb (AQIM), initially called the Salafist Group for Preaching and

Combat (GSPC) before becoming an affiliate of al-Qaeda in 2007, has established an effective base of operations in the Sahel, especially in northern Mali.

Both AQIM's creation and presence in the Sahel were born out of events in Algeria. The terrorist group suffered major setbacks at the hands of Algerian security forces in the late 1990s and was forced to flee Algerian territory into northern Mali by 2003, ensnaring the country in a vicious web of regional terrorism, drug trafficking, and organized crime.

AQIM has successfully embedded itself into Malian society, patiently building and expanding a network of familial ties, social support, political relations, and economic exchange. It imposed a toll on the transborder smuggling of drugs and extorted a large number of ransoms from Western governments, which has enabled the group to become a well-funded terrorist and criminal organization.

AQIM and its affiliates have upset social hierarchies and contributed to communal violence. In Mauritania, transnational Salafi groups have made some inroads among the Haratin—the so-called black Moors who are often illiterate and considered second-class citizens. While AQIM has so far failed to attract recruits within this community, there is growing concern that some Haratin might be tempted by its message of egalitarianism and denunciation of the stratification of Mauritanian society. This risk is heightened when combined with other driving factors such as the fragmentation of social structures, lack of access to education, and widespread feelings of unfairness.

Policy Recommendations for the International Community

In all of these countries, past approaches have focused on building the capacity of the security sector but have neglected the underlying institutional and social roots of insecurity. Of these, state fragility, corruption, and leaders' ambivalence are the most insidious. In light of this, it is clear that even well-meaning governments in the region are unable to simultaneously tackle the host of problems they face.

It is up to the international community, therefore, to help local governments prioritize and triage the necessary reforms. Much of this should proceed on a country-by-country basis—distinctive solutions must emerge organically from within each state. International actors can play a crucial role in helping fragile states address their internal stresses.

Promote Lasting Solutions to Societal Inequalities

To address high-level group grievances, governments must design strategies to promote social inclusion, political integration, and economic empowerment. To succeed, these policies must target groups—such as the Tuareg in Mali and Niger and the Haratin and black Africans in Mauritania—in addition to individuals. As the World Bank's 2011 *World Development Report* puts it, "Signaling change to groups with grievances is often a key early priority." This can help mobilize support for transitional justice and reconciliation.

Property rights and access to resources remain enduring problems in most countries of the Sahara and Sahel. In Mauritania, for instance, manipulation by local officials in the attribution of property rights contributed to social unrest, and Mali has been the theater of resource conflict over access to water, fishing rights, wood, and so on.

Policies that support community development programs that invest in basic social services (roads, clinics, courts, and so on) and promote equal access to land and economic resources can produce peace and security. Ensuring the equity of resource distribution and property rights can also help the underserved in both rural and urban areas. Governments must establish effective controls to protect against fraud, expropriation of land, and abuse by state officials. Anticorruption commissions should be empowered to exercise their auditing functions.

Groups' levels of political inclusion and cultural rights within these societies also need to be augmented. In Mauritania in particular, major efforts are needed to increase the representation of black Africans and Haratin in state institutions. This is critical to help break down the cultural and ethnic divide in society. International donors can play an important role by investing in development programs that help promote reconciliation and stability.

In any process intended to reform the distribution of power and resources, there will be losers and winners. It is critically important to carefully assess the political and economic implications of reforms and take into account the interests of different stakeholders when renegotiating the power balance between disadvantaged groups and powerful ones. It is essential to mitigate the adverse effects of reforms on powerful groups as some of them are bound to resist accountability checks on their power. For reforms to be successful, governments need to establish broad-based and inclusive coalitions with influential sectors in society as well as international donors and investors.

Build and Reinforce the Rule of Law

The failure to enforce the rule of law naturally affects the credibility of the state. This credibility problem is further compounded by gross levels of corruption and human rights abuses. The erosion of credibility leads to a loss of legitimacy that has negative consequences on stability, foremost among them the risk of seeing citizens shift their allegiance to malevolent nonstate actors. The loss of legitimacy can lead to rebellions and violence, and it can also prompt disgruntled citizens to establish their own security and governance systems.

Promoting good governance and reinforcing the state's capacity are therefore critical to improving economic conditions and building people's trust in national institutions. This requires responsible national leadership as well as determined international donors willing to link economic assistance to improvement in human security.

Address Youth Alienation to Combat Extremism

In Mauritania, the government has tried to delegitimize the ideological justifications for radicalism by hiring hundreds of new imams to preach in the country's mosques and by engaging extremist prisoners in a dialogue with state-sponsored Islamist scholars and clerics. It has also bolstered its legal system and modernized its military equipment. These efforts will be unsuccessful, however, unless the sources of youth alienation are addressed.

As long as the divide between the youth's expectations and the state's capability or willingness to meet them exists, the danger that disgruntled young citizens might look to nonstate actors for essential goods remains.

Bolster the Capacity and Professionalism of Local Security Forces

Building the capacity of fragile states to combat transnational terrorist groups and organized crime must be accompanied by preconditions for security-sector oversight and institutional reform. Security-sector reform is essential to promoting an environment that is stable and conducive to economic development. In cases where governments are willing to take on criminal and terrorist groups but lack the capacity to monitor their security forces, security-sector reform and capacity-building programs must be embedded in an overall strategy of good governance and development.

The reforms should focus on fostering civilian oversight of the security forces and effectively prioritizing security expenditures and the allocation of resources. Underfunded security forces are easily overwhelmed in conflict-ridden societies, and oversized forces are usually inefficient and fail to provide public security. The key is to design reforms that are affordable and efficient. It is also crucial that reforms to the security sector are accompanied by efforts to strengthen the institutions of justice, from criminal to civil law.

In states willing to engage in governance reforms and combat organized crime and violent extremists, the international community should, for example, promote youth employment and support anticorruption initiatives and security-sector reform. But assistance programs should be tailored to fit the specific needs of each country. In cases where high social and ethnic polarization is conducive to violence, the focus should be on adopting and implementing legal frameworks that ensure inclusive political participation and equal access to economic resources and services. In some situations, affirmative action policies in state employment and political representation are desirable. In situations of high criminality, the professionalization of the police, prosecution, and other actors in the criminal justice system is a must.

Leverage Multilateral Cooperation

The international community can help mitigate external pressures by promoting regional cooperation in sharing intelligence, monitoring financial flows from drug trafficking, and conducting joint military operations.

Thus far, international efforts have been hindered by several factors. First, Western governments and international donors have focused on propping up the capacity of individual fragile states but largely ignored that insecurity is a product not just of internal factors but of external ones as well. Second, international policy has typically overlooked the relationships and connections between conflicts in the region. And third, competition and differing perceptions of threats among neighbors hinders regional cooperation.

For instance, Algeria's actions, intentions, and calculations in its spheres of privileged interest have hampered regional efforts to quell conflicts in the Sahara and Sahel. Algeria's West African neighbors solicit its leadership but doubt its inclination to do what is right in promoting peace and security. Indeed, many see Algeria as not doing enough in the current crisis in Mali. The resources it has applied to fighting AQIM outside its territory have not matched its capabilities. In Mali, Algeria had hoped to stay on the sidelines during the country's latest cycle of insurrections. It focused on securing its own borders and containing the terrorist threat within the confines of Mali, Niger, and Mauritania, which neighbor Algeria to the south.

Until the sudden French military intervention in Mali in January 2013, Algeria was attempting to negotiate a political solution to the conflict by nudging the armed actors with whom it has connections. Algeria was especially focused on Ansar Dine, but when Ansar Dine withdrew from the negotiation process with Bamako on January 7, Algeria's efforts to secure a diplomatic solution to the conflict came to an end. Algeria opened its airspace to French military jet fighters and closed its southern border with Mali when the French intervention began.

In the wake of the January hostage crisis in which militants stormed the In Amenas natural gas field in eastern Algeria, near Libya, Algiers no longer has the luxury of staying out of the situation that is unfolding in Mali. Not acting will only compound Algeria's efforts to transform the many advantages it possesses in economic and military power into actual influence. Its efforts to gain acceptance as a responsible power in its region have thus far not been successful. Neither have its attempts to block external intrusion in its immediate neighborhood. The challenge for Algeria is to intertwine its goals with the needs of its weaker Sahelian neighbors and accommodate the interests of its regional competitors (Morocco and Libya) as well as those of larger powers (mainly France) while minimizing their interference.

Policymakers in the United States and Europe face the imperative to better understand the basis of Algeria's decisions, viewpoints, and approaches to its region and international alliances. Such an assessment and understanding is critical to identifying mutual interests and positive-sum solutions to the region's problems. The European Union and the United States should engage the Sahel in a way that is complementary rather than competitive to Algeria and to support regional security institutions. The Algeria-based General Staff Joint Operations Committee and Fusion and Liaison Unit need to become true forums for sharing intelligence and coordinating the fight against terrorism.

Enforce a Regional and International Consensus Against Ransom Payments

Western governments must design a coherent and clear policy toward the payment of ransoms to terrorist and criminal organizations and their local intermediaries. Such payments have contributed to the growth of a veritable criminal industry that emboldens criminal entrepreneurs and violent extremists. It also has had corrosive effects on fragile Sahelian societies like Mali and on regional cooperation. The use of intermediaries has fomented complicity between organized crime on the one hand and local notables and senior government officials on the other. And the paying of ransoms, at times accompanied by the freeing of terrorists in exchange for the release of Western hostages, has strained relations between the countries of the region. The rejection or criminalization of ransom payments is not currently feasible, but Western governments must not encourage this behavior.

Notes

1   See Luis Simon, Alexander Mattelaer, and Amelia Hadfield, "A Coherent EU Strategy for the Sahel," European Parliament, May 2011, www.europarl.europa.eu/committees/fr/studiesdownload.html?languageDocument=EN&file=73859.
2   USAID, "Counter Extremism and Development in Mali," October 2009.

Index

Page numbers in *italics* refer to maps.

Alambo, Aghali, 71
Algeria, 2, 4–5, *86*; geopolitical posture, 99–102; In Amenas natural gas field attack (January 2013), vii–viii, 64, 108, 195; intervention in Mali, 109–110, 195; Islamists in, 158; and Mali, 87–117; and Morocco, 166; multilateral cooperation with, 195–196; organized crime in, 63–69, 71, 74–75, 81–82, 170; radicalism in, 191; refugees, 102, 106; regional initiatives, 110–111; U.S. partnership, 100–101, 104
Algiers accords, 90
Altadis, 170
Ansar al-Sharia brigade, 17–18, 20–21, 24, 32n20, 108
Ansar Dine, 61, 75–76, 78, 92–95, 195
anti-Israel activism, 156
anti-Qaddafi struggle, 7, 158
anticorruption initiatives, 139, 192
AQIM. *see* Al-Qaeda in the Islamic Maghreb
Arab Gulf states, 149, 159
Arab Movement of Azawad (MAA), 78
Arab nationalism, 133
Arab Spring, 158
Arab-Tabu conflict, 21–25, 52
Arab tribes: marginalization of, 190. *see also specific tribes*
Arabic, 156
Arabicization, 22, 125, 130
arms smuggling, 63–64, 71, 116n53, 134–138, 170–171
Army of Barqa (Jaysh Barqa), 11, 13–14
ATT. *see* Touré, Amadou Toumani
autonomy: for eastern Libya, 11–14; for Western Sahara, 181–182
Awbari, Libya, 55
Awlad Buseif, 52

Awlad Suleyman, 42, 50–52
Ayittey, George, 135
Azawad, 91
Azuz, Abd al-Basit, 16–17

B
Baath Party, 158
Baida, Libya, 8
Bamako, Mali, 66, 88
Bamana, 126, 133
Barqa (Libya), 8–9
Barqa Council (Cyrenaica Transitional Council), 11–14, 31n4
al-Bashir, Omar, 153, 158
Belal, Mohammed Val Ould, 134–135
Belmokhtar, Mokhtar, 64, 133
Ben Bella, Ahmed, 116n49
Benghazi, Libya: airport, 44; importance of, 9–10; "Little Kandahar," 15; "Save Benghazi" campaign, 21; September 11, 2012 attack on U.S. Consulate, vii, 1 2, 8, 14, 18, 56, 97; University of Benghazi, 10
"Benghazi and her sisters" (*Benghazi wa akhawatiha*), 10
Benin, 64, 66
Benjedid, Chadli, 116n49
Berabiche, 73, 77
Berber nationalists, 99
Bertelsmann Transformation Index (BTI), 122–123
Bettou, Hadj, 63–64
bidan (white Moors), 126–127, 149–150
Bilhaj, Abd al-Hakim, 15–16
Bin Bayyah, Abdullah, 159
black Africans, 125–126, 128–129, 140, 141n13, 142n34
Black Battalion, 54
black market, 36, 38–43, 63–66, 71

Libya, viii, *6, 34*; Arab population, 49; black market, 3–4, 36, 38–43, 63–66, 71; border conflicts, 35–59, 189–190; Border Guard, 44–45; Chad campaign, 22, 47, 49–50; citizenship requirements, 48–49; civil war, 91, 158; Committee of 60, 25–26; constitution, 25–26, 30–31; current status, 186–187; Cyrenaica Transitional Council (Barqa Council), 11–14, 31n4; eastern, 7–33, 189; ethnic and societal divides, 3, 48–56, 190; General National Congress (GNC), 8, 11–12, 14, 23, 26, 30; General People's Congress, 47; hydrocarbon sector, 11; institutional development, 30–31; Interim Defense Committee, 38; Law No. 11, 45; maritime security, 39; military zones, 29; Ministry of Defense, 21, 44–45; Ministry of Finance, 38; Ministry of Interior, 17, 20–21, 28, 38, 40, 45–46; National Army, 38; National Transitional Council (NTC), 8–9, 11–12, 24–26, 29, 44–46, 51, 58n1; nationality rules, 39; organized crime, 71; post-Qaddafi, 1–2, 11, 158–159; Qaddafi regime, 10–11, 36–37, 43–47, 49–51; refugees, 58n5; Salafi extremism, 4; Salafi militancy, 14–21; security forces, 24–25, 27–29, 58n1; September 11, 2012 attack on U.S. Consulate, Benghazi, vii, 1–2, 8, 14, 18, 56, 97; state weakness, 2, 185–186; Supreme Revolutionaries' Committee, 29; Supreme Security Committees (SSCs), 17, 28; Tabu-Arab conflict, 24–25; as trafficking hub, 36, 38–42; Warrior's Affairs Commission for Development (WAC), 29

Libya-Chad wars (1975–1994), 22, 49–51
"Libya is Not Afghanistan," 18
Libya Minor, 9
Libyan Army, 24–25, 52–53; Fars brigade, 54; Tarq brigade, 54; 32 or Khamis Brigade, 54
Libyan Islamic Fighting Group (LIFG), 15
Libyan Muslim Brotherhood, 19
Libyan Shield, 21, 44–45, 52–53; Center Shield, 32n33; Eastern Shield, 24–25, 28–29, 32n33; Western Shield, 32n33
Libyan Unionist Party, 14
LIFG. *see* Libyan Islamic Fighting Group
"Little Kandahar" (Benghazi, Libya), 15
Lome, Togo, 64

M
MAA. *see* Arab Movement of Azawad
Maali, Mahmoud Abul, 130–131
Maali, Mohamed Mahmoud Abul, 133
Mabrouk, Siddiq, 45
al-Magariaf, Muhammad, 14
mahadras (religious schools), 130–131
Maiga, Ali Badi, 76–77
Majabra, 24
Mali, *86*; and AQIM, 73–77; border conflicts, 36, 105–106, 188–189; conflict in, 72–73, 75–78, 87–117; corruption in, 2–3; destabilization of, vii–viii, 89–92, 187; Development and Governance Centers, 90; as "donor darling," 79; ethnic and societal divides, 3, 93–97, 189; foreign aid to, 4–5, 187; foreign intervention in, 106–114, 195; as fragile state,

2, 72–73, 88, 138, 185–187; illicit
trade, 3, 63, 65–67; instability in,
87–89; kidnappings for ransom,
68–69, 196; natural resources, 192;
neighbors, 109–112; northern,
62–63, 66–71, 75, 82, 94; organized
crime in, 69–73, 75–82, 169–170;
radicalism in, 4, 168, 190–191;
refugees from, 134–135; Special
Program for Peace, Security, and
Development of North Mali,
79, 90; Touré administration,
90; Tuareg rebellion, 1, 54–55
al-Manqoush, Yusuf, 45
Mansour, Jamil, 150–153,
156, 158–162
marginalization, 141n13, 189–190
Mataly, Mohamed Ould, 76–77
Ma'tan as-Sarah air base (Libya), 38
Mauritania, *118*, 119–143, *144*;
anticorruption initiatives, 139;
Central Commission of Public
Contracts, 124; corruption, 121–
125, 186; current status, 186–188;
Department of National Security,
134; donor support, 80; drug
smuggling, 143n46; ethnic tensions,
3, 127, 190; external stresses,
134–138; foreign aid, 5, 107–108,
140; fundamental challenge facing,
186; geopolitical pressures on,
150–151; illicit trade through, 64,
66–67; institutional weakness,
121–125; internal stresses, 121–134;
intervention in Mali, 109–110; as
Islamic Republic, 147–148, 162;
Islamists in, 145–163; jihadism in,
159–161; kidnappings for ransom,
68–69; Law on Land Reform,
125–126; Ministry of Employment,
Access, and Professional Formation,
155; Ministry of Higher Education,
155; Muslims in, 147; National

Assembly, 157; National Human
Rights Commission, 124; Office
of the Inspector General, 124;
organized crime in, 70, 74–75, 80,
82, 170–171; political inclusion,
192; population, 126–127, 148;
property rights, 192; racial politics,
149; radicalism in, 4, 129–134, 168,
190–191, 193; refugees from Mali,
134–135; smuggling networks,
170–171; sociopolitical tensions,
125–129; state weakness, 2, 185–
186; urban population, 148; urgent
steps that need to be taken, 139–
140. *see also* Sahel-Sahara region
M'barek, Hakim Ould Mohamed
(alias Houdheifa), 170
mediation, 19, 24–25
Mediene, Mohamed, 104
Meydou, Mohamed Ould, 72, 77
migration, 65
milishiyyaat, 58n1
militancy, 14–21, 108, 169
military operations, 194–196
militias, 58n1, 77
Misrata, Libya, 10, 46
MNA. *see* National
Movement of Azawad
MNLA. *see* National Movement
for the Liberation of Azawad
money politics, 186
Moors. *see* bidan (white Moors);
Haratin (black Moors)
Moroccan cannabis resin
smuggling, 62–63, 65, 67, 70
Moroccan Western Sahara.
see Western Sahara
Morocco, 101, 111; and Algeria, 166;
ceasefire with Polisario, 174–175;
control over Western Sahara,
180–181; illicit regional flows to, 64,
66, 171; intervention in Mali, 110;

United States Consulate, Benghazi (Libya): September 11, 2012 attack on, vii, 1–2, 8, 14, 18, 56, 97
University of Benghazi, 10
urbanization, 137

V

Vall, Ely, 156
violence, 178–179; extremist, 132, 136, 138; Salafi, 8

W

al-Waal, Libya, 55
WAC. *see* Warrior's Affairs Commission for Development
Wadi al-Ahmar, 12–13
Wadud, Abu Musab Abdul (Abdelmalek Droukdel), 96
Wahhabism, 190
Walsum, Peter van, 180
Warfalla, 42, 50–51
Warrior's Affairs Commission for Development (WAC) (Libya), 29
al-Watan Party, 15, 19
weakness: institutional, 121–125, 186–188; state, viii, 2, 185–191
weapons trafficking, 63–64, 71, 116n53, 134–138, 170–171
West Africa Police Information System, 111
Western Libyan Shield, 32n33
Western Sahara, *164*, 165–183; autonomy, 181–182; calm of 2010, 167–169; conflict in, 172–179; ethnic and societal divides, 3, 189; Moroccan control over, 180–181; population, 174–175, 178; radical Islamism, 4; as region of concern, 169–171; state weakness, 2, 185–186; tensions, 180–182

white Moors (*bidan*), 126–127, 149–150
WikiLeaks, 143n46
Wolof, 126, 133, 149
World Bank, 123, 150
World War II graves: attacks on, 14
wujaha (tribal elders), 20

Y

Yemen, 108
youth: alienated, 4, 129, 136–137, 168–169, 176–177, 185, 193; AQIM recruits, 4, 129–130, 132, 136–137, 160–161, 185; criminal activity, 168–169; radicalization of, 121, 129, 132, 139–140, 150, 161
youth protests, 156, 167
YouTube, 157
Yunis, Abd al-Fatah, 27

Z

al-Zahawi, Muhammad Ali, 17–18
Zawiya, Libya, 10
Zintan, Libya, 10, 46
Zouerat, Mauritania, 121
Zubayr al-Sanussi, Ahmed, 11–12
Zuwara, Libya, 10, 40, 46–47
Zuwaytina oil terminal, 13
Zway, 8–9, 22, 41, 50–52
Zway-Tabu conflict, 21–25, 52
Zweila, Libya, 51

About the Authors

Anouar Boukhars is a nonresident scholar in Carnegie's Middle East Program. He is an assistant professor of international relations at McDaniel College in Westminster, Maryland, and the author of *Politics in Morocco: Executive Monarchy and Enlightened Authoritarianism* (Routledge, 2010).

Boukhars was a co-project leader of Carnegie's Mauritania Working Group, where scholars and policymakers gathered in four roundtables between January and June 2012 to discuss critical issues faced by the country and the response of the international community.

Boukhars is a former fellow at the Brookings Doha Center, where he published "Political Violence in North Africa: The Perils of Incomplete Liberalization" and "Fighting the Growth of Terrorist Networks in the Maghreb." His other publications have appeared in numerous journals and leading newspapers, including *Journal of Conflict Studies, International Political Science Review, European Security, Terrorism Monitor,* and *Columbia International Affairs Online.*

Peter Cole served as a special consultant to the UN mission in Libya (UNSMIL), mapping the emergence and functions of armed groups, both state and non-state sanctioned. Prior to that he was a senior analyst on Libya with the International Crisis Group (ICG) during the revolution and the ensuing transitional government, providing policy advice and background briefings to the UN, EU, governments, companies, NGOs, and most major media outlets. He is the co-editor of *The Libyan Revolution and its Aftermath*. He recently completed an MPhil in Modern Middle Eastern Studies at Oxford University, is fluent in the Yemeni and Libyan dialects of Arabic and studied Farsi for two years at Oxford.

Wolfram Lacher is a researcher at the German Institute for International and Security Affairs (Stiftung Wissenschaft und Politik, SWP) in Berlin. His research focuses on Libya, Algeria, and security issues in the Sahel/Sahara region. Before joining SWP in 2010, he worked as a North Africa analyst at Control Risks, a business risk consultancy in London, from 2007 to 2010.

Lacher studied Arabic and African languages and history, International Relations, as well as Conflict and Development Studies at Leipzig University, the Institut National des Langues et Civilisations Orientales in Paris, the American University in Cairo (AUC), and the School of Oriental and African Studies (SOAS) in London. Recent publications include: "Libye: révolution, guerre civile et montée en puissance de centres de pouvoir locaux," in Frédéric Charillon/Alain Dieckhoff, eds., *Afrique du Nord. Moyen Orient 2012–2013*; "Printemps arabe: trajectoires variées, incertitudes persistantes," *La documentation française*, 2012; "Families, Tribes and Cities in the Libyan Revolution," *Middle East Policy*, Winter 2011; and "Organised Crime and Terrorism in the Sahel: Drivers, Actors, Options," *SWP Comments* 2011/01.

Alex Thurston is a doctoral candidate in the Department of Religious Studies at Northwestern University. His research interests include Islam and politics, Islamic law, religious education, transnational religious exchanges, and use of new media by religious activists. In 2011–2012, he conducted field research in Kano, Nigeria, London, England, and Washington, DC with the support of fellowships from the Social Science Research Council and the Wenner-Gren Foundation. His dissertation, "Northern Nigeria's Arab-Educated Activist Intellectuals: Law, Media,

Politics, and Islam, 1954–2011," focuses on how study at Arab universities affected the religious identities, career trajectories, and political engagement of late colonial and postcolonial Muslim scholars in Northern Nigeria.

Thurston holds an MA in Arab Studies from Georgetown University and a BA in Religion from Northwestern University. In 2006–2007, he conducted research on Muslim youth movements in Senegal as a Fulbright Scholar. His writing has appeared in *Islamic Africa, Foreign Policy, Christian Science Monitor, World Politics Review, American Interest,* and other publications. He writes about Islam and politics in sub-Saharan Africa at Sahel Blog: http://sahelblog.wordpress.com.

Frederic Wehrey is a senior associate in the Middle East Program at the Carnegie Endowment for International Peace. His research focuses on security and political reform in the Gulf and North Africa.

His most recent Carnegie publications include *The Struggle for Security in Eastern Libya* (2012) and *The Precarious Ally: Bahrain's Impasse and U.S. Policy* (2013).

Prior to joining Carnegie, he was a senior policy analyst at the RAND Corporation, where he was the lead author of monographs on Iran's Revolutionary Guard, Saudi-Iranian relations, and the strategic impact of the Iraq War in the Middle East. In 2008, he led a RAND strategic advisory team to Baghdad, Iraq, focusing on post-surge challenges in support of Multinational Forces–Iraq. Wehrey is also a lieutenant colonel in the U.S. Air Force Reserve and has completed tours in Turkey, Uganda, Libya, Algeria, and Iraq, where he earned the Bronze Star in 2003.

His articles have appeared in *Foreign Affairs, Washington Quarterly, Current History,* the *International Herald Tribune, Survival, Sada, Small Wars and Insurgencies,* the *Christian Science Monitor, Financial Times,* and the *Chicago Journal of International Law.* He has been interviewed by major media outlets such as the *New York Times, Washington Post,* the *Christian Science Monitor,* PBS *NewsHour,* NPR, BBC, and CNN.

He is the author of the forthcoming book *Sectarian Politics in the Gulf: From the Iraq War to the Arab Uprisings* (Columbia University Press).

Carnegie Endowment for International Peace

The Carnegie Endowment for International Peace is a private, nonprofit organization dedicated to advancing cooperation between nations and promoting active international engagement by the United States. Founded in 1910, its work is nonpartisan and dedicated to achieving practical results.

Carnegie is pioneering the first global think tank, with flourishing offices now in Washington, Moscow, Beijing, Beirut, and Brussels. These five locations include the centers of world governance and the places whose political evolution and international policies will most determine the near-term possibilities for international peace and economic advance.

OFFICERS

Jessica T. Mathews, *President*
Paul Balaran, *Executive Vice President and Secretary*
Tom Carver, *Vice President for Communications and Strategy*
Charles Gauvin, *Chief Development Officer*
Thomas Carothers, *Vice President for Studies*
Marwan Muasher, *Vice President for Studies*
Douglas H. Paal, *Vice President for Studies*
George Perkovich, *Vice President for Studies*

BOARD OF TRUSTEES

Richard Giordano, *Chairman*
Stephen R. Lewis, Jr., *Vice Chairman*
Kofi A. Annan
Paul Balaran
Bill Bradley
Gregory Craig
William H. Donaldson
Mohamed A. El-Erian
Harvey V. Fineberg
Chas W. Freeman, Jr.
James C. Gaither
Patricia House
Jon M. Hunstman, Jr.
Linda Mason

Jessica T. Mathews
Raymond McGuire
Sunil Bharti Mittal
Adebayo Ogunlesi
Kenneth E. Olivier
Catherine James Paglia
L. Rafael Reif
J. Stapleton Roy
Vanessa Ruiz
Aso O. Tavitian
Shirley M. Tilghman
Daniel Vasella
Rohan Weerasinghe